FAITH WITHOUT DOGMA

FAITH WITHOUT DOGMA

The Place of Religion in Postmodern Societies

Franco Ferrarotti

Transaction Publishers
New Brunswick (U.S.A.) and London (U.K.)

Library of Congress Catalog Number: 92-17835
ISBN: 1-56000-074-0
Printed in the United States of America

Library of Congress Cataloging-in-Publication Data

Ferrarotti, Franco.
    [Fede senza dogmi.   English]
    Faith without dogma : the place of religion in postmodern
societies / Franco Ferrarotti.
        p.   cm.
    Includes index.
    ISBN 1-56000-074-0
    1. Christianity—20th century.   2. Christianity—21st century.
3. Postmodernism—Religious aspects—Christianity.
4. Secularization (Theology)   5. Sociology, Christian.   6. Religion-
-Philosophy.   I. Title.
BR481.F4713   1992
270.8'29—dc20   92-17835
                                                              CIP

To my Mother
who celebrates her 91st birthday in
Rome on March 25, 1993

Les dogmes de la foi ne sont pas des choses à affirmer.
—Simone Weil, *Lettre à un religieux*

Contents

Preface to the American Edition

This book is published in an American edition when a new encyclical letter by John Paul II has come to light and at the same time the debate about the theology of liberation, in both its Latin American and European versions, seems to have come to an end. It might sound paradoxical, but it could be easily demonstrated that the recent *Centesimus Annus* encyclical letter reformulates quite a few insights and points made by the liberation theologians. To be sure, words should not always be taken in their literal meanings. If critically analyzed from a strictly theological point of view, there is no doubt that the theology of liberation, as a doctrinaire corpus, leaves much to be desired. The same is true if it is taken as a political, iedological text as many American commentators—Peter L. Berger among others—have done. In this case, the theology of liberation is loosely linked with what it is supposed to be a Marxist orthodoxy without, unfortunately, realizing that this would be a blatant *contradictio in adjecto*.

In this book I try to show that the theology of liberation has been and still is a powerful movement of opinion that is rooted in the scandal of a Christian conscience vis-à-vis the subhuman living conditions in which millions of human beings are forced to exist. It has to do with a moral thrust rather than with a systematic doctrine or a political platform. In this sense, the connection with the pope's document is undeniable, especially if one considers those statements by the pope in which the law of the market is squarely confronted and essentially criticized because "there are numerous human needs that have no access to the market." In other words (and these words are underscored in the papal text), "*there exists something that is due to man because he is a man. . . .* This something that is absolutely due implies necessarily the possibility of surviving and of actively contributing to the common good of mankind."

The pope draws the logical consequence of such a statement: the aim of the business enterprise must be redefined; it cannot be confined to the mere production of profit. The very concept of profit comes under attack:

> The aim of the enterprise is not simply the production of profit, but the very existence of the enterprise itself as a human community. . . . Profit is a regulating factor of the life of the enterprise, but it is not the only one; the consideration of other human and moral factors must be added; these factors, in the long run, are equally essential for the life of the enterprise.

It would just be too easy to reply with the *bon mot* by John Maynard Keynes that "in the long run, we shall all be dead." Leaving, however, any diatribe aside, one may ask if, on the basis of the pope's statements, we are still in a capitalistic system or whether we are entering an unspecified postcapitalistic world.

In particular, one perhaps could be impressed by the fact that the overall perspective is still a Eurocentric one and that perhaps the logic of the Polish patriot is prevailing over and above the functional exigencies of a true ecumenical approach. While the pope recognizes the limitaitons of capitalism from a social and moral point of view, he seems to have some difficulty in conceiving an "open Church" and religious practice as a personal, inner experience, which seem to form a basic prerequisite for the future unity of all the positive historical religions. For a moment, this great ideal—perhaps the true utopia at the threshold of the third millennium—appeared to be within reach, especially with the Vatican Council II and with the interreligious meetings at Assisi a few years ago. At present, the idea of a universal religion not to be "administered" by any dogmatic church hierarchy but, on the contrary, to be lived as a personal inner experience seems to be losing ground. Yet, the future of mankind might well depend on its triumph.

Rome, 21 April 1992

FRANCO FERRAROTTI

Preface to the First Edition

Some years ago there was a ceremony at Louvain University to commemorate the thirtieth year of publication of that valuable journal, *Social Compass*. For reasons I have not yet been able to fathom, I was invited to give the opening address. My subject was that of the false alarm regarding secularization—a theme that is revealed only in retrospect as a rather provocative one. I argued for the persistence of the sacred and the imminent arrival of "Constantinian Christianity." Jean Séguy, who has an exceptional ear for such things, referred to my "heavy-footedness." Some time after at the Sorbonne, he mentioned an "event"—the end of Christianity—which was supposedly late in arriving. It certainly was. Nonetheless, changes in the world situation as well as recent discussions among theologians have, I believe, shown that I was right. The problem is still facing us and is made even more pressing by the deficiencies of the Marxian notion of religion, both theoretically and organizationally, which has now been demolished.

The risk now is of confusing the drama with farce—the "lay religion" and the "theology for atheists" I discussed in the first volume of the trilogy that is now concluding, with the vague drawing-room deism expounded by the omnipresent philistines of culture. These are the ready-to-use people of science, always available and willing, open to the best offer. Vico had already glimpsed, in his *Scienza Nuova*, the germ of a "lay religion" or, as I put it, a "civil theology" (see section 342 of the first volume). However, it was Nietzsche in his first *Untimely Meditations* who demonstrated, perhaps unconsciously, how lay (or as I prefer to call it, "everlasting") religion should not be reduced to serving as a prop for the current political and cultural situation. Nietzsche's portrait of the "champion of academic culture," "man of faith, writer" David Friedrich Strauss, was a merciless exposure, and in comparison even those worthy examples of Italian culture, the books by Giovanni Ferrara and Ruggero Guarini, are just bloodless handbooks. And yet the path they map seems to me the correct one. We shall have to locate it and pursue it with determination, as befits "men without myths in a world lacking predetermined certainties. One day, faith will teach them how to go onward without the refuge of dogma, so as to be reborn, transfigured after its apparent demise.

Rome, 8 December 1989

Preface to the Second Edition

Why is it that the reviews of this book have been unusually lively and plentiful? Does it touch an exposed nerve of our times, perhaps? Maybe, but it is also possible that it simply appeared at the right time—at first suppressed and whispered about like the "slander" in a Rossini opera, and then rapidly gathering strength, body, impetus, borne along noisily, even muddily, in the raging spate of fleeting cultural fashions.

Let me confess at once that I am immediately suspicious of large sales. Anyway, I am grateful to my reviewers, every one of them, even the least agreeable and ill-disposed ones (those who see the review as a duel to the death with the author, rather than as a service for potential readers). I think that even the toughest, most unyielding polemics are useful. I replied to Paolo Miccoli's occasionally venomous remarks (in the *Osservatore Romano*, 26 March 1990) that criticisms do an author good, especially when a book is blessed with a measure of success. They resemble the flax the ancient Romans burnt in the wake of the conquering general, the *imperator*, on his triumphal return to the capital, as if to say, "*sic transit . . .*" It's a salutary reminder that the author should not be overweening. Naturally, this also applies to the critic's need to be careful.

Concerning the *Osservatore Romano* review, I fear my stern and worthy interlocutor criticizes, and criticizes radically, what he has not read with the required deliberation. For example, to cite Hobbes against me without noting my remark on page 193 on the relation between Hobbes and Machiavelli in the terms once used by Leo Strauss (with whom I partly agree) is at least hasty, not to say superficial. And how much that passing remark implies for an insightful reader! So too it seems simplistic to blame me for the analysis and interpretation made by liberation theology (which is possibly the most mature combined political and theological expression of contemporary Latin American thought), closing off the question by saying that after all, nobody talks about it any more. Possibly my critic is unaware of this, comfortably relaxed as he is with his dogmas, but his line of argument is downright sinister if one thinks of the year's silence imposed by the Church on Leonardo Boff. You may ask, what's a year? It is certainly not the same as Giordano Bruno's "gag"—we've progressed somewhat from that, and we must give due credit: burning at the stake is out. However, his is an argument surprising in one who shows such contempt for the "hacks" and who merely earns himself the title of "honorary hack" when he so plainly equates success with truth.

Gagging apart, can it be that what is no longer talked about has thereby stopped being important? But from where then do these earnest and obedient guardians of orthodoxy get their criteria for evaluation—market research, perhaps? If we have to extract the value of ideas, and still more ideals, from their quotation on the stock market of current affairs, then we should indeed be victims of that "wearying horizontalism" my reviewer rightly complains of. One can be basically victorious even in defeat; Priam dies, but gloriously. There is splendor in failure. One should remember the revelatory, purifying function of certain defeats. It is odd that it should take a "layman," as my grudging critic never wearies of labeling me (as if to suggest a *non expedit* in dealing with subjects supposedly reserved for the attested ecclesiastical bureaucracy), to recall that practical success is no guarantee of anything. Indeed, it is almost always a portent of prevarication when it is not actually the product of deceit or violence.

Despite all this, paradoxically, there is some debt of gratitude. In an era when ideological divisions are collapsing and the term "ecumenicalism" is used in vain and on every street corner, it is a comfort to run up against a genuine exponent of the dogmatic mentality—in the strictest sense of the phrase. Moreover, my astringent critic is right on one essential point and twists the knife in the wound, with all the unconcerned cruelty of someone unaware of what he is doing. It is true: *A Faith without Dogmas* (*Una fede senza dogmi*) is presented after *A Theology for Atheists* (*Una teologia per atei*) and *The Paradox of the Sacred* (*Il paradosso del sacro*) as the conclusion of a trilogy on the sacred. But in my view it is little more than a skimpy preface, if not a surrogate or a book *faute de mieux*. It had in fact been my intention to bring together and discuss the points of similarity between the five great universal religions (Judaism, Christianity, Islam, Hinduism, and Buddhism). In the precious text of Tertullian, *De testimonio animae*, I find a loving, almost fearful search for the fragments of natural truths already present in the writings of pagan thinkers. Again, beyond this endeavor of spiritual archaeology that for Tertullian is not beyond suspicion, the bold attempt to plumb a new source of truth bewitches me. The impulses of the pre-Christian mind are there, the simples, the defenseless feelings reflecting common knowledge, the knowing wisdom of the illiterate, ordinary consciousness not burdened down by scholastic cultural sedimentations. I should call this soul, which Tertullian listens to with such humble attention, the "mythless soul"—if my interlocutor from the Vatican will allow. This echoes the way Felice Balbo talked of "men without myths"—purely human men, but thereby already men acting as priests to men. Tertullian put it: "Novum testimonium advoco immo omni litteratura notius, omni doctrina agitatius, omni editione vulgatius, toto homine maius, id est totum quod est hominis. Consiste in medio, anima, seu divina . . . seu minima divina . . . seu de caelo exciperis. . . . [S]eu post corpus induceris." Again: "Sentis igitur perditorem tuum, et licet soli illum noverint Christiani, vel quaecumque apud deum secta, et tu tamen eum nosti dum odisti."

I am well aware that my project, which proposes to grasp the transcendental unity of the great universal religions, requires that I should take at least another thirty years of full intellectual capacity, together with historical and linguistic knowledge I do not at the moment fully command. And yet there is a "seed text" (*lògos spermatikòs*) awaiting its speolologists and its careful, humble—and undogmatic—interpreters. This is the test before us, the ground on which our stature as people of the postideological age—for the first time universalistic in the global sense—will be tried. This will be effected in a context that appears *outside, but not opposed to*, the historic, positive religions. Only Umberto Galimberti among my many critics seems to me to have grasped this fully. The Church may well have its victories, celebrate its Canossas, and revive the fatal dream for Europe of a new Holy Roman Empire. No one has forgotten that it waited for centuries before rehabilitating Galileo. It has not yet accepted even in a restricted way, nor basically understood, the French Revolution, the tragedy of individual autonomy. *Homo religiosus* will not arise save on the ruins of the monopoly of the sacred peculiar to the bureaucratized churches.

To this point, with a few additions and alterations, I have adhered to the text of my "interlocutory reply" published in *l'Unità* (20 May 1990) and in *la Critica Sociologica*" (no. 91, Winter 1989–1990). But now I ask myself if my polemical hubris did not take me too far. What truth is there in Paolo Miccoli's remarks? I ought to be able to set aside personal feelings and irritation, the state of mind of an author who feels himself misunderstood and insulted. What is important in those remarks? I don't know if *Una fede senza dogmi* contains merely "illusory acrobatics on the metamorphoses of the sacred." I do know that it tries to respond to real needs on the part of today's individual. I don't think these needs can be reduced to "compromise proposals from a semiculture" or "neopagan sacrality." Such deep-rooted distrust of even the most timid effort to live religion as a profound personal experience can possibly only arise from too long a coexistence with a dogmatic spirit, which scents in every attempt at open, nonritualized, and simply human discussion a threat or a danger to be warded off.

As against the reviewer in *Osservatore Romano*, don Claudio Sorge recognized in *Famiglia cristiana* (11 April 1990) that I regard religion as a "necessary part for the completeness of man" and that I feel "acutely the desire for the sacred in the world." Naturally, I have many defects:

> For example, the idea of revelation and Church, conceived in the sense of a mysterious reality—but nonetheless a real, living, prophetic, and sacramental one. . . . The sociologist asserts the need for a religious spirit for the salvation of science, and the goodness of ethical progress, though he sees clearly the difference between ethics and religion. When I say "distinction," I don't mean

"counterposition," but a difference whereby one cannot equate nor reduce religion to the problem of ethics.

In other words, Sorge was reproving me for having an "incomplete conception of religion." Indeed, I am afraid I don't have one because his own "complete conception" of religion turns out essentially to be the one that the churches laid out in hieratic bureaucracies claim to monopolize, denying through their pastoral practice the ecumenicalism and interreligious spirit of Vatican Countil II that they continue to proclaim in theory (if in muted form).

In this regard, I draw attention to a strange coincidence with a part of the political left that sees in the sacred and especially in the "return to the sacred" only a vain search for a radical alternative to capitalism. In *Il Manifesto* (1 August 1990) Paolo Virno comments:

> The intention in grounding the critique of the capitalist mode of production on something "more essential" is only the sign of the extent to which this mode of production is in good health and has sorely reduced its opponents. The leap backward toward the sacred is symptomatic of a desperate poverty of theoretical instruments regarding the analysis of current social relations. It resembles the behavior of someone who is overwhelmed by debt and to keep going can find nothing better than contracting new ones, and still more, always for larger sums. He is convinced that in this way the initial due dates will be forgotten.

As regards the sacred as a value salvaged from the laws of the market and the logic of bureaucratic organization, we might say that we are faced here with two instrumentalisms, both unable to transcend the givenness of what exists. Does this involve the unpredicted but happy marriage of two contrary, symmetrical dogmatisms?

We cannot have too many doubts about the dogmatism of the official Catholic church when we look at the recent document published in the original Latin version in the *Osservatore Romano* (27 June 1990), emanating from the Congregation for the Doctrine of the Faith, and entitled *Instructio de ecclesiali theologi vocatione* (Doctrine on the ecclesiastical vocation of theologians). The prevailing concern in the document seems to lie in its reemphasising the infallibility of the Church and the request for an essentially "corpselike" obedience from the theologians. If a theologian should find himself out of synchrony with the teaching of the Church, far from turning to the mass media—as Hans Küng did not hesitate to do, together with Leonardo Boff and others—he should responsibly choose silence. He must suffer and pray; as we read in paragraph 36 of the *Instructio*, "the freedom of the act of faith cannot justify the right to dissent. In fact, it does not mean freedom as regards truth, but the free self-determination of the person in conformity with his moral obligation to accept a truth from without, not one's own, not one expressed from within. Yet it is claimed that an internally positive welcome should be prepared for this preconstituted truth, as if it was what it is not. It makes one, not too disrespectfully, think of the Stalinist show trials of the 1930s in Moscow, when the accused acknowledged their guilt and heaped ashes on their heads for not having immediately and joyfully recognized a truth—the truth, that is, of the dictator—as their own, internally self-determined, before the court of conscience.

It has long been made clear, by the twenty-two Tübingen theologians, echoed in Italy by the journal of the Dehonian Fathers *Il Regno*, how the whole of the *Instructio* is pervaxded by an authoritarian, paternalist outlook. "Without referring to existing communities, it is impossible to read the experience of the Church, and therewith both the teaching of the bishop and that of the theologian. . . . Anyone who hypothetically did not know the Catholic church and the richness of its life in the past decades and proposed a judgement based on the *Instructio* would get an impoverished, restricted picture." The central problem underlying the document signed by Monsignor Joseph Ratzinger was forcefully expounded by Monsignor Carlo Maria Martini, archbishop of Milan:

> Is faith necessary for a theologian? In other words, is an atheist theologian possible? The question is not an idle one. In fact, there are many activities undertaken by theologians that require no more than the honesty and capacity of a serious researcher. . . . But when the *Instructio* speaks of the "theologian" it means something more. . . . The theologian is thus the person . . . who reelaborates the content of faith in the conceptual, cultural, and linguistic context of his time. It is to do this that criteria of discernment are required. (C. M. Martini, "Ma quella del teologo è proprio una vocazione?" [But is the theologian's really a vocation?] *Corriere della Sera*, 1 July 1990)

True, one needs "criteria of discernment." Will that need be met by the hierarchy alone? Ernesto Balducci has some doubts in this regard:

> The document has a structurally authoritarian viewpoint, even though it is enlightened by a recognition of past errors. It is not enough to acknowledge incontestable errors. One must identify the reasons that made them possible, otherwise the conditions for repeating the mistake are reproduced. . . . Teacher and theologian are presented as figures isolated from the People of God, which is the object of their concerns; whereas in reality, the People is the plenary subject of the experience of the Faith, and within which we find both teacher and theologian. (*Corriere della Sera*, 28 June 1990)

The critical reservations regarding my book expressed by Carlo Cremona, however, seem fully in line with the authoritarian outlook expressed by Monsignor Ratzinger:

> I ask myself if Franco Ferrarotti is a sociologist or a theologian. The sociologist has the right to investigate the benefit or harm that faith bestows on man, on how today's individual or individuals in earlier times react to the indications of the faith. But investigating the nature of the faith itself is a job for the theologian, not the sociologist. (C. Cremona, "Senza dogmi, che fede è?" [Without dogmas, what faith is it?] *Avvenire*, 23 May 1990).

For Cremona, it's a sin that the rigid partition between disciplines—as though these were exclusive game reserves keeping out inquisitive, ambitious poachers—should carry no conviction for the more up-to-date trends in epistemology. These, on the contrary, are inclined to support multidisciplinary kinds of research strategy, if not downright postdisciplinary ones. A more appropriate, and urgent, critical comment seems to me to be that of Aldo Di Lello (*Secolo d'Italia*, 25 February 1990): "Ferrarotti's outlook is essentially that of the 'repentant scientist,' who is forced to reconsider his theories in the face of the damage caused by the dogmas of science itself." The definition of "repentant scientist" would not displease me, if only I had the slightest inclination toward repentance. I willingly acknowledge my mistakes, but I regret nothing and repent of nothing; it is not in my character. Di Lello goes on:

> The form of religiosity he . . . presents as the backcloth for his book is one profoundly recast according to the values expressed during the postscientistic era and in the epoch of "democratic" ecclesial experiences. In the wake of

Father Boff's liberation theology, these contest the authority of the hierarchy. The road lies open for a wholly individualistic vision of the "sacred," as though it were a private shelter against anxiety."

In view of my remarks about the "morality of the positivists" and the resumption of the critique of the "rabbi of sociology," Emile Durkheim, this individualistic interpretation seerms to me hard to sustain. On the other hand, the idea of a religiosity that is ultimately not left exclusively in the hands of bureaucratized religions seems to me certainly well-grounded. This is a point accuratly grasped by Francesco Erbani (in the "Mercurio" section of *La Repubblica*, 24 February 1990). He captures the deep correlation between ecclesial monopoly of the sacred and the poverty or absence of lay culture in this regard—a correlation that holds on the theoretical and also hitorical level, notwithstanding the exceptions of major figures such as Carlo Cattaneo, Aldo Capitini, Ernesto Buonajuti, Ferdinando Tartaglia, and most recently, Lorenzo Milani, Felice Balbo, and Claudio Napoleoni.

Although the exploration of this correlation is possibly the most important purpose of my book, I must acknowledge that it has escaped many otherwise sophisticated reviewers—a purpose whose goal is that of establishing what kind of person (also in the anthropological and temperamental sense) should be produced by the simultaneous presence of a dominant bureaucratized religion and a defective lay culture. For example, Giovanni Monastra (in *Diorama letterario*, April 1990) says that "the retrieval of the 'sacred' attempted by this well-known sociologist seems to be feeble. . . . [I]t is a flase 'sacred,' conceived of as an intimistic device, an individualistic consolation, a private refuge for someone escaping from anxiety, loneliness, and the depersonalization of modern life." Michele L. Straniero too concludes, in an obviously ironic vein (he is not forgotten as the author of an interesting study of Don Bosco, especially in the latter's difficult relationship with the Valdesi): "But why should this civil religion be more effective and bring salvation more than the traditional one, or be less deceptive? Frankly, Ferrarotti has not managed to explain this to us. Perhaps a fourth volume is required" (see the "Tuttolibri" section of *La Stampa*, 24 March 1990). One is tempted to reply, "If only one more volume would suffice!" However, the extent of the problem is neither mocked not superficially trivialized in the interviews and discussion by Pietro Greco (*L'Unità*, 24 January 1990), Aurelio Andreoli (*Secolo XIX*, 19 April 1990), Maurizio Ortolani (*Giornale d'Italia*, 22 February 1990)—and by N. Sergio Turtulici (*Eco della Valli Valdesi*, 16 March 1990), who acutely brings out the question of the relation between the time of man and the time of God (as do Antonio Saccà (*Tempo*, 1 March 1990), Maria Rosa Russo (*Giornale di Sicilia*, 2 April 1990), and Antonio Sambataro (*La Sicilia*, 4 March 1990). Turtulici writes: "Ferrarotti's idea . . . is that secularization, the time of man, does not necessarily exclude the time of the eternal and of God, a religiosity to be invested in the relation with others, in civil life, be it lay or illumined by the rays of faith."

Man's time, and God's time, then. Everyday time and eschatological time. Umberto Galimberti grasps the themes that I am concerned with, from Christianity and science to secularization and the sacred "in its dealings with the satanic." He sees that these themes oscillate between the two times, in an intermediate space where "events are considered in the context of their ultimate meaning by tracing their outline, which is eternal since it is grounded in the soul of man as its ineliminatable lineament." This is, to date, the most profound and penetrating comment on what I have tried to say in this book. It is a comment that is not congratulatory and gives me no grounds for self-satisfaction, but that on the contrary opens up new, demanding areas of study. Galimberti says, "History encounters the Eternal, and in this confrontation the Eternal yields up its marmorial nature and History its feverishness. This space opened up between everyday time and eschatological time is the precondition for the great osciallation of Meaning, wherein these subjects take on vibrancy and depth" (U. Galimberti, "Apriti, o scenario, a tutti gli eventi" [Open up, o scenario, to every event], *Sole-24 Ore*, 18 February 1990).

To comprehend the passages of temporality between these two poles requires an undertaking of analysis and interpretation that is daunting. It involves analyzing their interlinkage, which becomes the design of a life, and expressing their meaning, which, in the last analysis, is the meaning of life. In this, the individual's varied, unpredictable activity congeals and sets into that of the group; it becomes history, and by way of the multiform network of social

movements and historic institutions becomes crystalized into cus-
tom and socially determined culture. Notwithstanding this, I am
grateful to Umberto Galimberti for having made it so clear as to
make me understand its character as a necessary, and therefore
inevitable, theoretical transition.

Rome, 15 August 1990

1

Toward the End of Constantinian Christendom

The Demand for Renewal Starts from Below

Between the 1960s and the 1990s the destruction and scars of the Second World War appeared healed and about to be forgotten. Industrialized societies, powerfully driven forward by the needs of reconstruction, seemed launched on a path of pragmatically sensible development, without unexpected shocks. But beneath the smooth facade of formally codified institutions, deep pressures and forces of incredible power were at work. These included not only the preparation of the protet movements that were to peak in May 1968 but also capillary demands for renewal in the Catholic world traditionally tied and loyal to the directives of the Church's teaching. These requests did not come from the top. It is well known that the summit is rarely interested in the processes of renewal. Renewal, when it came, came from below and started out from the periphery. Think of the experience of Don Enzo Mazzi at the Isolotto in Florence, of that of the Abbot Giovan Battista Franzoni at San Paolo fuorile mura in Rome, not to mention the earlier Esperienze Pastorali of Don Lorenzo Milani.

The proposals of Pope John XXIII, in some ways prophetic, were an initial sign of opening up. Under this pressure, it was no wonder that the Catholic hierarchy finally decided to make a collective repsonse to these requests, which were mysteriously pressing at the basis of the church and in extraecclesiastical society. This response was the summoning of the Second Vatican Council. An old, already ailing pope, universally held to be a pope typical of transition, imprinted a decisive change of line on the Roman curia, with all the frankness of a true revolutionary.

Naturally, it cannot be said that the overall evaluation of the work of Vatican II and the directions emerging therefrom have been concluded. Rather, it has scarcely begun. It would be superficial and hasty to believe this represented only a reply by the Church to the protest movements of the postwar period. Undoubtedly, its roots concerned at least fifty years of history, and especially in Italy, one cannot overlook the "modernist movement" at the beginning of this century. This, with Romolo Murri and others, was to shake Catholics' consciences and disturb their age-old, Counter-Reformation acquiescence. Aside from this broad historical background, there was no pronouncement of the council that lacked a not-always limpid, and indeed often difficult, contorted story, of which it came to represent the problematic and far from definitive outcome. Indeed, what was striking in the history of the Church was its ability to wait and its serene calculations based not on the measure of a man's life nor on biographical chance, but rather its taking into consideration the logic of the development of an institution whose trajectory of change must be analyzed and evaluated in terms of centuries.

Little more than twenty years separate us from the council, twenty years, it has been usefully remarked,

> which in the course of three pontificates, Paul VI until 1978, John Paul I, pope for a month, and John Paul II, inaugurated that same year, are still probably a very liquid lava of tendencies and phenomena, pressures and counterpressures, to the point that one can perhaps say we are only at the end of an initial phase of the postcouncil. . . . It is thus a matter of attempting a partial, provisional balance sheet of the council, naturally not therewith claiming to write a real history of the Church in the twenty postconciliar years, since this would probably be a rather different—or, better, the start of a rather different—history from the previous one.[1]

This historian's caution is laudable and legitimate. Here, on the other hand, I shall try to grasp the significance of those events, with the courageous hope that the reader will not mistake this either for daring nor an excess of speculation.

On the death of John XXIII the control of Vatican Council II passed to the Montini Pope, Paul VI, perhaps the most intellectually prepared and subtle pope of this century. With great clarity, he outlined the aims of the council as: (1) self-awareness of the Church; (2) its renewal; (3) the reunification of all Christians; and (4) the Church's dialogue with the contemporary world.

It is hard to argue, as has been authoritatively attempted, that in the face of the precise clarity of these objectives Vatican Council II was none other than a work of codification and legal registration of changes already underway and set out. In his opening speech to the Ecumenical Council Vatican II in 1962, John XXIII was fully aware of the innovations being prepared and stated: "In the present order of things, Divine Providence is leading us to a new order of human relations which, through the intervention of men and moreover beyond their very expectation, are developing towards the fulfilment of Its higher, unseen designs. And everything, even human diversity, is laid out for the greater good of the Church." However, today, twenty years from its ending, can the council still be considered a radical, genuine turnaround in the life of the Church: or else, first discretely under Paul VI and then more decisively with John Paul II, as a process of slow but continuous emptying of its essential innovatory content, has it reached the point of justifying the suspicion that, in the letter and in spirit, it has been betrayed rather than enforced?

The question cannot adequately be dealt with just on the basis of suspicions and clues that mostly do not rise above the level of hearsay, capricious and fragmentary for the most part. Behind this question there lie problems of principle that concern the process of renewal of the Church and the interpretation of Christianity in depth. One must critically reconsider the image of man that lies at the heart of the positions taken by the most recent popes. For John XXIII, man is always, systematically, beyond the letter of the law. Man in flesh and blood wins over juridical and theological formalism. The first gesture of this unforgettable pope was at once simple and revolutionary: the visit to the prisoners in Regina Coeli, Rome. Moreover, the reminiscence of his own relatives, communicated with phrases colored not by holy writings but by the most immediate and intellectually unprotected everydayness—including recollections of how they were caught cutting wood one day on an estate and later imprisoned—was as though to say: I am one of you; I know by direct experience what your situation is; we are all prisoners, imprisoned in this world. This kind of "papal complicity" was an unheard-of act. There was the outstretched hand and embrace of one human being for another, rather than merely a sovereign on the throne of Peter. There was a deeply felt sense that no man is an island, no one can save themselves unaided, and that power is the occasion for blame.

John XXIII, more through his practical attitudes than through his explicit teaching, had started the Church on a process probably destined to continue into the first decades of the next millennium. This process it would perhaps not be incautious to call the "end of Constantinian Christianity." This son of a Lombard peasant family had in fact set up the council almost as a family council, a kind of informal family meeting with his bishops. All the experiences of the Church on a world scale would be discussed and used to bring the gospel in the same fashion to all the countries of the world. The age-old practice of secret Vatican diplomacy, in which the aristo-cratic Pius XII (a man unusually well-versed in canon law and at home in all the chancelleries of the powerful) excelled, was simply abandoned and forgotten. John XXIII, with his encyclical *Pacem in terris* established the basic points of a new world order of peace and justice.

The Church and the Individual

These new perspectives as regards the structure and government of the Church thereafter found their most authoritative expression in the "Pastoral Constitution for the Church in the Contemporary World." It seems certain that through his practical example as pope, John XXIII rediscovered and promoted the concrete truth of the "mystical body" in polemical tension with the hierarchically stratified and arthritic Church, exalting, on the contrary, the "People of God" as the basic category and foundation of ecclesiastical teaching. The formula *servus servorum* took on again in him all its value and penetrating power in everyday practice, beyond the purely liturgical connotation of the formal ritual.[2]

In practical terms, with John XXIII we have finally the confir-

mation of the gospels' promise that those who are last—the prisoners, the excluded, the segregated, and the emarginated—shall be
first. At the same time, this meant a break with the ruling circles
and social leadership that, historically, had often managed to com-
bine positions of objective privilege and moral authority with the
Church's blessing. Even more explosive were the consequences on
a world level concerning relations with the other universal religions.
One might say that with John XXIII the Catholic church's Counter-
Reformation had at last ended, and that the Church of Rome had
opened up on an essentially equal footing not only to the "separated
brothers" but also, as an absolute novelty, toward the "men
without myths."[3]

Felice Balbo designated with this formula those human beings
who, though belonging to no church or religious faith, expressed
through their simple humanity the basic convergence of the values
and transcendental unity of the positive historical religions.[4] Perhaps they might also be defined, in the light of Tertullian, as
"*naturaliter Christiani*," if the simplicity of their purely human
virtues did not consign them, as ideal citizens, to a broader, more
flexible and mobile historical and religious horizon than the Christian context. In this sense, whatever the future development of
John XXIII's teachings and the council he desired, the ecumenical
outlook linked to those teachings and practice will forever remain
exemplary. By this, the Church seemed to burn its bridges with
western European civilization as the sole repository of the values
of human civilization. It opened up to other cultures. It seemed
ready to see in men and women, independently of faith, race, or
culture, the unifying, creative center of value. The human person
had intrinsic value. No chrism could enoble or save it from without.
No blessing from above could enoble it. It was end, goal of history,
and of its own destiny.

To instrumentalize the human person, even for the goal of universal salvation, or with the prospect of the redemption of mankind,
so as to draw it from the original fall and free the individual from
the obsessive "remembrance of the forbidden fruit," meant to
mistake or betray its essential prerogatives. These belonged to a
creature capable of creation and self-creation, at least in the sense
of a self-consciousness that made up and guaranteed the autonomy

of the person: what we might call with a pardonable pun, the "personality" of the person.

The Break with the Church of the Pacts

How far we are from the Church that signed agreements with regimes that by principle and practice were hostile to the person—such as the fascist and nazi regimes or the more recent dictatorships that for years have bloodied Latin America! Is it not perhaps true that all absolutist governments have eagerly sought legitimation through the Church's approval on the basis of the principle "*A Deo lex—a rege lex*"? It is strange to have to observe how at all events, since the donation of Sutri, the Church has always systematically aligned with the established order, proposing solid reasons against critics of religion who took advantage of it to reduce the religious phenomenon to an "opium of the people," to a mass fraud, and in any case a poor, residual phenomenon, destined to disappear with the progress of rationality among men and in the world.[5] The situation had troubled not only the "strong" thinkers of the Enlightenment but also inspired the imagination of the poets: "For those to whom the earth has no more to offer, heaven was invented. . . . Long live this invention! Hail to a religion that pours into the bitter cup of suffering humanity some drops of a sweet draught, of spiritual opiate, some drops of love, hope and faith."[6]

Beyond the stereotyped and at times frankly vulgar anticlerical propaganda that has generally seen the priest in the service of the powerful and privileged social groups—wholly unmindful of the evangelist's *Vae divitibus!*—one must recognize that the Church established itself as an established social power only with the ending of the imperial persecution when in 312 of the current era it obtained the status of *religio licita* from the emperor Constantine. Constantine was a thoroughly ambiguous figure, inclined to every opportunism to triumph over his political opponents, to the point of making his own fortunes as military leader and last resource of power in an empire in crisis depend on the link with the Church and Christianity in general.[7]

That there may be a link of continuity between the new political Christian-imperial theology and the classical one that made the emperor the political and the religious leader of the empire, thus uniting religion and politics closely, seems to me a difficult question. It would require a detailed examination of the unfortunately incomplete texxts of Marcus Terentius Varro and other writers. They reflected on the *"theologia civilis"* that was the basis of the *"religio pubblica"* of the Roman state. This, even today, has a precise resonance in those jurists who tend to legitimize power in the name of its decisionism and sovereign autonomy as regards society—not on the basis of the demands of society but only of its ability and capability to decide. They thus confuse authority as authoritativeness with authority as clumsy authoritarianism.[8]

The breaking with this past carried out by John XXIII was explosive. However, for this reason its further development was to encounter significant obstacles. Caesaro-papal political theology had necessarily to confront the new orientation and try by all means (from condemnation of the liturgical innovations desired by Paul VI as devilish to the resumption of secret diplomacy, by definition subordinate to raison d'état), in order to slow down its development. The traditionalist bishop, Marcel Lefebvre, formerly military ordinary of the French colonies in West Africa, became the referent and rallying point of the most reactionary Catholic forces, fearful that liberty within the Church could produce the obscuring of the idea of the priest committed not only to celibacy but first of all to obedience and respect for the Church hierarchy; and that the pope's openness to questions of social justice would end by shaking the pyramid of existing power, sweeping away established interests.

While Paul VI, in the encyclical *Populorum progression* recognized the autonomy of third world countries and their right to dispose directly of the natural wealth belonging to them and tried to remove Christianity from the exclusive protection of western European civilization, he lost the battle for the renewal of the Roman curia. The Church continued to be goverened at the center, from above. The Catholics of dissent and the communities of the base did not break off their struggle, but undoubtedly the battle became increasingly difficult. It may well be that it is not quite legitimate to reduce the behavior of the official Church of this period to the single aim of saving the bureaucracy of the Roman curia, seen as intrinsically hierarchical and by definition antidemocratic. It may be that the doctrine of the *pars sanior* is in itself just a salutary corrective of democratic practice, so as to avoid bogging down and stagnating, caused by the mutual neutralizing of opposing, symmetrical forces, and so does not necessarily involve their destruction. It may be that a pluralism of prospects and positions even within the Church is a factor of dynamism and dialectical encounter, which in the end would find confirmation in the very fact that Catholicism is much livelier in the countries where the resistance to papel infallibility was stronger, as in France. In Italy, aside from a short modernistic period, nothing approached the open-minded militancy of men like Ernest Hello, Louis Veuillot, Léon Bloy and others like them.

The Wind of the Spirit Drops

Papal infallibility and customary obedience to the hierarchy certainly contributed to creating a bigoted catholicism, intellectually weak and inclined to opportunism. However, it is also true that neither should the democratic principle be absolutized, at the risk of negating it. Democratic practice is itself a problem, not the solution.

With Paul VI the spirit of the council began to decline. The wind of renewal dropped, and a certain weariness appeared. The sharp problematic acumen and intellectual refinement of Paul VI, a pope brought up on French culture, from Jacques Maritain to the personalist, communitarian Emmanuel Mounier, were easily mistaken for a congenital Hamletism; theological scrupulosity passed for weakness. However, the image of man held by Paul VI did justice to the complexity in which modern man found himself enveloped and in some ways imprisoned. Moreover, man himself was no longer seen as a given. It was argued that he had no nature. It was understood that man had history, developed and became, advanced and at times, suffered setbacks, and dramatically retreated in his history, and also was practical, immersed in the everyday, dripping with blood and sweat. In a way that could seem paradoxical only from a superficial viewpoint, Paul VI was "Sartrean." *He saw man in his situation.* One could not judge in the abstract. Sin itself lost its metaphysical absoluteness, its offense to the cosmic balance. Man must be judged in a specific situation, in specified terms, those of history, delimitated and delimiting, in which he lived out his life. It was hard to grasp that part of responsibility the bishops (in the *Report on the Faith*) bore for estranging the Church from the young in particular, without bearing in mind Paul VI's conception of man.

The Synod of Bishops took a position on two determining questions: a) social reforms in the outside world and renewal in the Church; and b) ecumenical understanding among the Christian confessions and the dialogue with all the main religions of the world.

As regards the first point, the Church had given proof of a coherent, explicit antiracist attitude; in favor of human rights; against the arms race and deprivation of the elementary freedoms; against contempt for the family and arms investment and cuts in social spending. Internal renewal was certainly marking time, but at least it had not, as some hoped, proceeded along the path of "restoration," whereas the need for collegial ministry by the bishops with the pope was confirmed. On the other hand, as regards ecumenicalism, a fine if modest victory for the spirit of the council was the one that impeded the incorporation (in an inevitably subordinate position) of the Secretariat for the Unity of Christians in the Congregation for the Doctrine of the Faith, directed by Cardinal Joseph Ratzinger, notoriously favorable to an extreme centralization of authority.

The document of the Synod of Bishops and the accompanying report by the cardinal, however, were silent on the vital questions. When they were not silent regarding problems, they were majestically silent on the practical ways to resolve them. It is unbelievable that there should be no acknowledgment of the questions most directly involving the everyday life of the faithful and more or less immediately respond to it: birth control, communion for the divorced, celibacy or marriage of priests, the position of women in the Church and society, ecumenical understanding. The latter concerned not only declarations of principle, but practical initiatives for dialogue, encounter, discussion on an equal basis of common problems, recognition of the communion service of other churches, the liturgy of prayer in common, and above all the promotion of ecumenical prayer. One has the impression that behind the curtain of apparently progressive words, open to the future, through its omissions and silences the curia of the center had worked out its plan, strategic and tactical, for recovering positions lost with John XXIII and only partly retaken with Paul VI.

Clearly, the conception of humanity had changed. We have gone back to medieval canon law, which had, moreover, never been abandoned but only modified for modern times. The individual returned to being a fixed datum, an object to control and watch, paternally,, from above. John Paul II, in his personal history lacking a democratic past, a pope from the trenches who one can well imagine advancing with the shields and armor of a new Julius II, for whom dogma is to be seen as an unchangeable given and sacredly ahistorical, admirably embodied the new course. The harshness with which he criticized and ultimately condemned the "new theology" (forcing some of its most fluent exponents into silence), the lack of understanding amply shown regarding the drama of the Latin American peoples, are its demonstration. There has been an attempt to give an apologetic interpretation of liberation theology, as though it derived from purely personal speculations, and so at the most expressed individual needs and frustrations. But the liberation on which this theology reflected critically has a social consistency beyond that of the histories of the individual scholars. It concerned the new awareness that human masses, from time immemorial submerged in poverty and beset by want and endemic precariousness of the means of subsistence, were inquiring about their right to a life that was not subhuman, to dignity, and to a decent quality of life.

Formerly, poverty was indicated and explained by the Church as a destiny, the mysterious work of a Providence as concerned about human beings as it was inscrutable in its designs and, if necessary, cruel. The truth underlying and driving the new theology of liberation was simple: the poor wanted to free themselves from the poverty by which they were constrained without fault or responsibility. The idea grew that the problems of the poor individual were not only an individual question. There is poverty caused by structural factors against which individual good will could do nothing, or almost nothing. Within the Church and with it, the poor were on the march, if necessary against the Church. The poor were tired of palliatives or nostrums, fine words and preaching resignation. The poor wanted their own liberation: a complete liberation. The first level was that of economic, political, and cultural liberation of the Latin American peoples, the second was achieved with the liberation of the individual, the specific person. The third was liberation from sin, at once communication with God and dialogue with his brothers, the crowning of the whole process of emancipation. They were three levels, distinct but not separate, united by a dialectical link. Each necessarily referred back to the others. By itself, none of these levels was the solution to the problem of dependence. Dependence was a global phenomenon. One could not be liberated economically without being at the samme time freed culturally and politically and without on the other hand recognizing oneself in the supreme equality that found fulfillment in transcendence.

Theology between Principles and History

The unresolved crux of liberation theology is the distinction between liberation from sin and recognition of transcendence and historico-political liberations. To understand the nature of this crux and start a process of its dissolution, description, and explanation, it is initially essential to determine what was liberation theology's deepest purpose. In the words of one of its most visible exponents, it "is an attempt to understand the faith from the viewpoint of the historico-liberatory and subversive practice of the peoples of this world, of the exploited classes, the despised races, and the emarginated cultures."[9] These meager phrases are sufficient to let us see how liberation theology appears as a theology antithetical to that of the classical, or traditional, one. Classical theology is a reflexive doctrine that presupposes the attainment of the discursive, scientific plane, in the full sense. Liberation theology, on the contrary, makes itself a practical instrument for intervention in a given historial situation. It does not start from the biblical world as absolute *prius* [in St. John's gospel: "In principlio erat verbum . . .] but rather from the given historical situation and is in fact a critical reflection "made from and by historical practice compared with the Word of the Lord . . . a reflection on and in the faith that is realized through an option and a commitment; through real, operative solidarity with the exploited classes.[10] Its starting point is neither the word of the gospels nor the teaching of the Old Testament. For it, the primacy of practice is beyond debate. The traditional attitude, which descended from principles to the practical level in order to absorb it in the sublimity of the principles from which it began, is reversed.

This makes comprehensible the attention liberation theologians give to the actual historical and economic circumstances of Latin America. They are theologians working, observing, and acting in a specific context. They are linked to political and workers' struggles of the short and middle range, not in order to escape from meditating on great principles, but to confront the present and its problems in the name of classical theology. In this sense, liberation theology is tied to the earlier catholic dissent and once more exposes the conservative functions of institutionalized religion.

This perspective is not content with a broad conceptual definition. It seeks examples, and finds eloquent ones, in Christian pedagogy itself, which "does not derive from the formulation of the Christian message, but from the process of institutionalization of religion. This process has developed at three levels: the faith, the intellectual definition of the religious message, and organization."[11]

At all three levels of pedagogy the dimension of individual and group self-determination is missing. The power structure dominates the religiosity of the person. Actual economic and political conditions are blurred by the discussion of questions of principle. It should therefore be no surprise that the existing social order is, thus, metaphysically legitimated. The revolutionary and utopian potential of biblical religion and Christianity have been blunted and subsumed into the logical schema of ancient Greek philosophical discourse. The subversive potential of these messages has been intellectualized and shifted back to the path of current philosophical categories.

Liberation theology breaks with this tradition. Theology is produced in direct contact with the actual circumstances of the people and the material relations of life. Leonard Boff in this way links traditional Christology with the immediate political struggle of Latin American men and women. Christ's declaration "My kingdom is not of this world" is canceled out. For Boff, Christ announces a "reply" that is already current and active in history being made. His reply is already for today. Christological formulas must thus respond to the demands of Latin Americans who are facing problems of social and cultural emancipation today. It does not involve humanity in general, to whom traditional philosophy and theology devote attention. Boff's argument is not essentialist but is historically rooted. It is immediately translatable into political initiative.

Perhaps the most interesting aspect of Boff's writings is his attempt to re-create the Palestine of Jesus's time, to put in context the words of Jesus by making them come down from the theological, eschatological level to that of the everyday. This historicization of Jesus is clearly a danger for the ecclesiastical hierarchy, which has mastered the art of indefinite postponement of practical commitment. This technique of deferment is rejected by Boff. The kingdom of God does not mean for him only the "liquidation of sin, but of everything sin means for man, for society and the cosmos. In the kingdom of God, pain, blindness, hunger, tempests, sin, and death will no longer exist."[12]

The Primacy of Practice in Liberation Theology

Boff's theological observation is to be understood only by bearing in mind the characteristics of the environment where it is unfolding: that of the Brazilian church. The basic experiences Boff underwent lead him to speak of a necessary "reinvention of the Church." In his view, in fact, "the Church starts to grow from the base, from the heart of the people of God. This experience puts the common way of thinking about the Church in crisis."[13] Here, liberation theology is related without a break to the experiences of the Catholics of dissent, in Italy and elsewhere, and to the struggle of communities at the base. Think of the example of Don Giovan Battista Franzoni. In the case of the ex-abbot of San Paolo Fuori le Mura too, "the category people of God and Church-communion permits a better redistribution of the sacred *potesta* within the Church. It obliges us to redefine the task of the bishop and the priest. It allows the rise of new ministries and a religious style of life embodied in the popular classes. The hierarchy becomes a simple internal service and not the constitution of ontological strata, which open the way to divisions within the body of the Church and to really different classes of Christians."[14]

Though emerging in the first instance in contact with Latin American social reality, it is noteworthy that liberation theology should have important forerunners in the demands for "new Christianity" (to use Jacques Maritain's formula), in other countries, and especially in Europe. Gustavo Gutierrez in particular worked out a conception of liberation theology that surmounted that of the Latin American environment. In his view, the world asserted itself increasingly as irreversible "in its secularity." Gutierrez states that "secularization appears as a distance from religious guardianship, as a desacralization": a valid but incomplete summary. It is mistaken and superficial to speak of secularization and desacralization, and how that simply confirms the disturbing confusion between sacred and religious, and the failure to understand how often, especially today, the sacred appears in disguise. Gutierrez aims better, making important modifications: "Secularization is above all the result of a transformation of man's self-understanding. From a cosmological vision one passes to an anthropological one, above all because of the development of the sciences. . . . This new understanding of man necessarily bears with it a different way of conceiving of the relation with God."[15]

In Gutierrez there is in this premise the paradoxical positive reevaluation of secularization that, initially, would agree with the Christian vision of humankind and, secondly, would promote a greater Christian fullness, at least to the extent to which it offers each of us the possibility of being more fully human. In his pages, Bonhoeffer's disturbing question is hovering: How do we speak of God in this "adult world"? First, in fact, one saw the world from the Church. Now one sees the Church from the world. The perspective is reversed. One must thus redefine the formulation of the faith. In other words, Gutierrez forcibly maintains that faith must find a new point "for its insertion in the dynamic of history, for its morality, style of life, language of its preaching, and of its faith."[16]

This typically pastoral perspective seems to have been underestimated by critics of liberation theology. Clearly, a concern for its assonance with Marxism prevailed. Recognition of practice as a point of departure has caused it to be suspected of ingenuous materialism. One must bear in mind the characteristics of Marxism in Latin American culture and the relative inexperience in practical politics of many believers, who suddenly find in Marxism, or believe they have found in it, a key for understanding and explaining the economic and political phenomena of an increasingly complex social reality. The theology of liberation has no difficulty recognizing the debts of the Christian tradition to Marxism.

This commitment to Marxism can be explained for Latin America by the particular place occupied by the Christian and Catholic tradition during the rapid, radical changes in the postwar period. There one first notes an oscillation between theology and the pastoral at the time of Vatican II, which we might define as a rapid "switch of fronts," from the enthusiastic defense of the Kennedy New Frontier to the radical critique of the North American model of development.

José Miranda's book[17] precisely reproduces the phase of the firsst acceptance of Marxism in 1974. There are two reasons for his enthusiastic acceptance of it: (1) the lack of a critical tradition among believers on the level of history and economics, indeed, a tradition of broad accommodation to the system of dominance in South America; and (2) wider difficulties or deficiencies, almost everywhere in the Christian tradition as a whole. Christianity does not in fact contain a precise political agenda and there have been religious proposals throughout history that do not distinguish between the political and the religious. One may state that as regards politics in Jesus's time, there is a clear nonidentification with both major movements and the choice of this or that sect. In spite of the fact that the kingdom preached by Jesus allows for various political choices, one cannot deny that the politics largely accepted by the Church for a long time has been that of the monarchy, the empire, or communities of states with religious aims.

This predilection for supranational-monarchic forms of power seems to respond better to the Church's higher needs rather than the more particularistic interests of its believers in society. The historica tensions between the Church and the expressions of its believers in society are well known. The very claim by the Church to the title of "perfect society" also marks the intention not to identify the higher values of the faith with political mediations. But this term was often abused to mean an identification with the real power of political control.

The Catholic tradition has been very slow to accept the democratic system as possible for religious inspiration, and even slower in accepting norms of a democratic kind in organizing relations within the Church itself, whereas their opposites, those of absolute monarchic system were better accepted. It is this that has led to the rather unpleasant separation of the Church from the historical processes of liberation in the West. One adds to these historical difficulties of the faith a specific unpreparedness in grasping the historical significance of contemporary changes on the historical and economic level.

The lack of both a critical and democratic tradition in the Church appears decisive in creating a readiness to accept, almost enthusiastically, various aspects of Marxism not only in the first phase of liberation theology in Latin America but still today. Nor should we ignore the influence on liberation theology of the particular condition of Latin American "subjection" to North American capitalist society; Marxism presents itself as a radical antithesis precisely in relation to a society with a capitalist structure. On the other hand, the religious tradition meets with many difficulties in understanding and criticizing it and seeing its high-risk nature for civilization.

In Latin America in the conciliar period Church and theological commitment were reemphasized in response to societal structural reforms permitting a religious distancing from the endemic condition of underdevelopment. Vatican II in contrast forcefully proposed commitment to earthly realities in the name of a renewed theology of creation and incarnation. Kennedy's New Frontier, offering not only a prospect of investments and economic development but also one of a partnership with the third world, seemed to respond to the new religious hopes.

The first great hope of liberation theology did not arise in the field of Marxism but from Kennedy's promise of a "capitalism with a human face." Many future liberation theologians were at first "development theologians," and this is where the special emphasis on economic reality was formed. Naturally, this was not a matter only or even mainly of theological work, but of movements, mobilization of social groups, and a concern for social welfare. But the uncontrolled penetration of capitalism in Latin America took on very different characteristics from the ideals imputed to Kennedy. "Real capitalism" with the autonomous or contrived connivance of military and civilian hierarchies devastated the development of whole societies. Political power became a vehicle for the appropriation and expropriation of national wealth. An unbridgeable gap was opened between elements involved at the base of the Church and the summit of society, as was a religious gap, when the Church hierarchy was silent as regarding this exploitation. One can speak of disappointment of messianic religious hopes, since the New Frontier was greeted as a commitment to liberation.

The depth of the disillusionment following the failure of the New Frontier explains the passage or "switch of front," to the enthusiastic reception of Marxism and radical forms of socialism. This switch, for example, led to the Brazilian episcopal conference, which at Medellin produced a very radical document, later also echoed by Cardinal Pellegrino's Walk Together, both standing in sharp contrast to the earlier accommodating attitude to the military hierarchy. When the radical *prise de conscience* against the unjust structure of society was supported by the bishops and other authoritative exponents of Church life, a shift occurred in the attitude of the ordinary pastoral work of whole dioceses to acceptance of liberation theology. In other cases, there was a tension between ordinary and alternative pastoral care. One may state that liberation theology in the last twenty years has been deeply inserted into the Latin American Church fabric. There are no comparable cases in the churches of the West, except directly in Vatican Council II.

Evangelical Demands, Existential Coherence, and the New Political Theology

Gutierrez has stated the South American position:

What in the last analysis drives Christians to participate in the freeing of oppressed peoples and exploited social classes is the conviction of the total incompatibility between evangelical demands and an unjust and alienating society. They feel with great clarity that they cannot claim to be Christians without taking on a commitment to liberation. But the way this action for a juster world is combined with a life of faith is still as the intuitive level, one of searching, and passes through difficult periods.[18]

In Brazil, and generally in Latin America, the "evangelical demands" Gutierrez speaks of are experienced directly and are never an alibi. They pose for the believers a problem of existential, not merely intellectual, coherence. A recent interview with Clodovis Boff, brother of the better-known Leonardo, helps us understand some situations in the church communities of the base in Brazil.

When you see the communities of the base that rely on the primitive community; there everything was in common, they put everything in common—their first move is to say, "So, why don't we live the Gospel, the suggestion of the Apostles? But we should have everything in common; so, let's do it." But they become aware at once—"But can't we sell, do like them? It's impossible." And they conclude, "So, we'll set up a common fund for the sick. We'll found a big community, a common work place, for all, etc." Aside from this, they say, "So, let's work until there is a society where everything is in common. We must found unions and parties so that this society will come." This means that the communities have a modernizing interpretation, are simply inspired by the community of the Acts. Only the intellectuals from afar say, "They are archaists, they go there and think of repeating, importing to today a proposal of two thousand years ago." One must interpret the language in its practical context, not outside its concrete context. It is precisely when you read their speeches and writings that you run the risk of making this interpretation. The people have much more common sense than the intellectuals because they feel the concrete constraints of the present, the social limitations. They know they cannot do like the Apostles because today's is a mass society, industrial, modern. So, the social problem is resolved not at the level of a communitarian consumer communism, but of a societal, productive one.

It is clear this does not arrive all at once. It arrives through reflection, discussion, talking. For the church communities of the base, the problem of archaism does not exist, it exists only in the interpreters' heads. We have learned we mut learn reality with our heads, yes, but also with our bodies, our feet. Reality isn't Cartesian, clear and distinct. . . . I think a second great challenge is this: the internal, or intrinsic organization of these communities. You see, they are spread all over the country, practically all the regions of the Episcopal Conference have experience of communities of the base. . . . The churches of the communities of the base in Maranhao, a state in North Brazil, worked, in the 1960s when I began until 1982, on the margins of the official Church and were tolerated, and also persecuted, by the Bishops. And from that time they have always worked as ecclesial groups, always offering dialogue with the Bishops even if the Bishops didn't want it. When in 1982 they had a big rally to reflect on their experience as communities, and I was present, the Bishops sent a Bishop as their representative to examine the experience. And the Bishop came back transformed, converted. He saw this was an ecclesial experience, evangelical. And then they designated a Bishop to accompany them officially. It means these communities have won the right to ecclesial citizenship. This is now a little the problem: if you enter the structures, you can be involved in structures, and the popular impulse then is broken.[19]

The problem as it is seen and experienced by liberation theologians, lies in preventing the prophetic spirit of the movement, once recognized by the Church hierarchy, to cool down and become sclerotic in bureaucratic routine. Gutierrez, perhaps the theologian who is most clearly aware of this problem, states: "What meaning does it have, then, this struggle, this *creation*? And what does this choice for *man* mean? What does *newness* in history, orientation to the future, mean?"[20] Gutierrez recalls Marx's phrase in "Social struggles in France 1848–1850": "The current generation is like the Jews who were led into the desert by Moses. Not only must it conquer a new world but it must also disappear to make room for men fit for the new world." And in the very moment Gutierrez poses his questions, he remembers Kant's famous questions in the *Critique of Pure Reason*, "What can I know? What must I do? What am I allowed to hope?"

This direct connection between moral clarity and practical decisions is the distinctive feature of liberation theology. There are no alibis. Subterfuges, postponements, and exemptions are not allowed: "The ways of God's presence determine the forms of our encounter with Him. If humanity, if every one, is a living temple of God, then we encounter God in the encounter with men, in the commitment to the historical future of humanity."[21] Here the "new political theology" takes off and becomes an ambiguous, as the liberation theologians themselves recognize, and as its principal theorist, J. B. Metz, deeply influenced by Bloch[22] and Moltmann,[23] and clearly admits. The point is that with this theology no longer can jesuitical distinctions break the unity between social and religious life. The privatization of religion and faith has been the historical response to the critique of religion as ideology worked out by the Enlightenment and Marx. For this reason it is not surprising that the first task of political theology lies in the deprivatization of religion, which prevents the gospel message from falling back into indifference to the political.[24]

From this premise there flows the practico-political positions of liberation theology. The Latin American Church is bound, is

obliged, to report every dehumanizing situation, against brother-
hood, justice, and liberty: every sacralization of oppressive structures must be reported. This reporting must be public. If the
institutional Church has been compromised in supporting these
oppressive structures it too must be publicly denounced. A constant, daily critical encounter must be maintained between the faith
and historical reality. Violence itself cannot be condemned in the
abstract. It must be put in context, explained and understood in
specific situations, grasped in its nature as *extrema ratio* for the
defense of the humanity of human beings.

In this way one rediscovers the vocation, both historical and
prophetic, of the poor. Gutierrez writes, "Only a genuine solidarity
with the poor and a real protest against poverty as it appears today
will be able to provide a concrete and vital setting for a theological
discourse on the poor. The lack of sufficient commitment to the
poor, the emarginated, and the exploited is perhaps the chief reason
for the lack . . . of a solid, effective reflection on the witness of the
poor. . . . [T]his witness today represents the inevitable and
pressing testing ground for the authenticity of its [the Church's]
mission."[25]

Notes

1. Guido Verucci, *La chiesa nella società contemporanean* (Rome-Bari: Laterza,
   1988), 423–424.
2. See my *Oltre il razzismo—Verso la società multirazziale e multiculturale*
   (Roma: Armando, 1988), 64–65.
3. Later we shall see that among the contemporary theologians more critical of
   "classical theology" one now speaks currently of "Christianity without the
   name."
4. See F. Balbo's *L'uomo senza miti* (Turin: Einaudi, 1945), 13–18.
      The little Machiavellis of the decadence say clearly with their beings that the
   Great Machiavelli needs heart and soul, that without prophets (who for Machiavelli are unarmed) the world cannot go forward, that the world is dying
   without saints. The Great Machiavelli is more than Machiavelli, he is the whole
   man. He is also a prophet because he is not content with saying "if men were
   good . . . " but makes them good, and even has himself killed by them to have
   them live and make themselves better. He knows men as they are only to make
   them be as they should be. Now, one understands that Machiavelli is only a
   means for man, and like his opposing prophet unarmed, is dust that is dis-
   persed, *vanitas vanitatum*. They are men without blood and animality without
   Man, unillumined men, men who do not suffer with the world, who condemn

themselves to nullity. . . . Faith in the unknown god of conscience today returns as in the earliest days of Christianity and the last of the Greco-Roman world, and opens up as the noblest, highest *prise de position*, the genuine attitude of man without Revelation, man alone.

5. The concept of religion as "opium of the people," a *topos* of Marxist propaganda in its ingenuous and popularizing form, has, along with the theory of secularization, taken a hard blow from postconciliar events and the resumption of militant religiosity, as morally intransigent as politically active against the economic leaders and dominant politicians.

6. H. Heine, *Historisch-kritische Gesamtausgabe der Werke*, vol. 11 (Hamburg, 1978), 103; see also my *Una teologia per atei* Rome-Bari: Laterza, 1983.

7. See, especially for my overall interpretation on Constantine, Santo Mazzarino, *La fine del mondo antico* (Milan: Rissoli).

8. See Carl Schmitt, *Politische Theologie: Vier Kapitel zue Lehre von der Souveränität* (Berlin: Duncker und Humblot, 1934)(????? 1922).

9. G. Gutierrez, *La forza storica dei poveri* (Brescia: Queriniana, 1961), 45.

10. Gutierrez, 75.

11. Antonio Sbisà, *Il primo dissenso cattolico*, (Florence: Le Monnier, 1976), 7.

12. L. Boff, *Gesù Cristo Liberatore*, (Assisi: Cittadella, 1982), 56.

13. L. Boff, *Ecclesiogenesi, le comunità ecclesiali reinventano la Chiesa* (Rome: Borla, 1978), 47.

14. L. Boff, *Chiesa e carisma* (Rome: Borla, 1984), 20.

15. G. Gutierrez, *Teologia della liberazione* (Brescia: Queriniana, 1981), 71.

16. G. Gutierrez, *Teologia della liberazione*, (Brescia: Queriniana, 1981), 73.

17. José Miranda, *Marx e la Bibbia* (Assisi: Cittadella, 1974).

18. Gutierrez, *Teologia della liberazione*, 144.

19. Clodovis Boff, "Chiesa, miseria, iniziativa popolare in Brasile" (interview by M. I. Macioti), *La critica sociologica* 77 (Spring 1986): 16–17.

20. Gutierrez, *Teologia della liberazione*, 145.

21. Ibid., 191.

22. The reference is to E. Bloch, *Geist des Utopie* (Frankfurt: Suhrkamp, 1964).

23. See especially Jürgen Moltmann, "Dio nella rivoluzione" (interview at the World Student Conference, Turku, Finland, 23–31 July 1968).

    (i) We live in a revolutionary situation; history will increasingly appear under the form of revolution; we cannot responsibly concern ourselves with the future of man save in a revolutionary way; (ii) the new revolutionary situation has provoked serious identity crises in Christianity; the Churches and Christians will stop being those who impeded the free realization of man and only thus will they reconquer their true identity; (iii) the eschatological and messianic tradition of hope may give rise to a rebirth of the Christian faith in our revolutionary age; (iv) the new theological criterion lies in practise; (v) Christians must align themselves on the side of the oppressed; the Church is not the divine judge of controversies in the world; (vi) the problem of violence or non-violence is not a real one; the only question is knowing if violence is just or unjust, and identifying the proportion means in relation to ends; (vii) the presence of Christians in the revolution may lead to their freeing from the constraints of the law.

24. See J. B. Metz's presentation at the Toronto International Congress of Theology, 20–24 August 1967, in *Zur Theologie der Welt* (Mainz-Munich: Queriniana, 1969), 99–116.

25. Gutierrez, *Teologia della liberazione*, 298. In this context, compare with the work of Giulio Girardi, especially *Sandinismo, marxismo, cristianesimo—la confluenza* (Rome: Borla, 1986); the book is chiefly concerned with the popular revolution in Nicaragua, but the questions dealt with are of general interest, as they concern the theoretical bases of Marxism and the theological ones of Christianity.

2

The Neo-Constantinian Temptation

The "Man in Rituation" of Paul VI

Despite its richness there is nothing in European Catholic dissent to compare with this hard, simple, coherent radicalness. Not even the Dutch catechism,[1] whose formulas were particularly explicated by E. Schillebeeckx's remarks and borne in mind by the more recent theologians of liberation, approaches this kind of commitment in society. K. Rahner's "anonymous Christianity," like E. Schillebeeckx's "Christianity beyond the visible frontiers of the Church" are important contributions to the renewal of the Church. They are decisive to bring it into the new phase of "post-Constantinian Christianity." The boundaries between the life of faith and earthly task have become more fluid. There is talk of a "Christianity without the name." Rahner applied the Johnian notion of People of God to the whole world. But none of these positions, though open and dedogmatic, can stand alongside (as regards the coherence of belief and experience) the experience of liberation theologists. They are Latin American experiences, but their significance goes beyond the historical and geographical context to present itself as an essential referent of universal importance.

It is not surprising that the reaction of the institutional Church has been hard. John Paul II and Monsignor Joseph Ratzinger have been stubborn. Butchers and victims have been put basically on the same level:

Situations of grave injustice require the courage of reforms in depth and the suppression of unjustified privileges. But those who discredit the path of reforms in favor of the myth of revolution not only feed the illusion that the abolition of an unjust situation is enough in itself to create a more human society but even favor the advent of totalitarian regimes. The struggle against injustice has no meaning unless carried out with the intention of setting up a new social and political order in conformity with the needs of justice. This ought to mark the stages of its institution. There is a morality of means. These principles should be respected particularly in the extreme case of recourse to armed struggle. . . . One can never admit, either on the part of established power nor by insurgent groups, recourse to criminal methods.[2]

Established power and insurgent groups, butchers and victims, exploiters and exploited: all are placed equally on the same level, judged by the same yardstick, outside any historical context with judgements that come down from above on the basis of premises supposedly atemporal and abstractly compelling. The "man in his situation" who seemed to be at the center of Paul VI's pastoral and theological concerns is wholly forgotten. As Don Enzo Mazzi, one of the first inspirers of Catholics of dissent in Italy, rightly fears, a return to the Middle Ages is always possible. With John Paul II a phase of restoration, covered by practical activism and showmanship that are certainly extraordinary, has been long started and pursued with great shrewdness. Don Mazzi notes,

So, bridges of gold to the churches, so that they let themselves be coopted into the new power system with the task of controlling and channeling this untrustworthy and fleeting aspect of human reality. . . . It has been called the neo-Constantinian temptation. The signs of yielding are before our eyes. One can not otherwise explain this tough centralizing ecclesiastical policy, the stifling of the periphery, the authoritarian intervention of the hierarchy in every ethical question, the inflexible rigidity of doctrine, the explosion of integralist crusades, and the uninhibited use of the crisis of public institutions to invade the fields of welfare and schools with religious preferences.[3]

Man in Movement, or Man under Guard?

It is often necessary to hunt the fine print of the news for the practical consequences of the positions of principle assumed by the Church hierarchy in the cloaked prose of official documents. The interview given by Monsignor J. Ratzinger to the weekly *Comunione e Liberazione* is valuable in this respect.[4] It is important above all because it restates with great clarity some principles of

Catholic moral doctrine that were rightly believed rather obsolete and that seemed at all events rather blunted by recent authoritative statements—especially in the light of Paul VI's uncertainties and the not-forgotten "openings" of Vatican II in its earlier stages. As regards that phase, dominated by John XXIII, one would say the official Church today is trying a quiet return to normality. The careful, circumspect replies of Monsignor Ratzinger leave few doubts in this respect. The image of man "in his situation" is flattened. We are distant from Felice Balbo's conception of "man without myths": "Man awakens in other men, conscience is aroused with his neighbor's by means man does not possess in his own right, does not construct, but *finds himself like birth: the personal or religious path.* But he does possess in his own right action and work, the way to liberation."[5]

Monsignor Ratzinger's integralism is wise. It is integralism suited to the times, which are electronic and essentially marked by the synchronic copresence that is made possible by the new means of transmission and sending of data.

> In reality, all information is either religious or adapts what it reports. This is all the more so for the Catholics and their media. The faith is destined to penetrate life in all its branches and expression: the faith is destined to become flesh and change the world. It would be a serious error to create a ghetto where one is concerned with matters of faith leaving the world as it is or dividing it into two sectors (what concerns the sacred and what the profane). From the incarnation and the cross (which is not a reduction of the incarnation but its full acceptance, going to the bottom of being, of death so as to change totally), the faith extends to the resurrection and transforms the reality of this world. . . . [U]nity (in the communion of the faith, Peter's successor, the visibility of the Church) and being free are inseparable. We believe liberty does not arise from the void, as Sartre thinks; for him, man is an absolutely indeterminate being, who has to create from himself, in a void of meaning, his own life. Liberty, on the contrary, is arriving at the truth, being united with the root of being, that is, God. We are free by possessing freedom. . . . One no longer believes that man has something to hope that goes beyond his doing. For that reason no limits are accepted.

However, this discussion, which is not without its stimulating sequentiality, is contradictory. On one hand he complains that man is reduced to doing for his own sake. On the other, he states man accepts no limits. Monsignor Ratzinger clarifies this: "There is something indefinite and gloomy in the optimism that comes from the progress of science and doing. No, human hope and greatness do not lie there. Rather, they lie in this very concrete relation with God who speaks to us, knows us, in the certainty that beyond our action there is a victory of the good and truth, which cannot either be produced or destroyed by us.''

The dialogue with God, what I should call the metahuman that illumines the human, is thus essential. Agreed, but what God? And through what mediations? The ancient Romans, both in the choice of their emperors and as regards the gods, were peculiarly alien to provincial pettiness. It has been remarked that in A.D. 193, when the legions of upper Pannonia, in agreement with those of the Rhine, acclaimed their general, Lucius Settimius Severus, emperor, it was an African who ascended the throne, more accurately, a Libyan. Severus was born in Leptis Magna, a city on the coast of North Africa the Greeks had named Libya. As regards religion, the ancient Romans had the same breadth of views. In their genuinely catholic or universal vocation, they kept an empty altar in their Pantheon, dedicated to the unknown God, as if leaving a place free at a great banquet for a guest who might by chance arrive late.

This must have been the spirit that inspired John XXIII's great ecumenical impulse and seemed to have found in the 1987 Assisi interreligious encounter its concrete, historic incarnation. Monsignor Ratzinger's words in this connection are like a cold shower:

An interpretation of Assisi that sees in Christianity, in the Catholic church, only a possibility for dialogue, only a platform, ends in relativism, in idology. Basically, when I started teaching philosophy of religion, I found in liberist [sic] circles themselves this same argument. It was said, ''We men cannot know the truth about God, they are all aspects of the intangible; we can understand them in symbolism, whose content ulltimately we do not know.'' This would be the end not only of Christianity but also of humanism, as by this hypothesis man has no recognizable essence. To say ''this is man'' would be absurd, and so arbitrariness would prevail. . . . This is precisely the deeply erroneous interpretation of Assisi, and yet the most frequent. It is said, ''No confusion, everyone retains his identity without syncretism, and we have dialogue because we know these identities are only historical . . . '' But this is the ultimate rejection of truth! This cannot be the model. There is dialogue when one moves toward the truth. Only by moving toward the truth do we respect everyone, respect ourselves, and can finally arrive at true peace, which without truth does not exist. . . . The category of truth and the dynamism of truth must be proposed again. The attitude that says, ''We all have values, no one possesses the truth''— this shows a static position, opposed to real progress. To accept these historical identities is to close oneself in historicism. One must oppose this vision with the dynamism of truth. And Christ is the truth, and so the dynamic force of history toward which we must move."

It could not be said more clearly. Monsignor Ratzinger declares he wants to move toward the truth but speaks as one who at the same time already possesses this truth, and along with that, the key to interpreting and explaining it to all. Interreligious dialogue thus seems, rightly to some extent, no more than an instrumental discovery. According to Ratzinger's reasoning, there is a well-grounded fear that the old intolerant dogmatism will triumph, in the name of antihistoricism—dogmatism unilateral and authoritarian, that one thought defeated forever by the spirit of Vatican Council II. Monsignor Ratzinger's interview bears precious witness that confirms the doubts and fears recently expressed by Hans Küng, Leonardo Boff, and other well-known theologians.[6]

These authors put us on our guard against the ever lively dogmatism of the "Roman ecclesiastical bureaucracy." This bureaucracy, in their judgement, "has never wanted nor liked Vatican II and has continued to lament the image of the medieval pope, Counter-Reformation and antimodernist, of the years before the council, so as to be able later to restore it as soon as possible, even with the aid of modern techniques, as was recently done for the frescoes in the Sistine Chapel."[7] Attempts are not lacking. Toward the end of January 1989, Norbert Greinacher, one of the "rebel" theologians of Tübingen, with the better-known Hans Küng, managed the initiative by three hundred theologians who drew up the Cologne Declaration, a manifesto that ended for the time being with the showdown between the local church communities and John Paul II, who in the end managed to nominate and have the bishops of his choice accepted *obtorto collo* at Cologne and Salzburg.

This was not just a local event. New support for the declaration has come from Louvain, France, and Spain. All acknowledge that Karol Wojtyla is an attractive person with charisma and manages to be lovable. There are no problems of a personal kind. The tension involves questions of principle. The Declaration of Cologne was accused of being impregnated with Enlightenment spirit simply because it defended the reasoning of the local communities against the unilateral decisions of the Roman bureaucracy. The summons

to obedience from the curia was very harsh. But Norbert Greinacher said he was convinced that the roots of the Enlightenment
and the French Revolution contain deeply Christian values: obviously, not just liberty, equality, and fraternity, but other values as
well, such as critical reason, individual rights, and freedoms. In his
view, it is important to remember that in the first phase of the
revolutionary process it was priests of the lower clergy who were
the ideologues of the revolution. It was a real tragedy of the
Catholic church, but also of the Protestant churches, not to have
recognized for so long these Christian roots of the Enlightenment.
Unfortunately, there was also an encyclical of 1832, where freedom
of religion was stamped as "*quasi deliramentum*." Still, according
to the Tübinngen rebel theologians, there is need to build a great
bridge between the Christian faith and certain Enlightenment values, as Thomas Aquinas built a bridge between the Christian faith
and Aristotle. But that needs, necessarily and initially, the recognition of the rights of the ecclesial communities of the base.

This recognition that implies the right first to understand and
then the duty to obey, and arrives at considering the protest against
the central Church bureaucracy as a kind of "prayer," is difficult
for this pontificate. As with the two *Instructions* on liberation
theology and in the attitudes of the hierarchy toward the Declaration of Cologne one notes at least two things. First, there is a
strange, paradoxical ambivalence to Pope John Paul II, who goes
on holiday in the mountains and swims for exercise like any man of
his day, who seems modern and even uninhibited in his use of the
mass media and intercontinental jets;[8] yet at the same time, when
problems are at stake on which the life of men and women hang
today—family, sexual, social, and political questions—Karol
Wojtyla appears decided, authoritarian, and immovable. He seems
a real pope of the trenches, firmly tied to tradition, unyielding and
hostile to substantial renewal. Second, there is the relative weakness of this "strong" pope toward the archaic heresy of Monsignor
Marcel Lefebvre, against whom, on the other hand, the "weak"
Paul VI inveighed. If it still exists, one must conclude that John
Paul II's ecumenicism is a hegemonic one, based on the indisputa-
ble primacy of the Catholic church and its hierarchy.

The Myth of Development

Aside from theological and internal disciplinary questions, the most recent positions taken by the Church deserve careful attention. On the social question, twenty years after the important encyclical *Populorum progressio* of Paul VI, on the occasion of John Paul II's encyclical *Sollicitudo rei socialis*, the organ of the Holy See wrote that

> history will say that toward the end of the twentieth century the idea of the development of humanity, which had enthralled European culture, was weakened and almost dropped from sight, and a pope from afar has taken it up and purified it and associated it with the spirit of the Christian message, calling to realize it not only Catholics but all Christians and believers in the great religions. I write in this way to show the novelty of the encyclical and at the same time the continuity of the teaching it contains, drawn from the Christian roots of what is burned into the fibers of the human heart. This encyclical is directly linked to the first by John Paul II, *Redemptor hominis*, which had put man at the center of the Church's attention. It integrates and makes current the content of Paul VI's *Populorum progressio*. It is also directly linked to the theme of central importance in the pontificate of John Paul II, who is, as it were, called back to his primary task, of developing and cultivating man, that is, to his original pedagogic-humanistic sense, after so much talk of culture in the anthropological sense.[9]

However, the *Osservatore Romano* does not stop here. With the usual, if sometimes crude, sharpness and the flowing pen of Monsignor Pietro Rossano, rector of Lateran Pontifical University, I am taken to task for having stated in the first volume of this triology[10] that the phrase "the name of peace is development" made me shiver with apprehension. This phrase appeared in the encyclical *Populorum progressio* of Paul VI. My reasons for concern are not to be sought too far away.

My illustrious interlocutor and critic calls to my attention that "the development of which the pope makes himself the promoter does not concern primarily or exclusively the economic or technological aspect of human existence, even if this concerns important and *indispensable* [my emphasis] aspects: it engages the whole man, and calls for individual and collective growth, and the dimension of transcendence or religious consciousness." Monsignor Rossano continues, quoting the encyclical directly, "A merely economic development is not capable of freeing man and indeed on the contrary ends by subjecting him still more."

Up until now, things seem clear to me; development is not everything, or better, development is not only economic but on the contrary must be understood as one aspect only of the human presence in the world. Agreed, but a few lines earlier development is defined as an important and "indispensable" aspect. Not by chance, the *Sollicitudo rei socialis* opens with an explicit reference to the *Rerum novarum* of May 1891, the famous social encyclical of Leo XIII, which, everyone knows, was set out and published as an authoritative response to the doctrine and organizational advance of the socialist movement linked to the premises of Marxian historical materialism. Moreover, *Sollicitudo rei socialis*, after duly recalling and summarizing the basic themes of *Populorum progressio* of Paul VI and *Mater et Magistra* of John XXIII, confronts explicitly and very vigorously, precisely the question of development. And the treatment of this subject is not merely doctrinaire or a priori. This encyclical opens with a series of assertions of fact that give the whole encyclical a robust structure and precise placing in the economic and socio-political reality of today's world.

No one would ever dream of thinking that the pope had abandoned the postulates of transcendence or the dogmas of the ultimate destiny of man, or the concept of the common good of all humanity, supported and driven by the concern for the "spiritual and human development of all" instead of the search for individual profit. But it is a fact that the *Sollicitudo rei socialis* rests on a sociological and politological analysis of the world situation that permits no optimism about the famous Program for Development followed and, one might say, paraded by the United Nations for over twenty years and today, in the view of unbiased observers, headed for a depressing failure.

As always, the pope's text is cautious:

> One cannot say that these religious, human, economic, and technical initiatives are useless, given that they have managed to achieve some results. But generally, bearing the different factors in mind, one cannot deny that the present situation in the world, in terms of this development, presents a rather negative impression. . . . Leaving aside the analysis of figures or statistics, it is enough to look at the reality of a countless multitude of men and women, children,

adults, and old people—that is, of concrete and unique human persons, who suffer under the intolerable weight of poverty. Many millions are without hope because, in many parts of the world, their situation has markedly worsened.

Let us leave aside transcendence, the common good, and so forth. Here it is not a matter of debating about unilateral or global development. The pope speaks clearly here. Whatever Monsignor Rossano thinks, it is a matter of economic development, started with financial means and through the application of various technologies and maintained by specific national and international lines of policy. This development has not worked. This development not only has not improved the existing situation or the traditional deficiencies, it has dramatically worsened them. Why? Where are the causes? To confine oneself to deplore the increasing "gap" between North and South and register the same inequalities within the individual countries between rich and poor can furnish the now aged "dependency theory" and that of "internal colonies." But it does not help us understand the dynamics of the problem and so does not offer the means or even the general directions for resolving it. The encyclical correctly analyzes the specific indices of under-development and stresses three macroscopic and disturbing crises, those of housing, employment, and international debt. The third world countries are themselves called to task. In the pope's words, there is no concession to demagogy, nor to the condescension usually accompanying paternalistic attitudes. He writes, "Noteworthy are the undoubted, serious omissions on the part of the developing nations themselves and, especially, of those who hold economic and political power there."

However, these papal admonitions are a valuable indication of an attitude of acceptance on his part of the logic of modernization and economico-industrial development as the sole way open to humanity to break the vicious cycle of poverty that reproduces itself and to ensure a minimum of well-being. This is the problem I had in mind when I raised a critical doubt about the formula in *Populorum progressio*, that "the name of peace is development." I was not thinking of exclusively theological and religious questions of transcendence. I was thinking of the terrible error and depressing outcome of the age-old thought that falls victim to the myth of development and that of organization. Later, after his encyclical,

John Paul II called to task the West and East, the two blocs, but that for me is scant consolation. The world situation has changed, and one can no longer conceive of it in terms of two opposite, counterposed, and symmetrical blocs. Even before the coming to power of Mikhail Gorbachev it was clear that a powerful underground force was working, an isomorphic tendency whereby the two blocs, though formally counterposed in ideological and institutional terms, were now rapidly converging from a technico-productive and distributive viewpoint.

The emarginated world, cut out, was that which, while it could not keep pace with the rhythm of development of East or West, saw itself fatally condemned to poverty and endemic hunger because it had meanwhile lost its original rhythms, its mode of life and basic habits. It is not enough to ask that capitalism or bureaucratic collectivism should distribute more generously to all peoples the product of their technical progress. One must ask them not to lay hands on the third world, respect its dignity and integrity, its habits and history.

Perhaps it is already too late. Some time ago I noted in my *Five Scenarios for the Year 2000* (Rome-Bari: Laterza, 1985) that the fall of the colonial regimes in Asia and especially in Africa did not mean a new phase of economic and political progress as everyone hoped. It simply left a void, hard to fill. Imitation and imposition of technically advanced models of life provoked a political and economic desert—and often also a moral one. In Africa what has already occurred in Latin America is happening—urbanization without industrialization. Uprooted human masses abandon agriculture ruined by pseudomodernization, and settle in bidonvilles in cities without elementary services, jobs, and efficient administrative services. On the other hand, the old dietary habits that found satisfaction in local products are changed in a western European direction, but thus intensified dependence on the outside even for basic foodstuffs. However, strong currency for purchases is lacking. Together with pseudomodernization there arrive mass poverty and chronic famine.

The city-effect and spurious industrialization are destined to make their negative effects felt ever more sharply in the next twenty years. As regards the West, the local populations will fall into a situation of structural imbalance, for a reason evident and cruel in its simplicity: these populations now need Western products and manufactures they cannot do without but will never be able to pay for. In this perspective, it is not a matter of taking to task, politically speaking the two blocs East and West, putting them on the same level—which in any case would be a case of economic illiteracy and relative political blindness—but rather of clarifying and critically attacking the technico-productive logic that is essentially one of convergence. To continnue to speak of liberal capitalism and Marxist collectivism is no longer sufficient. They are worn-out formulas. They must be revised in the light of real and deeply reshaped historical processes.

Meanwhile, in the current situation of third world paralysis, the question of violence reemerges. It is pleasing to note that in the text of the encyclical there is no longer the simplistic, exorcising rejection of a complex social fact that it is vain to think can be resolved through simply removing it. In the pope's words, there is a terrible question, to be seized and meditated upon: "The peoples excluded from a just sharing of resources . . . might ask: Why not respond with violence to those who use violence against us first?" For the first time in a pontifical document, the distinction between "slow" or institutional violence and terroristic, bloody, explosive violence as a response to the former, is contemplated. It is a hard question, which refers us to the original problem of legitimacy, the very foundation of the City in which it seems necessary that Romulus should kill Remus.

As we see, the problems are themselves difficult, and touch on subjects of different kinds, from theological to economic and political ones, and cannot be satisfied with simplifying responses, which would be deceptive. It will be necessary to return to them at a suitable time.

From Vatican II to the Vatican as Always

Meanwhile one observes the emergence of a powerful wave of restoration. Pope Wojtyla finds it hard to recognize autonomy, even if only relative, in local churches. He seems rather indifferent to historical and cultural variation. He displays a naturally centripetal preference that rewards faithfulness to orthodoxy and centralized control as against recognition of specific peculiarities and needs. At the same time one asks about the possibility of a liberation theology in Europe. Open theologians and the curial bureaucracy are increasingly on a collision path. This situation cannot be adequately evaluated from within, in theological and doctrinal terms. It is necessary to bear in mind the economic, political, and general historical framework.

Never before has the European consciousness seemed so in crisis. It is not just a question of the decrease of great certainties or the "triumphal march" of scientific progress in unison with accompanying social and moral progress that already marked the European societies at the end of the last century. This century is ending in the insidious mists of a general crisis of "rationalistic rationality"[11] and the total dissolution of the nineteenth-century points of reference and orientation. It is not only this. The entry into history of whole peoples excluded until now, or perhaps only acknowledged as passive raw material to be converted and shaped according to European cultural models, shakes the supposed European primacy and raises fears for its short- or medium-term fall. Nor can the precise referral made by liberation theology and Catholic dissent in the communities of the base be seen today as decisive. This referral has been expressed up until now with a series of philological and hermeneutic efforts that have assailed, with a vigorous blast of passion for spiritual perfection and faithfulness to the teaching of the scriptures, the bureaucratic organization of the Church. They have attempted to measure the gap in historical and theologico-doctrinal terms, with respect to the initial ideals.

It is not only this. To study and try to understand the deep purpose of liberation theology means questioning oneself on the effective possibility of a return to the evangelical, pre-Constantinian origins of the Church, beyond and against the Gregorian reform. In other words, it means asking oneself about the possibility of "re-charismatizing" institutions now definitively bureaucratized. The problem concerns the fact that one can obey persons despite their quality. Once bureaucratized, the Church poses the problem of an institutional charisma, if one can accept this strange contradiction in terms. No doubt in the course of its long history there has been in the Church a constant contraposition between personal, institutional-personal, and institutional movements. It is not in fact possible to have personal charisma that can avoid the formation of countermovements. Perhaps the only example of institutional charisma is to be found in the Church's administration of the sacraments. Even if there is in them a guarantee of salvation, there is not, however, the certainty of an institutional charisma. At the least one might speak of sacramentalization, but not charismatization. It is true that the administration of charisma inevitably involves its becoming everyday, and hence its decrease, since we know that charisma is always linked to a social or institutional deviance ("It is written . . . but I say"). The end of charisma, any charisma, always lies in liberation from the traditional, or social and family, ties current. In this sense, liberation theology is a passionate search for a way to recharismatize the Church that shakes it as bureaucratic structure and proposes bringing it back to the purity of its origins. Resistance to this attempt is not surprising. It has been remarked that the attitudes of European theologians to liberation theology are basically reduced to four:

1. Liberation theology is a mortal threat for the Church as it bears within it the Marxist ideology destined to unhinge and ultimately destroy it.
2. Liberation theology can have a positive function, but European theology must maintain its specific character and methods. Dialogue yes, but no fusion, or, worse, confusion: no convergence, especially as regards analyses of the religious phenomenon in and for itself, aside from political prises de position.
3. Some European theologians tend to see in liberation theology only a Latin American position, unleashed by those conditions and so without validity and universal importance.
4. Finally, there are European theologians and Christians who recognize in liberation theology not only a Latin American phenomenon but also a demand for regeneration of the Church, which perhaps more directly concerns Europe than Latin America. It is thus not exhausted in an analysis of individual countries, but involvevs and renews theological method as such.

It seems clear that the European attitude toward liberation theology is linked to the cultural and political interpretation of the situation in third world countries, in Latin America and Asia, and their chronic underdevelopment, worsened today by the debts they have contracted to the countries of the developed world. This underdevelopment—what does it depend on? On their psychologico-intellectual inferiority, or the objective position of subalternity that the asymmetrical market relations tend to reduce them to, once they have entered the cycle of world economic interdependence? There is a second question following this one, which has been put clearly:

> Does their [the third world countries] economic and cultural progress lie in approaching most closely the North American and European models, or in freeing themselves from subjection to these, and opening up their own path? The dominant culture in the U.S. and Europe replies decidedly in the first sense, and tends to impose this response on the third world countries. Its analyses are dictated by a subtle form of racism. They transform historical relations into natural hierarchies: . . . they tell the story of colonialization in terms of civilization. . . . Moreover, these analyses are often appropriated by the dominant groups in the third world and are impressed on their peoples through systems of education imported from Europe and the United States.[12]

The awakening of the ex-colonial people, even though amid tearing sufferings and contradictions, is posed today in terms of challenge to Eurocentric culture and the Church of Pope Wojtyla too. This seems every day to present itself as the basic pillar of the former. It is not surprising that for this reason the centralization and summons to order of the local churches in direct contact with the practico-political and cultural problems of the emerging countries are again dominant problems. The world changes, and not only in Latin America. The German theologians themselves, and even the Italian ones, traditionally more loyal to the central authorities, not to mention the U.S. episcopate and the strong resistance of Catholic universities all over the world, are aware of it and call centralized power to task. But the Roman curia, whose new constitution was published in *Pastor bonus*, clearly established that every document of the Holy See should have the doctrinal guarantee of the Congregation for the Doctrine of the Faith.

The triumph of Monsignor Joseph Ratzinger seems consolidated, perhaps beyond his own hopes. The man who was once among the founders of the journal *Concilium*, the international review of progressive theologians, in 1965 declared himself quite contrary to the closing of the Church "in the narrow ghetto of an orthodoxy that does not even suspect its own sterility, and in any case makes itself all the more ineffective the more it stubbornly it does its duty." He also states: "It is not by fleeing the world that one can renew the Church; the attempt was already shipwrecked when the zealous Paul IV wanted to suspend the Council of Trent to renew the Church with the fanaticism of the zealot." Moving on to the review *Communio*, ten years after the council he published from Munich what might rightly be seen as the manifesto of restoration: "A real reform of the Church supposes an unequivocal abandonment of the erroneous paths that have meanwhile led to catastrophic results. One must distinguish the spirit of the council— that is, the council experienced in its spiritual and theological essence—from the Antispirit."

The Antispirit is everything that concerns the material plane, the real relations of life, the everydayness of the faithful. All the social openings of the council are reviewed and reformulated according to the canons of a rigorous spiritualistic reinterpretation. The hope of the oppressed vanishes. The return of the Church to the poverty of its origins fades. The organisms created by the council, especially those that should be concerned with ecumenicalism, are virtually reduced to silence. The basic fear that seems to stimulate the feverish work of restoration is not new. It is the ancient fear that any contact with contemporary culture is a risk, and that every outside influence necessarily leads to heresy.

This also explains Wojtyla's weakness with regard to Monsignor Marcel Lefebvre. Lefebvre's schism was made possible first of all by another deeper schism—a division that tears the Roman church itself apart. It is the reflection of the division over the interpretation of the council. There is still talk of ecumenicalism. The pope continues to travel all over the world, to get off the plane, and to bend down to kiss the earth. The words are always those of Vatican II, but the spirit has changed. Ceremony prevails, the spectacle triumphs. The Roman church is stationary before the notion of the People of God. In other words, it is stationary before the practical, material liberty of the local churches and the communities of the base. Before the unforeseeable consequences of this freedom, the curia stops, comes to terms with the old integralism, against which

Paul VI had courageously and unavailingly fought. Despite the declarations of ecumenicalism, and even after the great Assisi conference, where, however, each religion had prayed separately from the others, there is a return to the dogmatic closure of *Extra ecclesiam nulla salus*. Despite the noisy disagreement of the North American bishops and faithful, the sexual morality of the most antiquated tradition was reasserted. But this time the struggle was not, as in the times of Pius X's condemnation of modernism, against a few isolated scholars and commentators. This time the situation was different. It has been eloquently remarked that "it was a global confrontation against the feelings of the faithful, against the People of God that does not understand the condemnation of contraceptives as a new dogma. . . . Is it possible not to see the gravity in a situation, that is, the depth of the divisions rising from the Church? Between a Roman curia that does not accept the council and the laymen, or by definition the laywomen, given the practice of the Church on the priesthood, the women? These wounds now bleed in silence: one day they will cry out."[13]

Neointegralism confirms for us that the spirit of Vatican Council II has yielded to the Constantinian Vatican as always. The immutability of the Church is exalted. Yet the Christian message, from the historical and doctrinal viewpoint, has undergone very interesting changes: from the Pauline interpretation stressed by St. Augustine to politicization and transformation into state religion under the Roman empire, until the painful construction of the temporal power that was to entrust to the bishop of Rome all the political and spiritual prerogatives. This was the happy crowning of a process of institutionalization that guaranteed the security of the Church as hierocratic structure while announcing its end as charismatic power. The risk of today's closures is so great it is hard to believe that in the name of discipline the process of innovation started by John XXIII is definitively blocked. At stake is the relation between the ethic as preached and the ethic as lived. The dogmatism of the hierarchy wanders in the void. It could simply transform itself into an alibi for mass hypocrisy.

The Revolt of the European Theologians

After Latin America, the Cologne Declaration, and the documents issued by French and Spanish-speaking theologians, Catholic historians and theologians in Italy too are are in ferment. In fact, when the discussion of the Cologne Declaration—signed by 163 Central European theologians against the Vatican's centralism and authoritarianism—was still at its height in Europe and the world, a document appeared, drawn up and signed by 63 Catholic historians, philosophers, and theologians from Italy. These were involved in universities, the mass meedia, and other Italian academic institutions.[14] With apparent modesty, this document was entitled, *A Letter to Christians: In the Church Today*. The form was much less peremptory than the German document, but its substance, even in an initial, swift reading, was equally demanding. The passages concerning the image of Pope Wojtyla's Church appear particulaly forceful:

> It seems to us that . . . there is a tendency to forget that the Church, not only at the individual level, but in its institutional structure, relations with states and the style of its preaching, should not let itself be influenced by worldly logic, but rather by the style of Christ, mild and humble in spirit, poor, come to save the lost sheep. . . . The conversion of our communities and the whole Church to this style of Christ's, to which Vatican II appealed, is a basic condition of obedience to our Lord.

This preamble, cautious in form but very determined in substance, prepares the ground for the central argument of the document, which directly concerns the organizational structure of the Church, though in the most diplomatic manner possible. "A basic point of ecclesiologial conciliar theory, even though a most delicate one, is the conception of the Church as a communion of churches. This will involve, inevitably, though not without travails, a change in the institutional equilibrium that, especially in the Latin church, has been solidifying to a particular degree in the second millennium of its history." The tone is so cautious it appears uncertain. It comes close to such conciliatory terms as to appear almost in doubt. "We are aware that there are no easy solutions whereby the unity of the faith and the 'great discipline' become an effective gift from the multicolored richness of the plurality of communion." The theologians and scholars who signed the document here make an historical aside, as though to comfort the hierarchy by reminding it that the Church has already lived through even darker and more uncertain periods than the present one. "It is enough to think of the very beginnings of the Church, the conflict between Paul and

James, or the times of Cyprian, and Pope Stephen, of Athanasius and Basil, Cyrillus and John Chrysostom, to be aware that the major conflicts in the life of the Church have been overcome only slowly, and through the suffering of everyone.

Here, we have reached the heart of the document. It concerns ecclesiastical teaching. More exactly, it concerns whether this is to be understood as an exclusive monopoly of the bishops or should also be open to laymen. "One of the lements that has entered a phase of 'readjustment' in the conciliar conception of the Church is undoubtedly the understanding of teaching," the Italian theologians state. Again, one observes their caution, which does not, however, prevent explicit statements: "One cannot ignore the fact. Moreover, the history of theology teaches us how the very term 'teaching' has undergone major semantic changes. Furthermore, one cannot deny that in the Church at its origins there was a teaching function not to be reduced to that of the guidance of the community. It does not seem to us that to define teaching as pastoral implies an attack on its dignity or necessity, and that, rather, it raises up its task of presiding over the communion of faith."

The Disquiet of the People of God

The theologians' revolt shows in the above its deepest purpose. First, it expresses the genuine disquiet of the faithful at the lower levels. Second, it aims at raising a question regarding the ability of the hierarchical Church to come face to face with the needs of the "new times." The language is cautious, much more diplomatic and veiled than that of their German colleagues. And yet, Monsignor Poletti, initially, and explicitly, and later the pope himself, more warily, criticized the public expression of this disquiet, and warned against the risk of a parallel Church. This would put the Church's existence at risk, along with its basic prerogatives, according to the letter of the Credo—*"unam, sanctam, catholicam, apostolicam, romanam."*

In the words of Cardinal Poletti, the official reaction of the Church was not long in coming, in his role as president of the Italian Conference of bishops. It was a harsh lesson, despite the air of general caution and respectfulness that marks the document of the Italian theologians. Poletti stated,

> The [Italian theologians'] "Letter" wishes to differentiate itself from other positions, through its less aggressive tone. . . . However, in essence, both the arguments advanced and still more the questions raised and the attitudes that appear make a statement of clarification on our part indispensable. . . . The charges and the claims, though put forward in forms more allusive than explicit, mainly refer to a supposed tendency to diminish the importance of Vatican Council II and to related regressive pressures said to run through the Catholic church. . . . However, the questions raised by the "Letter," still in a rather allusive way, regarding ecclesiology, the function of teaching, and its relation with the role of theologians, in reference to the interpretation of Vatican Council II, deserve more serious attention. Indeed, there seems to emerge a conception of the Church as "communion of churches" conceived of in such terms as to imply an alteration or attenuation of Catholic doctrine concerning the one, universal Church, and the primacy of the pope.

The response of John Paul II appears more indirect and certainly less drastic. The Italian theologians deal with some specific questions: "regressive pressures" and "worldly logic" in the Church; episcopal conferences; the appointment of bishops. The pope confined himself to replying to what explicitly involved the special role of theologians. More than a reply, it was a recall. We see the same prudence as inferred by the pope's silence regarding the French, German, and Spanish theologians. In Italy, the pope responded to the Italian theologians only because, possibly, he himself is an Italian bishop, the bishop of Rome.

However, it does not seem that the internal polemics in the Catholic church have seriously weakened civil commitment as regards Italy. Two Jesuits have for some time run the Istituto Pedro Arrupe (from the name of the late, lamented general of the Company of Jesus), in the heart of Mafia activity in Palermo. Their program, though said to be strictly apolitical and directed at religious education alone, are explicitly intended to create a new, local, ruling class—a ruling class in the broadest sense, that is, as governing class, class of influence.[15] The attacks on the Jesuit Bartolomeo Sorge, former editor-in-chief of *Civiltà Cattolica*, and Ennio Pintacuda, are innumerable. They also come from the Catholic hierarchy, from the bishops themselves, united in the assembly of the Italian Episcopal Conference. Political forces in government, like the Italian Socialist party, see in the supposedly pedagogic initiatives of the two Jesuits the secret inspiration of the "anomalous" local executive of the Comune of Palermo, which includes communists. However, the Jesuits, far from novices, historically, to intrigues of this kind, are holding firm and will probably win through. The wind is in their favor. The times when the cardinal of Palermo, Ernesto Ruffini, replied almost contemptuously to a discreet request for information from Paul VI that the Mafia did not exist, and that anyway it had been defeated by fascism (one of its merits that should, along with the punctuality of the trains, be acknowledged)—these times are far away. The current Catholic hierarchy has changed its tune. Not only is the existence of the Mafia admitted, but excommunication of Mafia bosses is requested: both for the chiefs and their followers, or *picciotti* (the foot-soldiers, in Mafia slang), as well as for their supporters, it is proposed that access to the sacraments should be prohibited. No church weddings, communion and confirmation, no baptism. Once Ruffini was dead, his successor Cardinal Pappalardo by 1982 was denouncing the Mafia as a social phenomenon, no longer only as individual criminality.

In fact, excommunication for "Mafia crimes" had already been threatened, at least for Sicily, since 1952. "Those who undertake robberies or sully themselves with premeditated murder—including those who order them, the material perpetrators, and accomplices—incur the excommunication reserved to the power of the Ordinary, that is, it can only be lifted by the bishop." This "punishment" was later confirmed by the Sicilian bishops on October 21, 1982. Currently, there are two novelties: excommunication has been extended beyond Sicily, thereby recognizing the Mafia as not only a local problem, but a national, even international, one. Aside from the crimes actually committed, those responsible for the organizations, the chiefs and their commanders, are also targeted. Three regions are directly involved, Sicily, Calabria, and Campania, with their related criminal organizations, Mafia, 'Ndrangheta, and Camorra. It is pointless to hide the difficulties that practical application of the ecclesiastical provisions involves. It will be hard for the many parish priests who live out their pastoral experience in the disarming honesty of Don Abbondio—"If someone lacks courage, no one can give it to him"—to refuse, for example, to let persons of notorious criminality act as godfathers at baptisms and communions. Now there is a "Church in the trenches" that will require of its priests and faithful an approach that goes far beyond the traditonal, all-in-all ritualistic, one.

Nor can one say that on the international scene the internal debates of the Church of Rome have for the present compromised ecumenical enthusiasm as regards the rest of the Christians. At Basle, about the middle of May 1989, all the European Christian churches, from East and West, met for a common discussion of "peace and justice." The choice of Basle as meeting place was not a chance one. In fact, we are in the heart of Europe, the "common house," even if still a divided one. Here, in 1431, the last great council before the Protestant breakaway of the following century was held, in a tormented phase of history where the doctrine of papal supremacy had to endure a heavy defeat. Erasmus of Rotterdam died in Basle and was buried, though a Catholic, in the Protestant cathedral. Again in Basle, Calvin drew up the first version of his *Institutio religionis christianiae*. Here, Dr. Falke opened the proceedings of the 1989 conference of all the Christians of Europe with a courageous search of conscience: "We come from a divided Europe; we come from separate Churches. We come from a Europe where the forces of change confront those of conservation. We come from a Europe that has made itself blameworthy before the world." Archbishop Cyril of Smolensk took the critical examination further into its historically specific terms:

> The 1917 revolution was born to create a new society for the good of man. But the fatal course of events, whose meaning we have yet to comprehend, produced the result that the accent placed on the construction of the future cancelled out the present, just as collective rights and aspirations to equality have obscured the rights and liberties of the human individual. In the name of the future have been sacrificed not only personal rights and the freedom of those who lived in the present, but often also human lives themselves.

The preliminary document of the assembly seemed imbued with this self-critical spirit.

> We have no right to speak as if we possessed the truth. The Church and Christians have often erred and have not lived in accordance with the word of

God. . . . We have sinned in considering Europe as the center of the world, and ourselves as superior to others on the earth. . . . We have too easily and often even justified war. . . . We have not overcome the divisions between the Churches and have often abused the authority and power we have been given. We must overcome the divisions between men and women in the Church and in society. We must recognize the gifts women have received for the life and management of the Churches.

Ecumenism is certainly not an invitation to an idyll. During his recent visit to the countries of Northern Europe, while he sharply criticized the widespread hedonism, John Paul II often said he was optimistic and found general confirmation regarding the progress of religious freedom.[16] The pope's optimism, especially in Denmark, collided with the coldness of a cutting logic. Luther's condemnation is still in force. The Church of Rome should withdraw it. However, a still more important condition is that we must recognize that visibility is not truth, and that the Church of Rome cannot proclaim itself ecumenical and at the same time continue to have of itself and of its own hierarchy a conception higher than that of Christ himself—one that puts it above all the other churches. Thus a basic theme that runs through all the theologies of liberation in Latin America as well as in Europe, underground and powerful, returns: what is under discussion is the Church as hierocratic power structure. The pope's primacy is itself called in question. The conviction that a critical doubt raised over papal infallibility could be an advantage for the Pope himself, and certainly for the Catholic church, is starting to make headway. Not by chance, the Church is more lively and socially open in those cultures where the dead hand of a dogma that by its very nature cuts off any discussion at its outset has not borne down.

Against Centralism: For the 'Open Church'

For these reasons, I do not believe that here we are dealing with a purely personal question, hingeing on the complex personality of the Polish pope, the traveling, television pope, and at the same time, the pope from the trenches. Undoubtedly Pope John Paul II poses a serious problem for anyone trying to evaluate his doctrinal and pastoral teaching on the basis of the customary frameworks of a crudely political interpretation—as pope of the left or right, innovative and socially "open," or conservative, if not even reactionary. These categories of judgement do not seem adequate; they correspond to ways of grasping ideologico-political orientations that are largely obsolete. With a considerable effort of imagination, it has on the other hand been suggested that this pope is the "first postmodern pope,"[17] and not an antimodern one, according to a tradition that runs from Pius IX to Pius XII.[18] In other words, John Paul II is said to provide a reasonable example of how to put the cultural emargination to which modernity has condemned the Church to good use. It seems he manages to reverse a situation of undoubted marginality to the point of making it a position of prophetic prevision. Here the most evident contradiction appears: we have a very mobile pope, a tireless traveler, a skier and a swimmer, who can use all the discoveries of most advanced modern technology according to the norms of a strategy of emotional mobilization that has undoubtedly produced some results on the global scale. Yet at the same time we have a closed, inaccessible, even dogmatic and authoritarian pope, when, for example, he is faced with such problems as contraception, even though he knows he has against him the mass behavior of the majority of Catholics in technologically advanced societies.

It is no surprise that in such conditions, those Catholic theologians who are most perceptive experience a growing unease and cannot bear a Roman centralism that is increasingly tinged with personalized judgement. One theologian has written:

> The pope we anticipate sees his function as a function of the Church. He would never be outside or above the Church, but, rather, in it, with it, for it. Then, there would be no more externalization, isolation or triumphalism from the pope, and so the pope would no longer be alone, but rather ever set on seeking unity wth the Church and perfecting it anew each time. Before taking important decisions or publishing important documents, he would assure himself of the cooperation of the bishops and the best theologians and laymen. . . . He would never consider the promise made to Peter as his personal inspiration, but rather as a special assistance in consultation and collaboration with the Church, to which the Spirit is promised as to a whole.[19]

Roman neoauthoritarianism has above all been demonstrated with regard to the government of the local churches. In particular,

John Paul II has used the appointment of bishops to guarantee himself centralized control without blemishes. According to some observers, a veritable *identikit* of perfectly suitable bishops is said to have been prepared, following John Paul II's orders: legitimate sons of Catholics, healthy, clearly opposed to female priesthood, oriented with the pope's position regarding the celibacy of the clergy. Recent events in Brazil and the U.S. are significant examples of the intolerance of the ecclesial base. In the United States, a black priest, George Stallings, was suspended by the archbishop of Washington for having celebrated mass without respecting the traditional liturgy. The substance of the disagreement, however, seems to affect deeper attitudes.

According to Stallings, this concerns the racism that marks the American Catholic church: "For the Catholic church the white priests come first, then the white priests who say mass in black districts, and finally, last, the black ghetto priests, like me." There was a deluge of denials, but it is hard to deny certain facts: only 2 million of the 54 million American Catholics are black. Of 19,000 priests, only 300 are black, and 13 of 314 bishops. The black priest of Washington is seen as a threat to the unity of American Catholics.[20] At the same time in Brazil a new dispute on the role of the "Church of the Poor" in Latin America has sprung up. At the fifth meeting of SOTER, the association of Brazilian theologians (5–7 July 1989), a statement denouncing the Vatican's measures against the Brazilian church was made public. It reads:

> Neither the people nor we understand certain measures taken against some of our bishops who have chiefly defended, and now defend, the poor. . . . The Church seems to be undoing the work done by Dom Helder Camara, the friend of the poor. . . . The people are confused and we are dismayed when certain bishops, without considering the episcopal commission on doctrine, launch suspicions and accusations through the mass-circulation papers against our brothers and comrades, like Leonardo Boff and Father Nesters.

With good cause, the Roman curia fears the rise of a "parallel Church." Instead, a real underground Church is developing, which views its legitimation in the attempt to seize the great transformations of human coexistence today and to link them with the spirit of the dogmas of Catholic morality, even at the price of historicizing them, by sweeping aside their ahistorical immobility. The institutional Church feels obscurely threatened by the growing requests for autonomy on the periphery, and by ever less docile ecclesial communities. In fact, it is not the institution in itself that is called into question, but rather the sclerotic institution, that is, the institution that falls back on itself to defend its own traditional image and supposed integrity. Paradoxically, at the moment when the maximum of flexibility seems necessary, when it should open to the new, it presents serried ranks against the "social" in ferment. It refuses to understand what is different, severs the ties binding it to transitional society—basically, its raison d'être. In the new situation, theology and the Church are forced to look reality in the eye: "How can we speak in the name of God in our time and respond to the reality of God as a community? . . . Who is it who we come up against concretely in history?"[21]

What was viewed by many and presented as an ecclesial matricide appears as the precondition for recovery and salvation.[22] One must be freed from the preconception that sees in Christianity a supremacy of values beyond discussion, the crowning of a necessary historical development, and the sole prospect to which human beings on a global scale can aspire. These are reflections of an unconscious ethnocentrism—from which one must escape, if one seriously wants to avoid the fatal collision between cultures—starting off, instead, a genuine intercultural dialogue.[23] One cannot deny that the Vatican Council II gave a decisive push in this direction. Equally obvious are the attempts to block the process of renewal. A Church with open doors is necessary. Perhaps opening the doors will not even be enough. It is the Church itself that must be opened so as to avoid dogmatic defensiveness and sectarian closure. It has been said,

> In the future, we must take the risk not only of a church with "open doors," but of an "open church." We cannot stay in the ghetto, and we cannot go back. . . . However, there is without an explicit doctrine, a series of proofs of the existence of a ghetto mentality, which tries to preserve clarity, order, piety, and orthodoxy by giving the Church a form that, in terms of the sociology of religion and political ideas, is that of a sect.[24]

The sterile purity of orthodoxy would be merely the antechamber of a spiritual desert and historical irrelevance.

Rather contradictorily, theological closure is joined in John Paul II with unexpected openings on the strictly diplomatic and political level. Thus Pope Wojtyla turned during the Lebanese crisis to the "Muslim brothers," an unheard-of historical gesture, or again, visiting the University of Pisa in September 1989, let it be understood it was time to review the trial of the "great Galileo," and that anyone who "opposed" him was "imprudent." At the same time, the pope urged the scientists to "respect nature," but without seeming to understand the radical difference between science and scientism—a real break. John Paul II explained: "I do not want my observation to be one that limits every just freedom or legitimate autonomy of those involved on the forward frontiers of modern science. Quite the reverse! The Church has faith, it promotes and encourages your commitment."[25] Indeed, the pope even managed to state, with the dithyrambic tone once used by C. P. Snow in his little book on the "two cultures,"[26] that "every true scientist is a priest." These are words that seem dangerously forgetful of the program daringly set out by Bacon at the outset of modern science, and which contrives to cover with a veneer of Machiavellian humility, a dream of universal domination: *"Natura nonnisi parendo vincitur."* It thus seems important to reopen the discussion of science, its ambitions of divine omnipotence, and the insurmountable barriers facing it when it is forced to respond to really human questions: the meaning of pain in the world, of birth, death, justice, and freedom.

Notes

1. See A. Chiaretti, in L. Alting von Gensau and F. V. Joannes, *Il dossier del catechismo olandese* (Milan: Mondadori, 1968).
2. "Libertà cristiana e liberazione—Il Istruzione della Congregazione per la dottrina della fede nella 'Teologia della liberazione,' " ADISTA, 10–12 April 1986, 12.
3. See E. Mazzi, "Il Medioevo nel nostro futuro?" *La Replubblica*, 28 April 1989.
4. "L'uomo vero? L'uomo in movimento," *Il Sabato*, 24–30 October 1987.
5. Balbo, 103; my emphasis.
6. Hans Küng, N. Greinacher, H. Haag, G. Denzler, L. Boff, J. P. Jossua, F. Klüber, W. Bartholomaeus, G. Schelbert, D. Mieth, J. B. Bauer, R. Modras, H. Häring, W. Godijn, E. Gossmann, R. B. Kaiser, H. Kühner, N. Copray, A. Schneider, A. Willems, L. Rinder, and A. Jensen, in *Contro il tradimento del Concilio* (Turin: Claudiana, 1987).

7. See Küng et al., 7.
8. See my *La storia e il quotidiano* (Bari-Rome: Laterza, 1986), where, dealing with the "charisma" of John Paul II, I refer to him as the "TV pope."
9. See Pietro Rossano, "La collaborazione ecumenica e inter-religiosa," *Osservatore Romano* 19 March 1983.
10. See my *Una teologia per atei*.
11. See the first chapter of my *Una teologia per atei*, the first volume in this trilogy.
12. G. Girardi, "Possibilità di una teologia europea della liberazione," *IDOC Internazionale* 14 (January 1983): 32.
13. See G. Baget Bozzo, "La curia e il popolo di Dio," *La Repubblica*, 6 May 1989.
14. "Lettera ai Cristiani: oggi nella Chiesa . . . , *Il Regno* (Bologna: Dehonian Fathers) no. 10 (15 May 1989).
15. Officially, the task of the institute is to "train the consciences and intelligences of a mature laity," but without confusing the sacred and the profane (a typically Jesuitical reservation, one might argue!).
16. "Pope Says Religious Freedom Is Progressing," *New York Times*, 6 June 1989; "Pope Sees a 'New and Better Era' on the Way," *New York Times*, 8 June 1989.
17. See D. Hervieu-Léger's contribution in *Voyage de Jean Paul II en France*.
18. For a recent account of these subjects, which intends to examine the evidence of the "struggle for world Catholicism," in some ways excessively conspiratorial in its terms (from the 1987 suspension of the Reverend Charles Curran from his post at Catholic University of America, Washington, D.C., to the censures against liberation theology in Latin America and the disciplinary proceedings against Archbishop Raymond Hunthausen of Seattle for his pacifism and against local Catholic churches the world over, from Holland to Peru), see P. Lernoux, *People of God—The Struggle for World Catholicism* (New York: Viking Press, 1989).
19. H. Küng, *Infallible? An Enquiry* (London: Collins, 1971), 201.
20. B. Drummond Ayres, Jr., "Black Priest Is Termed Threat to Catholicism," *New York Times*, 15 July 1989.
21. T. C. Ogden, *Beyond Revolution* (Philadelphia: Westminster Press, 1975), 111.
22. For example, see H. J. Blackham, *Religion in a Modern Society* (London: Constable, 1966); G. Szczesny, *The Future of Unbelief* (New York: George Braziller, 1961); G. Vahanian, *The Death of God: The Culture of Our Post-Christian Era* (New York: George Braziller, 1961); S. Rose, *The Grass-Roots Church* (New York: Abingdon Press, 1966); D. Pooling, *The Last Years of the Church* (New York: Doubleday, 1969); M. J. Irion, *From the Ashes of Christianity: A Post-Christian View* (New York: Lippincott, 1968); M. Boyd, ed., *The Underground Church* (London: Sheed and Ward, 1968); R. Adolfs, *The Grave of God* (New York: Harper and Row, 1966).
23. See, with special reference to the "syndrome of Christianity," R. McAlfee Brown, *Frontiers of the Church Today* (New York: Oxford University Press, 1973), especially pp. 34–39. Somewhat paradoxically, it is in the East European countries and Gorbachev's USSR that John Paul II's neo-Constantinian position seems destined to reap its most satisfying rewards although Gorbachev's initiatives have had a "liquidation effect." After decades, the Vatican has

reestablished in Poland normal diplomatic relations; in Hungary there is open talk of a rapid review of Cardinal Mindszenty's trial; recently (late July 1989), Pope Wojtyla, with the agreement of Gorbachev, was able to appoint a bishop in Byelorussia, at Minsk, the first for forty-four years. Perhaps the cases of "fruitful collaboration," or at least of "positive coordination" between Kremlin and Vatican will multiply in the near future, especially if, after the ideological failure of the "new Soviet man," the pope is disposed to make religion that precious glue that seems able to lessen if not remove the ethnic conflicts shaking the Soviet empire, putting at risk its cohesion with dreadful internal explosions. See my *Oltre il razzismo*.

24. K. Rahner, *The Shape of the Church to Come* (New York: Crossroad, 1983), 93. Despite the difficulties encountered by Vatican II regarding the practical renewal of the Church and the recognition of local autonomy, the ecumenical tendency seems to point to an historical movement on a world scale. From July 16 to 26, 1989, the Ecumenical Council of Churches met for the first time in Moscow on the invitation of the Russian Orthodox church. During its meeting the new Ministry for Religious Affairs' incumbent, Yuri Kristornados, and the USSR prime minister stated that "relations between the churches and the State are gradually becoming normal. . . . The future law on freedom of conscience will ensure juridically that believers have the possibility of participating in the life of society and its restructuring" (*Le Monde*, 28 July 1989).

25. See the report in *Corriere della Sera*, 25 September 1989.

26. C. P. Snow, *The Two Cultures and the Scientific Revolution* (London: Blackwell, 1960).

3

The Triumph of Science and Its Limitations

The Deferred Vendetta of the Sciences of the Approximate

It is strange that a critic as sharp and in some ways as farseeing about the Enlightenment as Friedrich Nietzsche was should have ended up espousing its interpretation regarding a basic theme, namely that of religion. Religion was presented as a mass deception, the "opiate of the people," an underhanded means for sending the masses to sleep. The corollary of this hasty view of the religious phenomenon may be guessed. The more rationality advances and the world is illuminated by the "luminaries" of reason, the more the circle of the religious will tighten, to the point of its complete, definitive disappearance. It may be that this superficial conception should be put down to the provocative statistical overabundance of priests and nuns, or again, more simply, to the systematic violation of the second commandment, which was supposed to forbid or at least discourage taking the name of God in vain, especially by those who have a daily trade and kind of professional jurisdiction over what relates to divinity.[1]

There is certainly some awkwardness through familiarity. It has been observed that Homer must have been irreligious, given that he was at home among his gods and behaved so freely with them, "like the sculptor behaves with his clay, that is, with the same unconcern that Aeschylus and Aristophanes possessed, and with which the great artists of the Renaissance in more recent times, and like Shakespeare and Goethe too, distinguished themselves."[2]

But the same author—Nietzsche—is ready to put us on guard against the claims of "religious sentiment" and its tricks: "Whoever today makes room anew in himself for religious sentiment must then also let it grow, he cannot do otherwise. Then, gradually, his being is changed, he prefers what is joined to and connected with the religious sentiment, the whole circle of judgements and sentiments is covered with clouds, traversed by religious shadows. The sentiment cannot stop itself. So, let us be on guard."[3]

Agreed, let us be on guard. But against whom? Against what? Internal imperialism, so to speak, would thus be a necessary and indelible attribute of religion. And this is the reason why "Christianity arose to lift up the heart. But now it must first oppress it so as to be able to lift it up later. As a result, it will perish." How can this forecast, whose display of certainty is so great it makes us fear for its basic fragility, be reconciled with the frankly scientistic idea that "the more the circle of religions and every art of narcosis tightens, the more seriously men are concerned to eliminate practically the causes of wrongs"?[4]

This notion, which tends to reduce the religious phenomenon to a mass drugging on which priests are supposed to have thrived for centuries, now appears at best as a conceptual trick, and moreover a fairly crude one. It well expresses an enthusiastic romanticism of science that, after Auschwitz, Hiroshima, and the current crisis of ecological systems, has had its day, leaving behind a related track of massacres, disasters, rage, and disappointment. It is then that precisely the dubious sciences, those it seemed hard if not impossible to accord full scientific status to, especially the social sciences, today enjoy a kind of deferred vendetta. The sciences of the approximate are those coming out on top.

Criticisms within Science

However, it would be imprudent to rejoice. The enjoyment could turn out to be premature. These always problematic sciences show serious deficiencies and limits. Their pathetic attempt to imitate the improperly described "exact" sciences has consigned them to a quantitavistic orientation that seriously reduces their potential, while it is pompously displayed as incontrovertible attestation of scientific rigor. It is enough to take one's distance to be aware of this. They always have all the answers ready. It is a real pity that they no longer know what the problems are. External signs of their disorientation are plentiful: the excess of instrumental activism, the blurring of the *telos*, their worldly success among the money-men devoted to wholesale trading on a world scale, among politicians, administrators, and the mass media. From a deeper, "internal" viewpoint, their faults seem impressive, and there stands out an unconsciously self-destructive tendency to discern in them the sure sign of social respectability and the confirmation of a completed consolidation. This entails the profaning of the other, the predetermined use of the not-yet-thought, and so, inevitably, the atrophy of thought and the decline of its native involuntary fluidity.

However, the whole of the scientific universe seems today dominated by the sense of an endemic precariousness that attacks and eats away the foundations. It is not only the neo-Pyrrhonism of Francisco Sanchez that casts doubts on scientific knowledge and its validity. The appetizing text of *Quod nihil scitur* should perhaps be seen in a pedagogic rather than strictly methodological sense.[5] The questions it raises remain open. At the end of his unceasing inquiry, the teacher turns to his young disciple to be in some way "taught." "If you ever acquire some knowledge, teach me it. I shall be grateful to you." The important thig is that problematic consciousness should not be quenched.

There is a quite different significance to the critical demands made of the sciences from within. Edmund Husserl noted at the start of his best know, if not his major, work, that "positivism as it wre decapitates philosophy."[6] But there is no doubt that if it has not decapitated it, it has seriously wounded the certainty of scientific procedure and shaken the bases of its legitimation. The question naturally remains valid for Nusserl and also for the legion of fashionable antipositivists, of how philosophy can be decapitated without producing philosophy.

Husserl's critical remarks reply to this problem by involving a specific historical and cultural background beyond methodological observation internal to scientific research. Husserl assumed the tone of an historian of ideas: "The exclusiveness with which, in the second half of the nineteenth century, the overall vision of the world of modern man accepted being determined by the positive sciences, and with which it let itself be dazzled by the 'prosperity' flowing from them, meant a distancing from those problems that are decisive for an authentic humanity.''[7] One has the impression that Husserl has known these decisive problems from the start. Husserl seemed already to know what the authenticity of man was even before starting his research. It coincided with his implicit, preferred principle. It was his metatheoretical assumption—a confining concept that directs and at the same time justifies his research by giving it direction. Husserl remarks, with ill-concealed and perhaps contradictory admiration of the "revolutionary upheaval" of the Renaissance,[8] on the basis of which he argues that "ancient man is he who moulds himself exclusively on the basis of free reason. . . . [R]eason is the explicit subject of the disciplines of knowledge (that is, of real, authentic, rational knowledge), of real, authentic judgement (authentic values as rational values), of ethical action (really good action, based on practical reason). Reason is thus a title under which 'absolutely,' 'eternally,' 'supratemporally,' 'unconditionally,' 'valid' ideas and ideals are collected."[9]

In this overexaltation of reason, Husserl sees a serious limitation, the very root of the crisis destined to weigh on humanity and so not only on science or the disciplines of theoretical knowledge, but as a threat of inauthenticity, and loss of the sense of orientation. In fact, "the crisis of philosophy means a crisis of all the modern sciences as branches of philosophical universality; it becomes a crisis at first latent and then increasingly obvious, of European humanity, of the overall meaning of its cultural life, and its overall 'existence.' "[10]

The Excess of Rationality

Where should the reason for the "crisis of scientific, cognitive reason" be sought? Husserl seemed to have no doubts: in the excess of rationality that has summarily executed, after first isolating it and deprving it of authority, the old metaphysics. The truly philosophical demand, the sense of a qualitatie value, by definition distinct and superior to that expressed by empirical data that are precisely measurable in a quantitative sense (everything that can be known without being exactly measured and which post-Renaissance science has set aside, relegating it to the sphere of an interiority not perfectly knowable)—this is what Husserl sees endangered by the new scientific "method" that may be said to be embodied, in his view, by Galileo.

The "promises" of science do not escape him.

> With the progressive and increasingly perfect ability of knowing everything, man also pursues an ever more perfect dominion over his surrounding, practical world, a dominion widened through infinite progress. This also implies dominion over the humanity included in the real surrounding world, and thus also dominion over himself and other men, a dominion over his own destiny that constantly increases, and so an ever more perfect "happiness," a happiness that men can generally conceive of rationally. . . . Thus man becomes truly the image of God. In a sense analogous to that in which mathematics speaks of infinitely distant points, of straight lines, etc., one may add, using a simile, that God is the infinitely distant man. Indeed, the philosopher, by mathematizing the world and philosophy, has in the same way idealized himself and also God.[11]

The first, basic critique of Husserl against modern science thus concerns its exorbitant "promises," its geometricizing enthusiasm, and ultimately its claim to omniscience. By making knowledge coincide with measurement, and measuring exactly in a quantitative sense, modern Galilean science has really performed a reductionist operation. It has reduced, in other words, the complex, not exactly definable human nature to the "unidimensionality" of "mere factual men."[12] By placing quantity above quality, it has reduced thought to quantifying. By obeying the imperatives of the cult of quantitative precision, it has canceled from human knowledge everything of the common knowledge, those ordinary, but essential, knowledges, which constitute the deep cultural structure of humanity, the knowing wisdom of specific, lived experience, the "flesh" of actual everydayness.

I do not believe Husserl arrived at the clear reevaluation of experience as actual everydayness, so ambiguous ultimately his position seems, between the still wholly idealist need for an infinite rationality and the ambition—wholly positivistic or neopositivistic—of rigorously delimited research. The rationality would challenge the merely mechanistic and quantitative level, while the research would be directed by hypotheses open to verification—

though in the awareness that there is no final verification, but rather every verification can only refer to other, infinite ones, by an infinite regression already seen as absurd by Kant. However, his judgement on Galileo is drastic:

> [T]he discoverer of physics and physical nature (or, to do justice to his prede-cessors: the one who completed the previous discoveries) *is a genius who both reveals and conceals*. He discovers mathematical nature, the idea of method, opens the way to an infinity of discoverers and physical discoveries. He discovers, in the face of the *universal causality of the intuitive world* what from then on was to be called . . . *causal law*, the "a priori form" of the *"real" world* (idealized and mathematical), the "law of exact legality," according to which any event in "nature"—of idealized nature—must be subject to *exact laws*. All this is a discovery and also a concealment, even if until today we have considered it a simple truth."[13]

At this point Husserl hastens to add, as if to avoid the impression of a simply demolishing, swingeing criticism: "Certainly I put *in all seriousness* Galileo at the head of the great discoverers of modern times, and so naturally in all seriousness I admire the great discov-erers of classical and postclassical physics, their *theoretical opera-tions*, which are not at all merely *mechanical*, but, rather, *astonish-ing*."[14] However, a reservation appears. From the Galilean interpretation of nature by his disciples and generally those who followed his methods, there necessarily were to derive corollaries that transcended nature, results and modes of argument destined to involve problematical spheres and environments not limited to or concerned only with nature.

I have stressed many times the limits of scientific research, especially when it yields to the totalizing proposals of scientism. This deplorable result is not, however, inevitable. A return to the classics of scientific thought itself would probably do rapid justice to those positions, intellectually lazy despite their triumphalistic tones, which tend to impoverish scientific research in the strict sense by stressing its specific techniques and procedures at the expense of properly theoretical concepts. As has been penetratingly observed,

> [F]rom the methodological viewpoint . . . the most noteworthy fact is that Galileo is well aware of the impossibility of direct verification, in experience, of the principles formulated through these concepts. Even the simplest definition

of naturally accelerated movement escapes such verification. This definition implies, in fact, that in the states closest to the initial one, velocity is infinitesimal—which seems to contradict direct observation. . . . Galileo's methodological awareness . . . appears still more clearly as regards the general principles of the science of motion. He well knew that these principles, whose formulation required the use of essentially theoretical concepts, cannot be directly verified against facts. The physicist must thus accept them in the guise of postulates, no differently from what the mathematician does for the principles of his own theories. However, he will add a requirement foreign to pure mathematics: that at least some of the theorems deducible from those postulated have an actual correspondence in phenomena.[15]

Scientism on the other hand fetishizes the facts beyond and outside the theoretico-conceptual apparatus, which for Comte too is essential if the "facts" are to begin to speak. The founder of positivism must not in fact be confused with the authors of the gross "factualistic" approach, which should recall, rather than positivism, the paleo-positivism widely imbued with sensism and ingenuous realism. For Auguste Comte, no research would ever be possible or even just hypothesizable without the "guiding light of theory."

The Arrogance of Scientism

What should we conclude? That science, as currently practices, is valuless and that it is better to turn to the alchemist or the witch doctor, if not to the charismatic, or, more simply, to the priest? In many western European cultures, especially the Italian, the question has often been formulated and until recently the reply given was not truly favorable to science. Dialectical, metaphysical rationalism in its Crocean version, which dominated Italian culture for about fifty years, believed science to be without cognitive value in the true sense, in that it considered the sciences provided not "concepts" in the rigorous sense of the term (i.e., philosophical-essentialist) but rather pseudoconcepts, or sectoral generalizations that might be useful but were not to be understood as logically binding. The Crocean and Gentilean neoidealists, many of whom in postwar Italy went back on themselves and went to swell the ranks of orthodox Marxists, tolerated the sciences as at most complexes of classificatory concepts, not without a certain practical utility, but essentially as "inferior means of intellectual life." Their hostility regarding science was one of principle. Their denial was radical. It concerned not only the social but all the sciences, including physics, chemistry, and biology. Only history was left standing, where moreover there joined up philosophy as well, as the sole acceptable truth concept was that regarding the action of man itself, who could, in Vico's sense, only truly know what he himself was doing, his *res gestae*. It is pointless to remark that the sciences were thus reduced to the rank of cognitive activities in the sense of a purely "mechanical" and "external" knowledge. But the question returns, where is the distinction between purely empirical practice, magic or witchcraft, and scientific activity? The distinction exists and should be well borne in mind.[16]

The tricks of scientism and its arrogance should not blind us. While magical-witchcraft practice is highly individual, linked to supposed extraordinary powers and gifts ("chrisms") in the uncheckable individual practitioner, scientific research is on principle open to all and checkable by all. The propositions it puts forward are verified or falsified by empirical data adduced by the research—data on whose consistency anyone can assure themselves. In other words, while magical or alchemical practice remains an essentially mysterious fact—precisely magical—scientific research is *essentially a public procedure*, and as such logically binding and intersubjectively valid.

I have already remarked on the defects of scientism and the need for a return to science as the means whereby we can put ourselves in a problematic relation to ourselves, others, and the universe, without which we risk falling into a neodogmatism that would mean the betrayal and death of science itself and the critical questioning that underpins it. It is as well here to stress that a wholesale critique of science—such as to equate science and scientism—is always portentous of a dangerous and arbitrary social situation, if not one of cruelty and ultimately of collective barbarism. This may arise in the name of "internal truth," of *élan vital*, or life-worlds seen as spontaneistic movements positive as themselves as signals and privileged fields of intellectually formless vitalism, and so on. The globalizing, dogmatic critique of science usually marks an involution at once cultural, social, and political. Never before as today,

perhaps, is it necessary to lend a hand to the apology for reason—
a reason that does not exclude reasonableness—or to the potential
of rational planning of which human beings are capable. Today, like
yesterday, it is true that the sleep of reason gives birth to monsters.
But at the same time, one must not forget that the dogmatism of
reason, like the tyranny of progress, is still more insidious than the
dogmatism linked to traditional beliefs, for it is a dogmatism that
deprives us of the only weapon we have against it. Both Husserl
and Geymonat seem to pass silently over, or at least neglect the
consequences of, the incursion of "time." The traditionalized
scientific categories formerly believed necessary, ahistorical and
primarily atemporal, are overwhelmed, dedogmatized, and made
fluid by it. In the end, the historicity of science is discovered—this
essential quality that seemingly degrades it but in reality restores
its basic characteristic, beyond any rhetoric of scientistic trium-
phalism, as a purely human undertaking, suffused with satisfactions
and tears, victories, failures, and blood.[17]

The Incursion of 'Time' into Scientific Reasoning

The incursion of time into scientific research brings it close to
common experience and manages to link scientific and everyday
discussion. For scientific categories as for the actions of everyday
experience, time presents itself as a decisive factor in establishing
and changing meanings, urgency, rhythm, planning, speed, and
delay. Today, in a society only averagely developed from a technical
point of view, we know that more haste means less time. Urgency
consumes time from the start. One can even die without having yet
lived. In the end there is no longer rushing, hurrying with a
meaning, a goal, but just running, without knowing where or why.
Pure urgency has become an innermost habit and way of life,
without an aim that gives it meaning. So, today there is "running"
but ever less "hastening" or running toward an objective with a
motive. Haste is no longer meaningful.[18] However, it has been
remarked,

At any rate, by evoking the circumstances of this discussion, we do not wish to
justify its all-too-obvious deficiencies by the haste resulting from it, as it is from
haste itself that it takes its meaning and form together. In fact, we have shown

by a sophistry exemplary of intersubjective time, the function of haste in the logical precipitation wherein logic finds its insurmountable condition. There is nothing created that does not appear urgent, nothing in urgency that does not generate its own transcendence in the word. But also, nothing that becomes contingent when for man the time comes when he can identify in a single reason the party he chooses and the disorder he denounces to understand in the real, and anticipate with his certainty, their action, which sets them in contraposition.[19]

Kant puts the categories of "space" and "time" on the same level. The philosophical logic of tradition is geometrical and spatial. But this means imitating the gods, to suppose ourselves out of time, freeze the moment, and in this limbo following the stopping of time, draw the aseptic outlines of a thought forever equal to itself, active in a vacuum, dehistoricized, dehumanized, and suprahumanized. The romantic enchantment breaks off at once if one introduces the passage of time: postponement, frozen movement, the anticipation of certainty, the anguished moment of the glance, the fatal sense of deadline.

The overriding concern of the person condemned to death is buying time, lasting longer. The anomaly of Gary Gilmore is in reality a stoic act, in consonance with pure violence: the refusal of postponement. Gilmore takes Hegel at his word—the criminal has the right to his punishment. Acceptance of death as the crowning act of a life of violence—meaning by violence the most suitable instrument for consuming the margins, canceling time, literally killing time, or killing the living of and in time.

The limiting-case does not exclude those of normality. Is a world dominated by technique not perhaps linked to rhythms counted with violent precision whose transgression provokes precise sanctions commensurate with its seriousness? It has already been remarked: ours could be defined as the time of the limit of mechanical resistance. Machines for arriving earlier and reducing distances have led people never to arrive. There is a present one cannot reach. It is the point of intersection between the urgency to save time and that which, by shortening time, annuls time itself. But here is a paradox that Chesterton in the *Return of Don Quixote* grasped well, and which at once makes the dispute between technophiles and antimechanicals fall into insignificance. Machines have become so inhuman that they seem natural, "remote and indifferent like nature.'' This dead system is constructed on such a vast scale that one does not know where it will stop nor how. This is the paradox! Things have become incalculable through being calculated. Individuals are tied to explosive devices so gigantic that they do not know where the blow will fall. Don Quixote's nightmare is coming true. The windmills *are* giants.

Who or what will save us? The grain of sand in the mechanism? The premature exhaustion of the primary sources of energy? Chance, or the distraction of the technician who slept badly the night before? Literary models have anticipated philosophical speculation. Lafcadio, the bloodless hero of *Caves du Vatican*, kills Fleurissoire whom he does not know, or hate, by throwing him from the moving train:

> If I can count to twelve *without hurrying* [my emphasis] before seeing a light in the countryside, the man is saved. I begin: one, two, three, four (slowly, slowly!), five, six, seven, eight, nine, . . . Ten, a light . . . Fleurissoire did not even let out a cry. Under Lafcadio's thrust and in front of the abyss suddenly opened up before him, he made a great embrace, to hang on. . . . Lafcadio felt a terrible scratch on his neck, lowered his head and gave a second shove, more impatient than the first. . . .[20]

Lafcadio's crime is born of the interference of chance in the space-time traversed by the train running through the nighttime countryside. When someone asks him the reason for his crime, he replies with great naturalness, "How can you ask I should explain to you what I have not understood myself?" Not action, then, as practice and project, but absurd action, action that denies at its root human meaning as planned temporalization. Here in fact there is deployed, as has been said, what is understood in all the details of the argument and the structure, temporality:

> If Discourse and structure are not uniformly spread on the uneven surface of the system and have to deal practically with the different, then it is precisely in fracture and breakdown to which they cannot but orient themselves that they tumble into the void of temporality. In this void the continuum of the existing structure cracks into the discontinuity in which a structure on new or different levels emerges. It is exactly in the act of this emergence that, as a break in the body of a text with uninterrupted writing, one discovers what the existing structure cannot bring into view because it would discover what it has no interest in discovering—*its end and its passing to no longer being structure.* Thus, as regards the Discourse, time is present in it, but not insofar as the

Discourse speaks explicitly of it, *but rather because it is silent and interrupts itself* so as later to resume with a differently plaited plot. Time is the difference in the identity of the Discourse, the break in which the meanings of the language are broken and recomposed.[21]

And yet, in art, becoming and passage have no meaning. The time a piece of music spans is not real time because as regards development (or succession) in a work of art one cannot speak. It is definitive or it doesn't exist. On the other hand, the experience of condensation in the instant of what will be realized in later states is one of the most common experiences (for example, when one begins a speech, what one will say is, if only summarily, condensed in the very instant of the beginning). Mozart put it that for him a melody was all condensed in an instant: the tempo of the melody was in a sense, eternal.[22] For this reason, tempo (time) and rhythm must not be confused. Rhythm is only the order of movement. Time is the means of planning the order of things to do, their meaning.

The observation starts from elementary experiences, memories of childhood fixed on the inner record with the deceptive simplicity of the black and white sketch—an endless summer afternoon with insects, lizards, grass snakes, playing in a dry moat, and then suddenly it's evening and time rather than being lived has been drunk in a single gulp. Or the reflection begins from impressions of a journey, for example, out of time, the timelessness of an Indian village like Sing-Pura a hundred miles from New Delhi, the soft "yielding" to things that seems to mark the world of acceptance, ritual repetition, not yet dominated by the mechanical precision of the watch or utilitarian competitive drives.

On this half-conscious background cultural information is grafted. There was an age when time was a qualitative duration, an existential quality, whereby it flew away or it never ended—independently of its quantitative mechanical measure. It has always amazed me that Giovan Battista Vico mistook the year of his birth in his autobiography. John U. Nef, the famous historian of the coal industry, observed that we do not know Rabelais's dates. This is not just a scholarly curiosity. It marks the great transition from time as duration to time a discrete sequence of phases. We are in time. We cannot escape it. We *are* time. The very function of religion is in decline as cure for the ills of the time, the "century," in the name of and for the "eternal." The sense of the eternal changes. In the age of consumerism, God is replaced by the supermarket. The peasant adage "God abideth, God provideth" no longer holds good. The traditional results of historicity no longer stand up. We are therefore time. But if time is atomized, segmented, exhausted, what are we?

Thrown into a world crushed by publicity and immediacy, we register the dominion of the present and the disappearance of critical distance and perspective. Time expiring, and urgency, are in direct relation with the fall of the sense of perspective, or "sense of distance." Instead, the myth of the immediately observable and sensible gains ground. But it is too close an immediacy to be authentic and meaningful. A mode of life dominated by "snapshots" is a world of images without history, depth. As we can see in the fearful presentism of films: how do we live, or stand still, under the blinding third-degree lights of a questioning that never ends and at the same time is rigorously logical and humanly meaningless. Here, scientism reveals all its arrogance. It had the presumption to offer only truths outside time. Instead, it suffers all the wearing away of time.

Secularization as a Product of the Scientistic Mentality

The concept of secularization as it has been expounded in recent years by theologists and sociologists of religion is possibly the most obvious result of the scientistic mentality, the involuntary ally of its bigoted counterpart. There is no doubt this concept has been used in an insufficiently discriminating way. Its critico-linguistic determinateness has been lacking. Perhaps the most conscious attempt has been undertaken by Howard Becker, who distinguishes "sacred societies" from "secular societies." However, whereas the former seemed quite easy to define, the task of characterizing the latter was symptomatically much less so. For Becker, "sacred society" is the one whose members seem constantly hostile or at least reluctant in the face of any change. This refractory attitude as regards innovations seems to result from the fact that "sacred societies inculcate in their members ends easily classified under the label of security, response, and recognition, with security in many cases as first priority. . . . The societies that instill types of conduct in their members producing a high rate of resistance to change are for me sacred societies."[23]

However, Becker is not content with a really rather elementary division, between sacred and secular societies. Along with the traditional sacred societies, he introduces the type of "prescribed sacred societies" characterized by a series of sanctions, well defined and without exceptions. As regards "secular societies," Becker is very cautious. In his view, in a completely secular society, "secularization would have the ultimate result, the emergence of a heterogeneous grouping of human units with no common end."[24] Such a result would make us think, rather than of a society, however fragmented and disorganized, of a mere herd of subjects without any link or relation. It is on the other hand a common-sense remark that societies—even the most secularized ones—always preserve a certain degree of stability and organic character. These characteristics of stability and organicity indicate in his view something "sacred." For this reason he suggests speaking of "secular societies, " "societies in the process of secularization."[25]

The most refined treatment of the concept of secularization is probably that by Peter L. Berger. He anticipates the unsettling criticism that hinges on the lack of distinction between the process of secularization and social change in a structural sense.[26] Berger distinguishes very clearly those aspects that are truly cultural and linked to subjective perception, from the changes occurring in the structure of society. He is thus able to put himself above the immediate polemic by referring to the basic concept of religion, on which moreover the concept of secularization necessarily depends.

For Berger, the possibility of treating the process of secularization from a flexible intellectual viewpoint, permitting him to distinguish the various social and cultural contexts (Europe as against the U.S., for example), derives basically from his concept of religion as a complex of meanings. These contribute decisively to the construction of the world, or social reality, as well as to its preservation and indefinite perpetuation. In other words, the particular phenomenological approach of Berger's general analysis[27] allows him to historicize and make a critical definition of the secularization phenomenon that is denied to others who uphold this argument. According to Berger, we are surrounded by the social reality we ourselves have created, since society in dialectical terms is just a product of the individual, who is, however, in turn a product of society. The dialectical structure of the person-society relation involves three basic moments that follow one another in logical, not chronological form: externalization, objectivation, and internalization.

This relation seems to resemble the Marxian dialectical approach. In reality, it is essentially distant in one basic point, the prioritarian moment of the grounding of historical experience. For Marx, the prioritarian, basic datum is linked to structure as a complex of social relations as material, essentially extra-subjective relations of life, conditioned by relations of production. For Berger, on the other hand, priority must be given to humanity, an archetypal idea of the person, which refers to a metahistorical subject of undoubtedly religious extraction, in a transcendental metaphysical sense.

Social Structures and Human Awareness

Thus, according to Berger, individual humans "produce" society. But in the process of internalization, society, the product of our *externalization*, is not only something "external" but also "internal," part of our innermost ego. Berger's tone, and the conceptual and expressive modality, seem to be aligned with Durkheimian language. Society not only determines our actions, it informs and moulds our identities, thoughts, and feelings. Here there is a curious exchange, which we might define as a dialectical reciprocity on a purely horizontal plane, suggesting a "mirror" reflex between two equivalent realities.

According to Berger, the structures of society become those of consciousness itself (note that Berger never uses the Durkheimian term *individu*, but that of *man*, as though to avoid the suspicion of primacy of society over individual, a concern that clearly did not even touch Durkheim). Berger's prose becomes poetic but does not thereby manage to resolve what seems a genuine puzzle in his argument: "Society does not stop at the surface of our skin but penetrates into us to the extent to which it enfolds us."

The "knowledge of society" thus pervades the individual, who finds his "production" objectified in the social order. Thus the "social construction of reality" is completed, according to a theoretical apparatus that Berger and Luckmann essentially borrowed from Alfred Schutz, with considerable assistance too from native American culture, especially from George Herbert Mead and his concepts of "role" and "generalized other." But it is prima facie clear that this objective social order is precarious. The radical break with the social world—the condition of anomie—is a permanent threat and an ever-open possibility, given the essentially psychologistic nature of the process of forming social reality. The individual risks losing the sense of his identity and at the same time that of the social reality in which he is inserted. Durkheim's anomie, suitably corrected by the interpretative contribution of Robert K. Merton, provides Berger with the theoretical possibility of avoiding the concept of deviance and the problem of its causal derivation. If indeed the individual produces society and society in turn produces the individual, how could there be deviance, that is, "deviation" or "gap" in this game of mirrors of high, preordered precision?

Society reacts to anomie as a source of absence of meaning and a break in the person-society relation. Chaos is warded off by society, which helps its members to stay "oriented" or "return to reality" by recognizing the "facts of life," the law, the *nómos* established by society, which is also created by the individuals. In this braking function, that of reorientation and leading the strays back to the fold, with the marginal too, so to say, the function of religion is essential according to Berger. As administrator of the sacred it points to a reality that gives meaning and at the same time transcends humanity, enfolds the individual, connecting him to a surpassing order and an otherworldly and highly meaningful design. For the sacred is not only counterposed to the profane but to chaos. It is thus the supreme guarantee of social order, the "awful contrary" of disorder and of violation of cosmic harmony.

It is easy to see at this point why Berger withdraws from, and does not link himself to, either of the two basic conceptions of religion. He rejects both the *substantive conception* of religion whereby it is defined and located in the social system in a structural sense as one of its more or less important aspects; or in the psychological literature as one of the basic impulses or needs of individuals. And he rejects the *functionalist conception* that is the prevailing one in the social sciences, from Durkheim and Malinowski, and which consists in describing and explaining what religion is: that is, what function it performs for the individual, the social group, and society itself overall.

However, the two conceptions are not rejected with the same conviction. Whereas the functionalist conception is basically criticized, one can say that Berger puts himself in a neosubstantive position, anxious to guarantee the reality and weight of the phenomenon of religion.

The criticisms directed by Berger against the functionalist conception are illuminating in this regard:[28]

1. Functional definitions tend to have a very wide significance and so violate an important methodological premise concerning the need that "every human meaning be understood from within."[29]
2. Functional definitions are vitiated by an implicit "ideological use": whereas in fact substantial definitions contain a single meaning or group of meanings that refers to transcendent units in a conventional sense, such as God, gods, supernatural beings, and worlds; functional definitions refer on the other hand to meanings like nationalism, revolutionary faith, life styles, and so on.
3. The functional approach to religion helps provide a series of semiscientific legitimations to a secularized vision of the world. Relgion is equated with other social phenomena and thus diluted into the uniform greyness that, according to Berger, marks the secularized reality where every display of transcendence is without meaning. But thereby, says Berger, social order, here revealing all his orientation as conscious conservative, runs the risk of losing its basic legitimating support—religion as a specific fact.[30]

From this conceptual framework there arises the conception of the process of secularization. Further, there derive from it the perception and evaluation of the liturgy, the sacraments, and generally of all the ceremonies and "external" ritual behavior, whose importance is often stressed to the point of making it, in practical terms, the equivalent or at least proof of a presence of the sacred.[31]

It is no surprise that in speaking of secularization Berger should have in mind "the process by which sectors of society are removed from the domination of religious institutions and symbols."[32]

A Reenchanted Disenchantment

As observed above, Berger avoids the oversimplification of a notion of secularization that makes it the equivalent *tout court* of the process of social, structural change produced by the industrial revolution and the advent of capitalism and urbanization on a vast scale. However he does not escape certain ideological traps that make him idealize certain isomorphic tendencies, extrapolating generalizations from little or no empirical evidence, to the point of incautiously asserting, though with enchanting irony, that atheistic and religious propaganda are equivalent in certain politico-cultural situations both in socialist and nonsocialist countries. It is clear that Berger could not have foreseen the extraordinary political effect of an essentially religious position as regards its basic legitimation, of the case recently emerging in Poland of the Catholic union Solidarność. It is perhaps enough to make us understand the extreme fragility, conceptual as well as an interpretive key to politico-cultural situations, of a hybrid and confused notion like that of secularization.

Naturally, Berger is cautious: "The religious factor must *not* be considered as operating in isolation from other factors but as standing in an ongoing dialectical relationship with the 'practical' infrastructures of social life."[33] But it seems clear it is not enough to invoke the "dialectical relationship," unspecified and basically equivocal from the viewpoint of the priorities and general theoretical framework in which its dynamism is supposed to develop, in order to escape from a puzzle that requires, rather than linguistic skills or subterfuges, a truly theoretical resolution. The stimulation of some insights should, however, be kept. It is especially worthy of note, as an idea that eems to herald the concept of a kind of "permanent religion," that in the multidimensionality of religious experience of everyday life, there is an anthropological constant that always emerges against and beyond the position of the official world that denies it.

In reality, in technically advanced societies that are believed to be based on rational calculation and scientific mentality, the signs of the "beyond" multiply. It would be superficial to dismiss and pass them over as simple displays of irrationality. At all events they have the value of a symptom. I have tried elsewhere to show that the relation between rational and irrational is not a dichotomy but rather a polarity. What seems irrational today may also be the prefiguration of tomorrow's rationality or the analogous expression—seemingly unreal and unintelligible—of a very real, widespread need in the primal phase, of a demand from society that for now lacks an adequate response.

Rationality is not itself an unchanging given. Rationality is what is sedimented through values that are historically variable. Reflection on the sacred and its ambiguous nature, which at the same time feeds and burns, helps us understand the social function of utopia. Religion as power structure administering the sacred has been understood as the basic instrument of legitimation of the existing social order. But the sacred may also prefigure a social order yet to be built, a community and morality that are different or even alternative. Religion is not only the codified one, variously linked to the power of the day, at once dominant and subjected. The future of religion is probably subordinate to the possibility/capacity of living religious experience in a different way—less formal, more intimate, less external, personal, and deeper.

It is true that previsions on the definitive disappearance of the religious experience and the sense of mystery have not come about. The signs are more plentiful than ever. In the very heart of Europe, where the Enlightenment was born and technico-scientific civilization was developed, old beliefs and new myths are consolidating. If in the Italian south there are still those affected by tarantism, recently in Norway 102 girls had themselves exorcised; in Germany, 11 out of every 100 Germans say they believe in witches; and in France 57 percent go to fortune-tellers and believe in horoscopes.

Some commentators have reduced all that to an act of envy of science. In other words, it is a shortcut. Scientific procedures, wherein everyday rationality is realized, are supposed to be too complex for the common person, not just to be practically duplicated and thus productive of objective results, but to be known in their theoretical and operational details. This knowledge is now the fief of a tiny elite that has thus become the holder in practice of huge power and that today in fact disposes of humanity's future, if only because it could produce its annihilation.

It has been remarked:

> The power of science is visible to everyone, but the keys of power—scientific competence and its use—are still very far from the masses and individuals. For humanity, it is still a mystery how science and technology achieve the results that astonish and shake the world. The distance of humanity from the sources of power starts from the seemingly most simple things. . . . In this situation, frustration is inevitable and people look for a substitute for the power that eludes them and that is wrapped in the mystery of conceptual complexity and military secrets. People seek a power that each individual is capable of controlling, accessible even to the poorest and weakest, and whereby everyone can still feel himself at the center of the world. And people find from time to time the substitute in that cluster of attitudes, also very different one from another— which today is called "the irrational": religion, drugs, violence of all kinds against social rules, the TV transfert where millions of people identify with the symbols of real power, magical practices, the occult, parapsychology.[34]

This argument, however, can easily be reversed. Might it not be that on the contrary it was science that desperately imitated the omnipotence of magic, the abolition of friction in space, and of the monocausal logic that is at the basis of the experience of drug-takers, the peace attained by those who have reached stoic ataraxis, or the Buddhist state of nirvana?

In fact modern society, suffused with technology and after the undeniable, amazing triumphs of science, is more than ever in need of collective meanings and is anxiously bewitched by mystery. After three centuries of enlightenment and scientific rationality, this society asks to be comforted, feels abandoned and like an orphan, on the point of turning to the little gods of astrology and fortune-telling. It is too easy and rather ungenerous to state that this is only the expression of a malicious, peevish envy of those who do not know or cannot understand. It is true that basic human needs have been left unsatisfied and that science, after overturning the revealed religion of tradition, with its values and ritual forms, and after criticizing its premises radically, has not been able or known how to fill the void it had dug with its own hands. It cannot manage to satisfy the hunger for substantive truth the world increasingly seems to suffer from.

Probably scientific truth expressed in a standardized proposition believed to be checkable by all and that is presented as empircally verified does not tell all the truth that human beings need. Despite the great successes of science, an extrascientific world continues to throw its troubling shadow upon them. The ostracism of this world in the name of rationality is understandable but not sufficient. Medieval figures like angels and devils, which one could think were forever ostracized from the mental and moral scene of contemporary man, in reality continue their eventful career, more overbearing than ever, in today's "lay" society.

Notes

1. Historically, God entrusted the name of Jahvé to Israel to glorify, and to make it known to other peoples. . . . Holy Scripture makes it clear that God's name must be invoked not abstractly, but according to concrete historical moralities. Salvation history, narrated in the Scriptures, provides us with examples of how the name of God has been pronounced at times in vain, at times with devotion: that is, made historically vacuous or pregnant with saving greatness. . . . In the Scriptures, God is begged to sanctify his name. What does this mean? God is asked not so much to sanctify his name, which is already wholly, fully holy, but to make us holy so that we can bear witness to the holiness of His name in our existence. When in the Hebrew prayer (Quadis) and the evangelist's (Matt. 6:9; Luke 11:2), God the Father is asked that "Holy be Thy name," He is being begged that He make our existence a plain witness to His pity. T. Goffi, "Nominare il nome di Dio," *Rivista di teologia morale* 16, no. 64 (October–December 1984), 535–538.   2. F. Nietzsche, *Umano, troppo umano*, vol. 1 (Milan: Adelphi, 1965), 101.
3. Nietzsche, 100.
4. Nietzsche, 89.
5. See Francisco Sanchez, *Il n'est science de rien* (Paris: Klincksieck, 1984); this is the French translation (ed. André Comparot) of the 1581 Latin original, revised and corrected on the basis of the 1636 edition.
6. E. Husserl, *La crisi delle scienze europee e la fenomenologia trascendentale*, (Milan: Il Saggiatore, 1961), 39. For some remarks on the "crisis of scientific rationality" see my *Il paradosso del sacro* (Roma-Bari: Laterza, 1983), especially chap. 3.
7. Husserl, 35.
8. On the idea of "scientific revolution," see Bernard Cohen, *La rivoluzione nella scienza* (Milan: Longanesi, 1988). The book, in six parts, deals with revolution as dynamic concept in Copernicus, Bacon, Descartes, Galileo, Newton, and Harvey; with Lavoisier's "dynamic revolution," the "Copernican revolution" of Kant, Darwin, St.-Simon, Comte, Marx and Engels, and Freud; and finally with the revolutionary century par excellence, the twentieth.
9. Husserl, 38.
10. Husserl, 41–42.
11. Husserl, 94–95.

12. It is not without significance that the term "one-dimensionality" should have been adopted by a leftist Hegelian like Herbert Marcuse, (see his *One-dimensional Man* of 1964, the bedside reading of the 1968 youth and student contestation).

13. Husserl, 81–82.

14. Husserl, 82.

15. L. Geymonat, *Per Galileo—Attualità del razionalismo*, (Verona: Bertani, 1981), 165–167.

16. According to Cassirer, science and magic have an aim in common: the discovery and dominion of reality. (E. Cassirer, *An Essay on Man*, [New York: Doubleday, 1944], 101).

17. For some considerations on the critical demand as regards essentialism, grounded on the category of "temporality," see my *Il ricordo e la temporalità* (Rome-Bari: Laterza, 1987), especially chap. 1. For a first, impressive account of the deep, revolutionary change of perspective that involves all the sciences, see Ilya Prirogine, *Dall'essere al divenize—Tempo e complessita nelle scienze fisiche* (1978). In this book, which precedes and prepared for that written with I. Stenghers, Prirogine argues we are living today through a scientific revolution not unlike Galileo's. His evidence should not be sought in specific discoveries, however important, like those of the pulsar or quark. The current scientific revolution goes much deeper. Whereas classical science seemed always concerned with describing and explaining the world from outside, and thus with an aseptic viewpoint, as if dealing with a reality extraneous to the researchers, outside and beyond any time factor, current research gives great importance to and recognizes the significance of time. Along with astronomical time, internal time is asserted, that which controls reversible and irreversible dynamic processes, which can still be measured by a clock, and which has a completely different meaning.

18. See my *Storia e storie divita* (Rome-Bari: Laterza, 1983), especially pp. 4–9, and *Il ricordo e la temporalità*.

19. J. Lacan, *La cosa freudiana* (Turin: Einaudi, 1972), 87–88.

20. A. Gide, *Les caves du Vatican* (Paris: Gallimard, 1922), 195–196.

21. F. Totaro, *Produzione del senso* (Milan: Vita e pensiero, 1979), 81.

22. E. Castelli, *Pensieri e qiornate* (Padua: CEDAM, 1963), 62.

23. Howard Becker, *Through Values to Social Interpretation* (Durham: Duke University Press, 1950), 63–64. Becker acknowledges a debt to Robert E. Park for the term "sacred society" ("Human Migration and the Marginal Man," *American Journal of Sociology* 33 [1927–1928]: 881–893). For an overview of the problem, see D. A. Martin, *A General Theory of Secularization* (Oxford: Blackwell, 1978).

24. Becker, 39.

25. It is scarcely necessary to mention Becker's baroque typologies, to which he devoted most of his analytic force; he classified sacred societies into traditional sacred (two subtypes), or prescribed (six subtypes), and as normative secular (eight subtypes) or abnormative (fourteen subtypes).

26. Among others, see Daniel Bell, "The Return of the Sacred? The Argument on the Future of Religion," *British Journal of Sociology* 28, no. 4 (1977): 419–449, where Bell criticizes the concept of secularization in that changes in religious beliefs are first of all of a cultural kind and do not depend on social structure.

In his view, the return of the sacred takes place according to a threefold
modality: moralism, religion of salvation, and mysticism.

27. See Peter L. Berger and Thomas Luckman, *The Social Construction of Reality*
(New York: Doubleday, 1966).
28. See P. L. Berger, "Some Second Thoughts on Substantive Versus Functional
Definitions of Religion," *Journal for the Scientific Study of Religion* 2 (1974):
125–153.
29. Ibid., 27; "Any human meaning must, first of all, be understood in its own
terms, *from within*, in the sense of those who adhere to it."
30. For a critique of Berger's position in this sense see, among others, P. Bourdieu,
"Genèse et structure du champ religieux," *Revue française de sociologie* 12
(1971): 3–21: "Berger's sociology is a sociology of order, whose too-static
vision cannot find room for this dimension" (i.e., of the various forms of
contestation in the modern world).
31. So Protestantism would be more "secular" than Catholicism: "Protestantism
can be described in terms of an immense shrinkage of the area of the sacred, in
fact, if compared with its Catholic opponent." Peter L. Berger, *The Social
Reality of Religion* (London: Penguin, 1973), 117.
32. Berger, 113.
33. Berger, 116.
34. E. Severino, "Per invidia della scienza," *Corriere della Sera*, 30 June 1982.

4

Secularization as a Problem: The Reenchanted Disenchantment

A Case of Intellectual 'Transformism'

As remarked above, from this viewpoint the concept of secularization appears as the most ambiguous and contradictory as regards
the sociological approach to the religious phenomenon. It oes not
seem by chance that there are clamorous incidents of intellectual
"transformism." Scholars deployed on opposing sides unconcern-
edly change allegiance, which is certainly legitimate, as long as the
reasons are given; and then as swiftly as it is unforeseen, they take
sides with their former adversaries. Some change sides with style,
taking the trouble to legitimize, with doubts and questions, the
gradual change of positions. Others change views and position
much more brusquely, in the course of a page: that is, passing from
the end of one chapter to the start of another in the same book.[1] It
is not even worth quoting the most obvious examples more fully,
linked to the two models of behavior cited. Scholars in this field
know these references well, and it is not worth repeating them
precisely so as to avoid a further round of tedious, useless polemics, with no empirical referents.

At any rate, it should be noted that despite the variously false
denials that have recently gone on, there are still those who aim at
secularization so as to have space in the scientific debate and in the
attention of a wider public.[2]

75

For this reason too of simple convenience, the moment of clarifying in detailed and less cloudy terms the character of the supposed phenomenon of secularization has arrived. It should be spoken of in linguistic terms, but historical ones as well, without neglecting the weight exercised by some theological currents in direct connection with the developments of certain interpretive sociological suggestions. From the start of its use the concept of secularization has in fact undergone a series of misunderstandings and upsets that have substantially changed its meaning and importance.

To retrace the itinerary of its destiny may be enlightening so as to grasp some salient aspects of the current debate. It derives from the Latin *saeculum*, which, much later than the classical age, becomes "secularization." *Saeculum* meant the time of a generation or cycle of life of a person. In other cases it referred to a specific temporal event. And yet the dichotomy, or better, polarity, between *sacer* and *saecularis* bore the semantic and cultural bases of the later concept of secularization. Indeed, the distinction between what is consecrated to the divinity within the sacred precinct of the temple and what did not belong because it was outside marked the difference between "initiates" and the "profane," between priests and laypersons. We probably owe to the Christian writer Lactantius the first attempt to legitimate this distinction theoretically, in the fourth century, when he speaks of those "distant from the truth of the faith." In more explicit terms, St. Avitus spoke of the pagan writers as *saecularii*, but was preceded by Eustatius Afro who saw all pagans as *saecularii*. One may place in the same period St. Girolamo's view, which tended to separate those who dedicated themselves completely to the religious life from all others, Christians and non-Christians. Here there is already implicit a value judgement regarding the superiority of a monastic choice, almost foreseeing the emblematic role of the hermitic and cenobitic life as the maximum form of religious expression, far from the despised world (*saeculum*).

Therefore, when reference is made to the "secular" one is using a pejorative, negative adjective. It is symptomatic that since the third century there is evidence of this attitude in the words of the bishop of Carthage, St. Cyprian, who condemned the (contemporary) fashion of dressing secularly, that is, in a way not consonant with the model of honesty, decency, and reserve of the perfect Christian.

The Slow Progress of the Term 'Secularization'

The application of such a criterion is not, however, an exclusive prerogative of the Christian world. Even in the world of the pagans themselves, as otherwise defined, we have seen, as pagans, there are echoes of a similar kind. Think of the Georgics, where attention is drawn to the *empia saecula,* or Tertullian's *"videmus saeculi exempla!"*

Along with the negative connotation, one should also record a less well defined meaning, an uncertain one without an evaluative definition. This is *saeculum* as a succession of years, an historical phase, a group of several decades, to the point of indicating a full century. Despite the not infrequent use of the word *saeculum,* our Latin forebears did not use the locution *saecularizatio.*

More than a millennium was to pass from the end of the empire in the West before we first encounter in an official text the term "secularization."[3]

Indeed, it was in 1648 that the concept emerged, during the preliminaries for the peace of Westphalia. There were negotiations to end the Thirty Years' War. The struggles between Catholics and Protestants had been relentless. The situation was also complicated by some defections among the Catholic clergy passing to the Protestant side, but without losing their former benefits or means of subsistence. To this historical phase there belong some reversals with not easily foreseeable results: the setting up of an "evangelical union" and a "Catholic league"; the Bohemians' choice of a Catholic to replace their Protestant king; Spain's help to the Catholics and France's to the Protestants; the "holy slaughter" by Grisons, a true massacre of Protestants by Catholics; the failure of the Hapsburg attempt to wipe out the Protestants. In the end, Mazarin forced the opponents to stipulate the peace of Westphalia. The "secularizations" were legitimated in this, that is, the usurpations of ecclesiastical goods. The French legate Longueville coined the term to indicate thereby the expropriation of ecclesiastical goods, masking the operation by using a new concept in a nominalist sense, but essentially to correspond to a deprivation-confiscation. Despite the Catholics' opposition, the secularizations were sanctioned and recognized as valid.

The need for secularizations arose from a specific incident. The elector of Brandenburg had been forced to yield some land to the Swedes. In exchange there was thought of giving him some properties belonging to the Church, but without these losing the title of principates of the Holy Roman Empire. Thus the elimination of ecclesiastical property was concealed under the word *séculariser*, which in fact removed the property of the areas in question while formally respecting their status as ecclesiastical principates.

Consequently, secularization seemed to respect the rights of the Church, even though concretely it asserted and sanctioned the change of property. All this had the look of a temporary solution, since the formal part was not discussed.

In other words, this concerned a lawful expropriation, concealed by an ambiguous terminology that suggested the idea of a correct submission as regards the HRE but meanwhile eroding at the roots the basis of its power structure. In practice the new owners were Protestant but their lands remained ecclesiastical and so Catholic in name only.

This shows how already on the level of its historical origins, the process of secularization was accompanied by widespread misunderstandings and attempts (not even well concealed, given that Catholics reacted vehemently against them) at mystification.

It is not, as has been suggested, neutral to have recourse to the concept of secularization, which clearly shows its real value as trick and domination. But it should above all be stressed that it has an illicit use, intended not to come to terms with the essential truth of the empirical fact—that is, the change of ownership.

From type to type of secularization, the Church itself used the term structurally by dividing the "secular" clergy from the regular clergy, by secularizing, for example, a Benedictine monastery and some property of the Jesuits to found Munster University (with the pope's approval in 1773) and accepting the secularization of members of the clergy formerly belonging to orders of a monastic type.

From the treaties of Westphalia on, the spread of "secularization" as a word in common use is fully open to documentation. There is no gap as regards the original meaning, but there are some negative connotations not cancelled by diplomatic strategems intended to diminish their significance. The ambiguity remained and by itself determined many institutional procedures within and without the Church. We are not thus witnessing deep changes of meaning, or semantic distortions. In fact the tendentially negative perspective applicable to secularization did not change, despite the appearances of conceptual neutrality.

So, Longueville taught a lesson. And a little less than two centuries later, the great secularization of 1803 saw the series of confiscations, transfers, and expropriations at the expense of institutions and organisms of the Church being repeated. If Longueville's Catholic opponents had gotten very little in terms of damages, the nineteenth-century Catholics repeatedly stigmatized the frauds suffered and condemned secularization as unjust, unmerited, and illegitimate. This was possible also through the fact that this time it was much more the Church itself that suffered damage, seeing others direct the injustice of secularization and stand up to the aggressive action of the usurping state.

There was a marked difference as regards the past. The state had not remained in the service of the Church's interests and no longer was its "secular" arm. In fact the reciprocal legitimating support had diminished, which the French Revolution had wished definitively to end. Consequently, the two former allies had become irreconcilable adversaries. Above all the capacity for decision making was reversed: no longer in Church hands, it had passed to the state.

Analytic Models and Specific Historical Contents

In the course of recent centuries, moreover, secularization of a sociological kind has been marked by complex, changing situations. If English Protestantism enjoyed a "splendid" isolation also favored by geographical motives, the northern European one seemed too distant from the heart of Europe and Rome to be trapped by Catholic influences and pressures. Events and crucial historical results occurred with the English civil war ending in 1660, the

American Revolution of 1776, and the French and Russian revolutions of 1789 and 1917, not to mention the Swiss and Scottish reformations and the failed revolution in Lutheran Germany.

Thus it was that the American model of secularization had rather a moral nature. The British one led to an institutional crisis if not a collapse of beliefs. The French involved a strong link between the political and religious dimensions. Finally, the Latin American one favored the marriage between Marxism and religion.

The emergence of secularism created problems both on the institutional and fideistic planes. Especially in Russia the conflict between the orthodox world and the new socialist reality gave rise to an absolute secularism by the state with the confining of religious experience within private or monastic circles.

A case apart is that of Calvinism, which demonstrates a certain secularization of ethical, but not structural, aspects, as against the Catholic and Anglican model where the institutions felt the effects of secularization considerably.

In the Lutheran field, finally, only the convergence between Marxism and secularism opened significant gaps in the institutional framework.

Ultimately, the meaning already pointed out as regards the Peace of Westphalia finds obvious confirmation in the following centuries. At all events, we see a contraction of spaces formerly belonging to the "set" of metaphysics and religion. Secularization thus continued to show that something was taken from the dominion of the Church. Possibly the object, the content of this removal changes. First it was a material good, a property, a territory, and then there was a move to less manifest aspects, less empirically verifiable but equally important from a sociological viewpoint: values, ideals, orientations, principles, attitudes, choices. At first sight the availability of ecclesiastical property is at the mercy of state management, afterward it is the turn of morality, politics, economics, freeing oneself from religious guardianship to become training grounds of the individual will for contingent interests of a family, organizational, and community kind.

The drive to secularization even found a formal operational instrument when in 1846 George Holyoake founded his London Secular Society, whose objective was the rejection of any kind of church or religious intervention. In this view, secularism took on the character of a practical popular philosophy, intended for the depriving of authority of every religious structure. The aim was to distance the church from all sectors outside religion. Secularistic militancy was a characteristic of the members of Holyoake's society.

However once more one must recognize that the secularist drive must in every case come to terms with its counterpart in that the very expression "to secularize," while in fact a frontal assault on the ecclesiastical dimension, also represents its indirect recognition. The confessional reality is not wholly negated. Rather, it is legitimated. Basically one was restricted to assign it a role different from the past, more specific, more pertinent. Religion thus was outside many sectors of social experience, except that this means also that the Church is concerned with questions far above mere everyday problems. Thus the ultimate sediment of secularism does not seem to annihilate the religious fact but rather to exalt it— giving it a prestigious space, since it is the most significant one to provide a meaning for experience.

There is no conflict and still less hostility between secularism and religion, but just a definition of fields of action. This was in the intentions of the London Secular Society's founder, whose followers nonetheless revised the original positions and descended to a more conflictual area that could only arouse lively reactions from the ecclesiastical side, fearful of the dangers inherent in the secularist current. Successive events have, however, diluted the polemic to the point of a recognition of a positive role for secularization, according to the argument in 1953 of the theologian Gogarten, who saw in it the natural destiny of religion.

At times there has been discussion of the emergence of the contemporary concept of secularization. For some the suggestion was born first among sociologists; for others it came from theologians. In reality, the subject of secularization was not alien to the development of sociological thought. However, if at a certain time, especially in the 1960s, secularization became a constant[4] in reflection on the religious phenomenon, the favorable opportunity was provided by some theological works to which other considerations of a sociological kind were gladly attached.

Once it was clear that secularism was an excess of secularization, the latter was even effective for the purposes of the survival of religious belief. So, this should be seen as a necessary updating of faith itself, otherwise relegated to playing a rearguard role.

For Gogarten too, secularization was a solution that allowed a display of liberty as regards hypotheses of incursion into not strictly religious fields—for example, with the creation of Christian parties. It was a tension toward liberty from ideological—including ecclesiastical—mortgages. So secularization was to be seen as legitimate and even desirable for the openings it offered in the light of a recovery of space for the religious.

Bonhoeffer's prophecy in this regard is very shrewd.[6] He spoke of a nonreligious reading of the biblical texts, convinced of the uselessness of a problem-solving or stopgap God. This was the abandonment of God, the same absence that by permitting secularization created the premises for a full life in contemporary reality, with a spirit effectively outstretched to humanity without the shield of a protective and reassuring God, good for all occasions.

J.A.T. Robinson's suggested approach, in *Honest to God*, is of a different tone. A complete revision of the conceptions linked to traditional discussions of God is demanded.[7] The gap between the religious and secular worlds is so deep that only a new arrangement of religious thought would make possible the reopening of dialogue between the two realities. On the other hand, with the decline of some customary paradigms, salvation did not belong exclusively to Christians, and indeed many non-Christians would be quite close to the kingdom of God thanks precisely to their rejection of too narrow a conception of the relation with the supernatural.

The exhaustion of basic terms in religious debate is a favorable sign for an about-face, producing a modernized reading of the sacred texts, a reconsideration of the most typically human and social contents, and a reconversion of structures in a secular direction.

Giving a hand to the position favoring secularization there came Harvey Cox's *The Secular City*, which gave important stimuli to the debate on the contrast between sacred and secular, giving widespread exposure to a subject otherwise secluded in the usual channels of academic debate. The spreading of theo-sociological theories of secularization passes primarily through Cox's successful book, which in brilliant and captivating ways speaks of a new advent of a secular stamp, new divinities made popular by mass communications, and a rediscovery of politics by religion (God is said to be more interested in state than Church questions). The Old Testament and politics are taken as central pillars of the new interpretation of contemporary society (a similar operation is also suggested by van Buren in *Il significato secolare dell-Evangelo*).[9] Consequently, the starting point for the believer is no longer the Church but rather the world, from which to acquire the impetus to reach—in time—an understanding of the role of the Church in the world. The end of old-style religion is the condition for reproposing Christianity in a secularized society, which poses the human being as the protagonist of history and not as the succubus of metaphysical manacles and complicated and meaningless liturgies.

The argument of Cox's essay turns on biblical sources and especially episodes in the Creation, Exodus, and the Mosaic alliance, as moments of passage and so of transformation, whose innovative nature is compared to that of secularization.

It is true that secularizing action brings with it the fall of myths and symbols, but it is also true that one cannot speak of a death of God, in the wake of other contemporary scholars,[10] in that the category of the supernatural cannot be canceled.

Centrality is given back to the individual and his work in history, having as its goal the transcendence of fatalistic, resigned conceptions.

We do not find ourselves before the end of Christianity, for the secular city does not wholly abolish the places of the sacred. However, it transforms the use to which they are put, or better, it creates new ones with less formalized, more dynamic, characteristics, especially as regards the relativity of every belief and religious organization, connected, at all events, with specific, particular sociological contexts.

Traditions must be subjected to criticisms, discussion, and revision. This does not imply the rejection of every religious problematic. It is only a change of viewpoint. It turns us toward this world, in this age (in the double meaning that refers to the Latin root of *saeculum*). In this way the believer is able still to cherish hopes for a future otherwise denied and discounted by the processes of rationalization and urbanization.

It is clear that a metaphysical God has no more motive for placing himself in the secular metropolis. However, when he presented himself as historical actor, fully involved in the secular future, subject-object of a renewed language, tied to concrete contents of existence, he would have had full right of citizenship in the secularized age.

The evidently optimistic view of this Baptist theologian is certainly sociologically "ingenuous," but is not without stimulating points that indicate well-grounded itineraries related to the continuity of religion.

The array of sociologists of secularization, already crowded, continues to increase still with fashionable schemas and tedious repetition. Indeed, some of them are so bound to this subject that scientifically they would almost cease to exist once their customary and most exploited object of study was removed. It is furthermore strange that the majority are incurable theorists with little experience in the field.

Larry Shiner has suggested a systemizing of sociological categories applied to the phenomenon of secularization. His attempt at synthesis is therefore useful in place of a long sequence of citations and authors.

There are thus said to be six contexts in which the various conceptions concerning secularization can be located.[11] The first is linked to the loss of meaning in religion, its institutions and symbols. The second concerns the adjustment of the Church to new secular demands and dominant models of life, with an emphasis on pragmatic and realist solutions. The third looks at society's taking its distance as regards religion, the progressive autonomization of public sectors, the individualization of religious belief, and the placing of religious motivation in parentheses (or its barring). The fourth brings out the tendency to broaden the weltanschauung far beyond the wholly religious view of reality by giving a leading role to the actions of the individual in society so as to refute the supernatural roots of institutions: thus religion too is made less divine, more human and anthropological (the case of Calvinism is exemplary: according to Weber,[12] its secularization is said to have created at least the premise for the capitalist spirit). In the fifth category there is disenchantment regarding the myths and mysteries of the religious reality that is "desacralized" as an essential component of society. The last context marks the transition from a sacred society to a secular one in terms of widespread social change and rationalization.

Invisible Religion

However, the book that has been most quoted and discussed in recent decades is probably Luckmann's on "invisible religion," concerned with the presence of "new subjects" as functional substitutes of official, institutionalized religion.[13] These subjects include individual autonomy, self-expression, self-realization, sexuality, familiarism, and free time—all spaces in experience made ever more free from fetters of a religious type. With the decline of traditional sacred values, the new cosmos is equipped with the alternative subjects just mentioned. Choices occur in a situation diverse from that of the past, especially as regards the visibility or invisibility of systems of attitudes and behavior. The chief result of invisible religion is precisely the internalization of every decision related to the cosmos considered to be sacred.

Recently Thomas Luckmann has tried to clarify his view that religion can only be an individual fact.[14] Indeed, religious institutions are only the expression of thoughts and actions of individuals inserted into the institutions themselves. The German scholar warns us against banalizing his argument to the point of believing that culture and religion are the mechanical aggregate of individual psychologies. In fact, individual thoughts and actions are said to have an essentially social character, in that they derive from an intersubjective relation (thus putting forward again the theorizing of the social construction of reality). So, the Church, in its historical interconnections, is said to have helped to model individual consciousnesses so as to orient them toward it. Recourse to a specific "social form of religion" is an approximate and temporary solution because of the impossibility of living in an "ideally" religious cosmos, that is, a symbolic universe in which there is no break between everyday existence and dreams, fantasy and experience, life and death. The historical development of post-Constantinian religion has enabled an increasing specialization of the religious function through special structures and liturgies.

As has already occurred for other theorists of secularization, including Italians, Luckmann has taken on over the years a more cautious position, with questionings and doubts. In fact, he now asks if the coming of "privatized religion" is only a beginning, or at any rate a partial phenomenon of replacement of the social form of specialized religion. In fact, the author of *The Invisible Religion* does not come down in favor of the possibility of a total victory of private religion at the expense of the institutional. Rather, he specifies that privatization is not complete. It is then also probable that there will be a resocialization of the Church in relation to new demands of society, whereby the ground lost will be regained. However, it is certain that the methods used up until now are becoming extinct.

Luckmann further damps down interest in the new religious movements that for him are banal, rather privatized, and of little importance for readaptation to modern industrial society. Rather than vanguards, they are uninfluential rear guards.

Some passages in Luckmann's argument may seem too assertive or didactic. It even anticipates possible objections, but in a way that again emerges as not explanatory, weakly reasoned, and empirically feeble. However, this approach preserves its value as an intelligent, practiced observation, certainly stimulating. It is not the time to go back over individual statements, which perhaps err for their partisanship, more nominalist than substantive distinctions, and for—conscious—Western-centeredness, and for its slender use of field research.

However, there is at least one opening that makes one hopeful, as it contains warning signals of great importance: the well-indicated usefulness of investigating the religious phenomenon not by questionnaires and quantitative data but through qualitative approaches, interpretations of biography, and narrative interviews.

Ultimately for Luckmann the sole acceptable definition of secularization involves "the processes by which the chief institutional circles of the social structure have been 'emancipated' from *specifically* religious norms."[15] This means in practice making the process of secularization correspond with that of industrialization (and/or rationalization?).

Is a distinction between sacred and secular societies after Howard Becker's formula really practicable?[16] Behind this dichotomous vision of Becker and Luckmann there is a latent idea of wanting to conserve, as it were, the given situation, rejecting different solutions (whereby the new religions do not bite on the social fabric). Moreover, Weber had sharply opposed clear distinctions. In addition, certain positions regarding the subject of secularization sound too near the influence of a wholly Western approach.

The Versatile Persistence of the Sacred

In reality, the sacred doess not seem to run risks of crisis, nor even of simple temporary eclipse. Its function, in fact, is kept lively, even though it is complex and not easy to interpret.

The processes of rationalization advance within the Church itself, whose dogmatic pronouncements cannot deceive because they only serve to mask the ongoing updating, the compromise in progress, the taking note of an enforced change. Secularization is thus not the work of the Evil One, as though this had crept into the very folds of the institution so as to wear it away and destroy it from within. Even if there were crisis and the hierarchico-institutional level, it would not be impossible to manage and could rather produce seemingly deviant phenomenologies that in reality were in collusion. Thereby, the mode of divergence-dissent itself, within limits, would manage to maintain solid ties with the institution, at least as a parameter of reference, even for groups and individuals otherwise destined to complete dispersal. The discovery of religion as a private fact cannot wholly depart from the previous experience of belief and socialization. For this reason the prophecy by Luckmann on the erosion of the social form of religion does not seem to have concrete proofs. The so-called "eruption of grace" has no need of ecclesiastical mediations. It seems then clear that church religion does not absorb all the potential of the sacred, whose multiple expressions give the lie to the idea of a diffused secularization. The sacred finds new, wider spaces. It would not be totally groundless to think that there may be a nonreligious view of the sacred.

The process of secularization has often been connected, apart from with industrialization, with urbanization. However, it is not certain that the expansion of urban centers always and despite everything favors secularizing developments. Among others, the case of Poland is symptomatic. Here, the number of believers and practicing Christians has even been increasing, espcially in the larger cities. It is quite true that in the specific case other socio-political variables have an influence. Nonetheless, the phenomenology in progress gives unmistakable signs of developmental asymmetry between secularization on one hand and urbanization on the other. Indeed, in addition, it is the growth of the cities that mostly favors religious socialization, participation in services, mass liturgies, large pilgrimages, and a more effective devotion to activism and religious militancy.

The example of Poland is not an isolated one. In the United States, it is the most populous cities that witness the flowering of religious groups, movements and cults, whose significance, whatever Luckmann thinks, certainly are not a sign of the end of the sacred.

Further, from another viewpoint, the very process of secularization, when it exists, becomes a source of development of the churches in that—as in the U.S. case—it allows the participation of members otherwise distant from any fideistic prospect. In other words, the level of language, content and philo-secular attitude of the churches becomes an excellent reason for acquiring new memberships, aided by greater proximity and affinity in the religious world—whose basic models are not perceived as wholly extraneous to the profane ones.

Paradoxically, as Becker has argued since the 1950s, secularization is turned into a privileged mediation for accepting new religious suggestions. Not by chance, tele-evangelism in North America manages to form links where perhaps the specialized social forms of religion have failed. The spectacular, charismatic, telegenic raiment of the TV preachers is undoubtedly a phase of secularization of the religious message (and instrument), but at the same time it provides a more attractive—because secular—image that breaks and overcomes customary resistances and diffidence.

At this point one should establish more homogeneously and comprehensibly the meaning of the concept of secularization. The possible definitions are many and at times conflicting (even with the same author). So, it has been attempted to simplify the complexity of the question by a simple use of adjectives as neutral as it is misleading. The differences of usage have made us imagine a multidimensionality of secularization, such as one might deduce from the list of 248 articles on the subject, accurately examined by Karel Dobbelaere.[17] The Belgian sociologist starts from the remark that the term secularization has been more often used in German (in some way taken for granted, given that we have seen it was first used in this context in the preliminaries to the Peace of Westphalia), but also in Italian, Flemish, and English. In France, the other derivatives are usually preferred—"laicization," or "de-Christian-ization," or "religious change." And yet the inventor of the term secularization was the French legate, Longueville, speaking in French. So, how can we explain this tendency to reject the term above all in the linguistic "set" it arose in? Perhaps it was and is so obvious a semantic muddle and the ambiguous implication inferred that other versions, more explicit and clear, are chosen. Above all, to speak of secularization involves a basic imprecision not removed, as it should be—what do we mean by secular? and secularization?

The presumed and claimed pluridimensionality of the concept does not remove its hermeneutic ambiguities but rather legitimates them by accepting them as they really are.

Despite the attempt at a *super partes* synthesis, Dobbelaere is at the same time critical and hasty as regards Luckmann's position. He shares the latter's idea of autonomization of the social as regards the religious, but by stressing its assumption of its own sacred cosmos diversified according to the individual institutions. In short, whereas one is freed from the religious and thus laicized, nonetheless the institutions maintain or create their own sacred universes. The sacred cosmos is no longer unique but fragmented, made complex in the various social and institutional branches.

As we see, the last approach, Dobbelaere's, ends to some extent by agreeing with Luckmann, especially as regards the fall in religious practice and the credibility of religious institutions and contents. Ultimately laicization is said to correspond to the de-Christianization of contemporary societies. So nothing new has been added to what is already known and discussed.

The Supposed Bankruptcy of the Religious

The author most convinced of the catastrophic thesis on the fate of religions is undoubtedly Bryan Wilson,[18] who aside from the deceptive appearances of a punctilious and careful style, lets his thought on this clearly spill out. We need only ask what interest there is in dealing so at length with a phenomenon destined to become a residue of the past. But there it is. And he explains secularization by lack of solidarity, increase in social mobility, and the depersonalization of social relations. The new religious movements themselves are to be seen as rather marginal and without sociological importance (so, agreement with Luckmann). It is very odd to read this in a scholar who deserves to be remembered for his well-supported interest in the sociology of the sects, which even in their marginality have meant much in the history of dominant religions. Basically, Christianity itself was a sect at the outset, with the typical typologies of a nascent group, forced to protect itself even with parasecret methods.

At the other extreme, there is talk of a permanence of religion, which will survive any attack of secularization that is unable to undermine its vitality and unpredictable ability to adjust and renew itself. Peter E. Glasner for his part easily demolishes the argument of secularization as product of a social myth, set up and guaranteed only by motives of an ideological kind.[19] Parsons[20] deals with it still more simply by enfolding secularization in a more general social change. In his view, it was a mistake to see secularization as a one-way process, concerning only the prevalence of secular over religious interests, where it would be permissible to invert the development and think of a rapprochement of the secular to the religious model. Certainly this is a paradox, but Parsons is deliberately provocative and marks a trend different from the usual one: that is, not the loss of ground by religion, but rather its "occupation," as it were, of secular contexts. Thus a double direction is reestablished that permits the religious to flow back into the secular, and not merely the latter into the former. In short, secularization marks the triumph of religion, but in forms different from those of the past, even if there is no immediate break, so that old and new coexist for a long time before a definitive change.

Robert N. Bellah,[21] a perceptive student of Parsons, essentially follows his direction. For him, religion is not being directed toward the periphery of modern societies but is rather reaching the center of individual and social experiences.

Here, we have rather unexpectedly arrived at an inversion of the starting positions. Religion is not about to end. It is going along its set path. Probably, rather than speaking of a reversibility of secularization, it is useful to define religion as irreversible. The sacred does not disappear, as it is closely tied to social experience. Without having necessarily to fall back on Durkheimian arguments, one must infer that, given the current premises, the concept of "permanent religion" will long be a usable one.

Notes

1. See D. Martin, *The Religious and the Secular* (London: Routledge, 1969), and for an earlier example, his "Towards Eliminating the Concept of Secularization," in J. Gould, ed., *Penguin Survey of the Social Sciences*; and for a change of direction, his *General Theory of Secularization*.
2. See, for a now distant example, S. Acquaviva and G. Guizzardi, eds., *La secolarizzazione* (Bologna: Il Mulino, 1973). Nonetheless, the first of these authors has often returned to the subject with less systematic contributions.
3. See for example H. Lübbe, *La secolarizzazione* (Bologna: Il Mulino, 1970).
4. P. L. Berger and T. Luckmann, "Secularization and Pluralism," *Internationales Jahrbuch für Religionssoziologie* 2 (1966): 73–86.
5. See F. Gogarten, *Destino e speranza dell'epoca moderna: La secolarizzazione come problema teologico* (Brescia: Morcelliana, 1972), *passim*.
6. D. Bonhoeffer, *Resistenza e resa* (Milan: Bompiani, 1969).
7. See J.A.T. Robinson, *Dio non e' cosi* (Florence: Vallecchi, 1965).
8. See H. Cox, *La citta' secolare* (Florence, Vallecchi, 1968).
9. See P. van Burean, *Il significato secolare dell'Evangelo* (Turin: Gribaudi, 1969).
10. See T.J.J. Altizer and W. Hamilton, *La teologia radicale e la morte di Dio* (Milan: Feltrinelli, 1969).
11. L. Shiner, "The Concept of Secularization in Empirical Research," *Journal for the Scientific Study of Religion* 6, no. 2 (1967): 207–220.
12. See M. Weber, *L'etica protestante e lo spirito del capitalismo* (Florence: Sansoni, 1966).
13. T. Luckmann, *La religione invisibile* (Bologna: Il Mulino, 1969).

14. T. Luckmann, "Religiosita individuale e forme sociali di religione," *Religioni e Societa* 1 (1986): 33–39 (replies to new questions from Carlo Prandi, who takes up the argument in "La religione invisibile—Un riesame del contributo di Thomas Luckmann," pp. 40–48 of the same issue).

15. T. Luckmann, 38.

16. H. Becker, "Current Sacred-Secular Theory and Its Development," in H. Becker and A. Boskoff, eds., *Modern Sociological Theory in Continuity and Change* (New York: Dryden, 1957), 133–185.

17. See K. Dobbelaere, *Secularization: A Multidimensional Concept* (London: Sage, 1981).

18. See B. Wilson, *Religion in Secular Society: A Sociological Comment* (Baltimore: Penguin, 1969).

19. See P. E. Glasner, *The Sociology of Secularization: A Critique of a Concept* (London: Routledge, 1977).

20. T. Parsons, "Belief, Unbelief, and Disbelief," in R. Caporale and A. Grumelli, eds., *The Culture of Unbelief: Studies and Proceedings from the First International Symposium on Belief Held at Rome, March 22–27, 1969* (Berkeley: University of California Press, 1971), 207–245.

21. See R. N. Bellah, *Al di la delle fedi* (Brescia: Morcelliana, 1975).

5

'Lay Religion' in Dynamic Societies

Forms of 'Civil Religion': From Rousseau to Robert Bellah

Bergson's approach to the religious problem may also run the risk of seeming a psychologizing one. In fact, it lends itself to reflections that go beyond the mere individual fact and mark orientations and peculiarities that others thereafter, with or without reference to those ideas, have developed in more complete terms from a sociological viewpoint. From just a rapid reading of some pages of Bergson's *La penseé et le mouvant*, there clearly emerges the global conception of existence and the superinvididual in the sense of religion as "social sentiment." Bergson warns us to notice that a science, in the fluid state of its origins, is always ready to dogmatize. Having available only a limited experience, it works less on the facts than some simple ideas, maybe or maybe not suggested by facts, which it deals with "almost deductively." Plato, however, still according to Bergson, undertook an operation that one might define as protosociolinguistic: he used the "concepts deposited in advance in language as if they had descended from heaven and would reveal to the mind a suprasensible reality." Furthermore, Plato's "good" and Aristotle's "thought of thought," the god of mythology and of Christianity, do not always appear with the same attributes. At any rate, it is in fact toward these entities that "prayers rise." "Be it static or dynamic, religion regards this point as basic."[1]

The same tone is heard again in *Les deux sources de lar morale et de la religion.* Here Bergson clearly sees how ideas on divinity help to smooth the path to social and individual action. He knows well that knowledge and experience are closely linked but is equally aware of the fact that the sum of probabilities may lead to a suspicion of certainty. The final outcome, as is well known, is that of mysticism as reinforcement and completion of the results already achieved. In fact, the mystics have arrived "with an individual effort added to the general work of life so as to smash the resistance that opposed this instrument, to triumph over materiality, and finally to find God again."[2]

Divinity is thus beyond the barrier, which only mystics manage to cross. Despite this, it is a common ground of reference. Religious feeling, insofar as it is socially diffused, thus comes to have connotations similar (but not completely) to those of Rousseau on "civil religion," later taken over explicitly by the analysis of Robert Neelly Bellah who applied them to the American case viewed along the parabola of the diachronic development of the U.S. as a nation. Then, Rousseau's statement whereby the principle of *action* lies in the desire for liberty is almost imperceptibly transformed into the assertion that the principle of the (American) *nation* lies in the same will to be free. Liberty as a value is experienced in terms of a predictive absolute and is, still in Rousseauistic terms, accompanied by the supposed "innate principle of justice and virtue" seen as a criterion of judgement applied to action. It is the sentiments, always following Rousseau, which evaluate and preexist ideas and are the voice of conscience, "a divine instinct, celestial, immortal voice," as we see in book 4 of *Emile*, the profession of faith of the Savoyard pastor.

The first formulation of the concept of civil religion by Bellah is in the text of a lecture in May 1966, later published in *Daedalus*.[3] The author refers to the existence of a "civil religion worked out and well institutionalized," said to accompany the churches but well distinguished from them. At all events, this is not a new form of church but a new "religious dimension," with its own characteristics represented by the "subordination of the nation to ethical principles that transcend it."[4]

The concept of civil religion, as mentioned earlier, derives from Rousseau, and especially from book 4, chapter 8 of the *Social*

Contract. The particular aspects of civil religion are supplied by divinity, life beyond the grave, judgement with rewards and punishments, and the practice of religious toleration. References to similar ideas can be found also in Benjamin Franklin's *Autobiography*,[5] as well as in George Washington's Farewell Address, where paradoxically Bergson's thought is almost literally reflected: "Religion and morality are indispensable supports of all the tendencies and customs which belong to religious prosperity." Reference to God, as a generic and thus undefined entity, therefore not belonging to the Jewish or Christian context alone, is a kind of connecting tissue that connects different solemn statements, official ones, in symbolically very portentous moments, by various U.S. presidents. So, the Declaration of Independence, Washington's inauguration, and to take examples distant in time and mentality, Kennedy's inauguration, as well as those of other important leaders of American politics, have appealed to the "God of Nature," the "Creator," the "Supreme Judge of the world," the "Omnipotent Being," the "Invisible hand," and so on, with a multiplicity of titles that not even a mind of feverish imagination could join together, even in a diversified series of circumstances and occasions. However, it should again be made clear that this is not a specific God, but a god more one than three, more inclined to the severity of the law than the readiness of love.

Then there is a persistent synthesizing of America and Israel. In fact as we shall see later, the U.S. seems almost to present itself as representing the new chosen people, whose members are the new protagonists of the "biblical alliance." So America succeeds in being the "promised land" too, where those of the chosen race have settled after leaving the "Egyptian" Europe. President Johnson seemingly echoed this idea in his inauguration speech: "They came here—the exile and the stranger, courageous beyond all fear—to find a place where man can be his own master. They have made a solemn pact . . ." It could not escape Bellah, a careful observer of symbolic dynamics, how proposals concerning the emblem of the U.S. had a particular meaning—Franklin suggested Moses, Jefferson the children of Israel. Despite this, Bellah stresses that in these operations there was no intention of subjecting the state to a specific religion or that this in turn should be directed at the political level. Only thus, in fact, could civil religion maintain its function as "genuine vehicle of a national, religious self-understanding."[6]

Thereby, civil religion is embodied in the values experienced in the everyday. In this perspective, it differs from church-religion. It is a personal fact, divided from politics, nonritual. However, this does not remove the common layer that accompanies the lived experience of millions of people and hinges on rites and beliefs, symbols and festivals. One thinks especially of Memorial Day, created after the Civil War and functional especially for inserting families into civil religion through community ceremonies, solemn speeches, and visits to the monuments of national heroes. It is moreover from the Civil War that the issues of the holocaust, of death and resurrection, are confronted in civil religion. Lincoln himself was compared to Christ, as a man chosen by God. Later, the institution of national cemeteries still more enforced the idea of a common religion.

And yet Lincoln never belonged to any church, even if his ideas were as firm and deep as a religious faith. In fact, as Tocqueville had rightly seen (as quoted by Bellah), "A political institution that contributes in a specific way to maintaining a democratic republic" was precisely the religion of the American Church, defined by others as the "poetry of civics." It scarcely needs saying that all this was made possible through time thanks to the lack of principled conflicts between religious and political structures. For this basic reason, civil religion could adopt symbols of a national kind able to stimulate and enliven great masses of people. Once the problem of independence was overcome, and partially that of slavery, there remained, however, unresolved and open, the problem of the role of America in a universal reality traversed by revolutionary pressures. It was then that the democratic republic of the United States was called on, says Bellah, to struggle against dictatorship, aggression, and armed conflict. Here and elsewhere the author, though passing from a dominant optimism to a widespread pessimism, lets himself fall at some points into an incurable ethno- or Americocentrism, which perhaps makes a scholar of great scientific and mental openness, coming from studies on the Apaches,[7] the religion of the Japanese shoguns,[8] and Islam,[9] lose credibility.

In Bellah's defense, it must be said that his feeling American is less accentuated than the "normal" attitude of his U.S. colleagues. And if the accusation that has been made of him as worshipper of the American nation is unjustified, an extenuating (or possibly not) circumstance is his dissolving of the discussion into a universal scale:

> As Americans we have been much privileged in the world, but it is as men we shall be judged. . . . It would be necessary to put into our civil religions a vital international symbolism; or perhaps the result would be better if American civil religion simply became part of a new world religion. . . . Fortunately, since American civil religion is not the faith of the American nation but an understanding of American experience in the light of an ultimate and universal reality, the reorganization produced by a new situation of this type would not necessarily destroy the continuity of American civil religion. A world civil religion could be accepted as a lament and not a negation of American civil religion."[10]

Social Crisis and Religious Points of Reference

The Vietnam War and other events destroyed many of these illusions, but in fact Bellah was quite conscious of the existence of "miserable interests and abject passions" that have instrumentalized, for the end of consolation, American civil religion. His proposal then involved a "continuous operation of reform," able to make civil religion grow and become rich with new content.

In another publication on civil religion in the 1970s there is a return to, and rethinking of, the subject.[11] This article arises from the fact that the concept of civil religion had had much resonance, to the point of becoming an element of common reference, known also to the nonspecialist public.

In this article Bellah states that "all politically organized societies have some type of civil religion."[12] He then goes on to make clear that civil religion is not always to be seen positively (he had attacked the German theologian Moltmann on this point), just as it is not his intention to "glorify civil religion in general or American civil religion in particular."[13] The opportunity provided was the example of Richard Nixon, promoter of an American *fides* ("We shall reply to God") but also of a conflict Bellah defines without half measures as "the most criminal war in American history."[14] However, civil religion managed to keep its vitality in George

McGovern's election campaign against Nixon, and McGovern's oratory often used biblical quotations.

The new youth and feminist experience seemed to call in question many of the traditional values. Bellah thus suggests: an inquiry into the whole civil religious tradition; a severe critique to discover positive and negative elements wherever they are; a widening of the inquiry to grasp the direction also of different traditions. In practice, the tradition of civil religion could not stay autarkic. On the other hand, it seemed obvious to him at the time that "each community is based on the sense of the sacred and requires a context of higher meaning."[15]

The conclusion of the discussion, before the postscript on the Watergate scandal that brought down many hopes, remains in the vein of the opening premise: "Religion, morality, and politics are not the same thing and to confuse them may lead to still worse distortions. The concept of civil religion simply points to the fact that in all societies there seem to exist some connections between them."[16]

The premise thus almost latently dominating the whole treatment of civil religion is that Bellah considers the West and the U.S. in particular as (relatively) less problematic contexts, especially in comparison with other developing countries. As regards this, as other statements, the reactions of some sociologist colleagues have not always been pleasant. David Martin in his contribution speaks for all of them, when he says he is in total disagreement, because Bellah "also seems convinced that his personal conception, which as he himself recognizes is very American, is the way in which things in the world are destined to go. . . . Bellah puts us all in the American melting pot and presents us with the consensus of the values not of the medieval but of the electronic village."[17]

On his part, Talcott Parsons finds an affinity between the Durk- heimian ethic of society and Bellah's conception of civil society. Parsons's approach is as usual peculiarly refined. Weber spoke of a consensus of values based on beliefs understood both as knowledge and as devotion. Durkheim was "blocked" on the institutional existence of a moral community, seen as an *object* whose founding elements were, precisely, morality and sacrality. Where Durkheim stopped, Bellah is seen as starting. Thus both the author of the theorization of "civil religion" and Luckmann, theorist of the "invisible religion" in some way present a common front, beyond the slender or nonexistent notes of reference to the single enlightened master. Parsons is authoritatively witness to this in writing that "wide reference has been made to a 'Durkheimian' viewpoint that, it is perhaps right to say, Luckmann himself has stated in its entirety."[18] But the central point is different. Durkheim identifies the moral community with the Church. And Bellah "has again managed to show with greater clarity in the case of America, that these distinctions are in no way incompatible with a societal community that is at the same time 'secular' and still endowed with a 'religious aspect'. In this sense, naturally, Durkheim was right."[19] But what are the distinctions involved? First of all, there is the one concerning the "State Church" distinct from the secular world. Then there is the more typically American one that shows a "confessional pluralism" and also a clear disagreement between church and state. Therefore, Parsons adds, morality and social community are not given by a church. And separateness does not seem to prevent the existence of an ethical community, as civil religion would confirm.

The latter, furthermore, has the capacity to "produce new forms of possible fusion between personal and social visions."[20] Bellah recalls in this regard the example of the so-called Peace Corps, a movement whose members took a vow of poverty and gathered recruits mainly among the young in search of "authenticity" in commitment to the suffering. Members of the Peace Corps simply refer to the founding values of civil religion in America. Bellah adds that this same argument may hold good for those young people who go abroad and take part in the sufferings of other parts of the world. They seem the incarnation of the continuous religion of mankind. In reality, this does not have full and concrete confirmation, as the "international moral community" so dear to Bellah "is not the result of any objective creed or imposed dogma. It is the greatest current example of how an account of interior autonomy and authenticity may also have the deepest social and moral effects."[21]

Critical Remarks

One of the most telling criticisms of the concept of civil religion (and thus of Parsons's and Bellah's functionalist approach) is undoubtedly that of Roland Robertson. He stigmatizes the intellectual operation related to the "religion of Americanism," "secular religion," or "civic religion" as if it were a mere exercise in sophistry, in that the theory seems to cling to a basic definition that is functional and nominal, as well as to systems of action seen in quite abstract terms. In concrete cases there is a switch toward definitions deriving from common sense and the everyday. Further, the notion of civil religion is unconvincing because it is inconsistent and out of conformity with conventional criteria of definition. One can thus speak of a show of relevance derived from the association of the two terms "religion" and "civil."[22]

In Robertson's critique there emerges also an unusual rapprochement with the theologian Altizer, one of the theorists of the death of God (seen as the only condition "that can make possible the coming of a new humanity").[23] It is curious to note that Robertson in citing Altizer should refer to another contemporary theologian, Moltmann, who as founder of the theology of hope has been one of the harshest critics of civil religion. In fact, Altizer believes the paths of the sacred cross the profane, and tend to sacralize it. This ultimate result is said to rejoin Moltmann's eschatology. However, probably the affinity between Altizer and Bellah, if it exists, lies essentially in the common field of application—America.

In fact, the author of *The Gospel of Christian Atheism* sharply polemicizes with American *dehumanization,* reconnecting itself thus with Bellah's optimistic pessimism (or pessimistic optimism, a flaw really more prevalent today than yesterday). Altizer's expectation is of a *coincidentia oppositorum*, or the union of sacred and profane. So it is that civil religion seems precognizant of this advent of Balek's "great divine Humanity," as one of the last century's "prophets."

Robertson recalls that the consonance between Altizer and Bellah occurs in the common attribution of meaning to American society seen in terms of redemption or apocalypse. Redemption concerns the historical role of America and its original promise of liberation extended to all humanity. Apocalypse involves the hope of a new order, that is, the final victory with the advent of the "kingdom of God." As we see, Bellah's thought emerges enriched in this way with new value, or rather, by clarifications of a theological kind. Bellah, with Parsons, is not a theologian, but in some way he uses the process of incarnation when he separates civil from institutional religion and sees America as a chosen nation, a new Israel in exodus from Europe, arisen by passing through the holocaust of civil war. However, the next phase of diffusion of civil religion at the international level had been slowed down by tragic experiences like Vietnam, so that the religious promise of America was blotted by it, lost face. Here Robertson shrewdly anticipated what was to be a further in-depth analysis by Bellah in the book symbolically entitled *The Broken Covenant*.

In a final comment, Robertson for once takes a position on civil religion, reserving this exception for those cases only where the religious dimension was directly connected with a political structure (as with Shintoism in Japan until 1945). On the other hand he quotes a very suitable passage from Charles Long:

> "From a religious point of view the American experience expresses what Rudolph Otto described as *misterium fascinosum*. He meant by this the quality of the religious object that attracts and arouses the desire for comfort, union, and identification with the religious object. The opposing attitude, *misterium tremendum*, the quality that indicates the distance of the object of religion from the faithful, has been reduced to a residual category in American experience. The deistic orientation of the Founding Fathers already gave us a *deus otiosus*, a god who had removed himself from the centre of this new world."[24]

It hardly needs stressing how close Long's argument is to the *Secularity of American Religion* recalled by Robertson, which undoubtedly once more shows his greater familiarity with contemporary theology than Bellah, more expert in the historico-religious field.[25]

At this point one can infer that civil religion is none other than a functional type of response to the impossibility of offering a single religious structure to a people as multiform as the American. If, as Susan Budd maintains, only ethnic identity can favor to the utmost the formation and historical continuity of a church, clearly civil religion must be only a sociological label given to a deeply secular society. Thus the Founding FAthers might even not have had a clear choice of a religious kind and so used a god for labeling purposes in relation to an American society needing unifying symbols. Civil religion is thus a container of values: individualism, hard work, freedom, and even anticommunism.

Again, Susan Budd recalls an expression of Eisenhower that defines American society as one based on religious foundations—it doesn't matter which. Thus it is possible to distinguish between a conventional and a civic religion, but both have rituals and ideals that serve to legitimate public affairs, also pervading foreign policy (think of Bellah's "international moral community"). In this regard it is right clearly to stress the existence of an exceptional mythopeic capacity, one of fable making, accompanying America's brief, crowded history.[26]

The 'Broken Covenant'

After the coedited volume *Religion in America*,[27] Bellah resumed the theme of his civil religion on the occasion of the Second International Symposijm on Belief organized in Vienna by the Agnelli Foundation in 1975. There, the American sociologist faced the problem of the new religious movements, especially the youth ones, and already had to record a change of direction, the result of rethinking. The subject was contestation (agitation) in culture and politics, followed by the birth of different groups and movements, which undermined the legitimation of the existing status quo and especially bible religion and utilitarian individualism, which had marked the history of the U.S. up until then. Now it seemed that national sentiment had entered into crisis and that the old roots no longer held. Changes had also occurred in civil religion itself, perhaps unable to withstand the shock.[28] It is not by chance that the first reference indicated by the writer is to his most recent book, *The Broken Covenant*, which dreams continually of a kind of rupture, as the dynamic sociology of civil religion had been sorely tested by the further developments in American policy and national religious consciousness. Now there was clear talk of a promise not maintained, a covenant broken, but the way was left open for further recoveries that might accompany the solemn moment of the

U.S. bicentennial. New myths were superimposed upon older ones, though for Bellah the game was still open in the light of a human freedom more shared within the country, and outside.[29]

The Broken Covenant is a historico-sociological analysis of the relation between civil religion and the mythological support structure in America. In the preface, the author also traces his personal history: his doubts about American society began about 1945 and grew thereafter to the point of leading him to take an attitude of rejection as regards his country's reality, as a love-hate relation in constant tension. The result was never a real, overall abandonment of the American moral and religious tradition. Bellah then became aware of the decline of many forms of compulsory belief but additionally recorded an increase in the sense of distributive justice. Both these phenomena were traced back to a common system of values based on individual freedom.[30] The new fact derived from the marriage of utiliarianism and science, which had developed latterly with a utopian impetus Bellah read in terms of the possibility of total technical control in the service of individual interest and freedom.[31]

The Berkeley sociologist in this book intervenes further to clarify the concept of civil religion, but this time too does not do so with the usual procedure. I prefer to show its utility, instead, through an excursus on myth. The latter is not useful for describing reality so much as for transfiguring it, to allow individuals and societies to use moral and spiritual meanings. Consequently, civil religion remains essentially an interpretation of the historical experience of a people in the light of transcendent reality,[32] which can be traced also in the new American myths that adopt, through the rational or ecstatic dimension, modalities that are constant through time. It is worth pointing out that in this case Bellah, just like Bergson, appeals to the Platonic vision of the "good" and adds to it the Spinozan intellectual love of God, as well as love of being and of all beings in Edwards.[33]

Bellah's work concludes with a chink of hope. A great "awakening," able to heal the rupture in progress or recover the spirit of the original myths—despite the conviction that from when the Pilgrim Fathers touched American soil, there began the breaking of the covenant of virtue and the spread of the series of nonvirtuous actions.

The accusation against Bellah, of wanting to generalize his argument, typically American, to other contexts could involve other scholars, such as Parsons, Swanson, and Herberg.[34] There is more than a simple convergence between them regarding the argument. In particular, Peter E. Glasner, who rigorously criticizes the concept of secularization, finds Bellah's perspective rather "similar in many ways" to that of Herberg and Parsons. He calls to his aid Tocqueville's "religion in general" and identifies a common American model of life that includes Herberg's tridimensional system (Protestants-Catholics-Jews) and the notion of American democracy. This would then mean that civil religion is not simply a "religion in general," given its typically American referent.

In truth, Glasner does not grasp one problem in his complex estimate (and ambiguity): that of the possible generalization of the concept of civil religion. According to Glasner, in fact, the approach of Bellah works *in America* (the emphasis is Glasner's). He thus neglects the idea of the "international moral community" that draws its foundation precisely from civic religion.

Later, there occurs a tendential dichotomy between Herberg and Bellah. The former seems more specifically American in his orientation, and the latter shows a more Judeo-Christian outlook, or at least a Protestant one. In other words, Herberg's conception is broader and less exclusive than Bellah's, whose basic formation certainly influences the content of his thought. This, however—and Glasner does not take this in a good light—seems increasingly disenchanted and critical.[35]

The critical contribution of Robert Towler seems, instead, more careful and detailed. He traces the concept of common religion to Robin Williams[36] in its meaning of designating a common set of ideas, rituals, or symbols capable of functioning as a clotting agent, even in societies torn by conflicts or divergences. It must be emphasized that the adjective "common" is not to be connected in this context with the religion of the common man but rather to the religion common to a nation. Bellah's suggestion is close to this viewpoint. Robert Towler maintains that it is coherent with Herberg's, without showing many distinctions.[37]

A Country without Prehistory

To understand the importance of Robert Bellah's proposal fully, which is certainly an attempt at recovery much more than an original suggestion, it would be essential to take up once more some basic characteristics of the formation of the U.S., its structure and genesis. This is typically a "country without prehistory," a "nation of nations," where the empirical datum has traditionally coincided with the supraempirical ideal, to the extent of making it appear to be "God's country," a biblical promise of earthly prosperity, the "promised land." In other words, beyond the sociological studies that often do not rise above the merely sociographic level, it still is left to us to explore that sense of "givenness" that has not escaped the analysis of some North American historians.[38]

When the pilgrim fathers managed to touch the shore of the state of Massachusetts as it is today, and which then was, not by chance, called New England (as though it meant a rebirth in pure and renewed form, especially bearing in mind the dangers of a long sea voyage with the illnesses and storms of those times), it is no surprise that they should perceive their experience in miraculous terms. Their landfall was not on a land without significance. They had managed, obviously with God's help, to reach it. They lived and had built their new homeland there, free from the religious and political tyrannies of the Old World, a new community as if it was, literally, the New Jerusalem.

The wide-open spaces, the magnificent sunsets, the great snow-falls, and the dense, mysterious forests all seemed to show them that this was the country God had reserved for them, where there was nothing to invent, where no value was unrevealed or needed expounding. Everything had already been given, presented by grace, and everything must be accepted. Perhaps it is hard for the reader today to recapture and relive that sense of mystical adventure that was instead the everyday experience of the Pilgrims, the founding fathers of the New World. One can also understand, in this viewpoint, that the New World could not let ideologies circulate, still less allow the struggles to invent and have triumph new values in ideological terms. By ideology is meant not only "false consciousness" but rather as "weapon" an instrument for interpreting the real, but above all as the means and strength for its transformation, the realization of a different society. Ideology is essentially a product of history. It lives in history and feeds on it. It describes its terms and tries to change its horizons, penetrate its shifting frontiers.

The New World, on the other hand, was already all in place. There was nothing to add to it, no new value to valorize. The ideas and principles that open the Joint Declaration of the Thirteen United States of America of 4 July 1776 in the famous Jeffersonian text already contains them all, explicitly, as "self-evident truths" that cover, like fixed stars, all possible historical development. For this reason any ideology or political action that tends to change the dominant values is seen first as an erroneous claim, a scandalous project, blasphemy, or as unAmerican. In the New World, in fact, hostory is taken for granted beforehand. Therefore it is useless, it has no place. One can only work to make the community ever more perfect, more functional. Its guiding principles are already given and are part of an original givenness: our more perfect union!

This makes clear, therefore, how America is a world without ideology. It has no need of it. It is a country without background, not historical in the real sense, at least unless one considers the native peoples, as one should. It is a world constructed coolly, with a constitution written and perfectionist, dictated by country gentlemen who knew Latin and Greek—perhaps the only really enlightened country ever known, even if it has been said, by the historian Charles A. Beard for example (not to speak of historical novelists like Gore Vidal who work in an openly iconoclastic vein), that some weighty, practical reasons were not absent from its construction.[39]

It is interesting that Daniel Bell should have been able, in the late 1950s, to write widely of the "end of ideology"—but more for Europe and the USSR,[40] which had experienced firsthand the defects of ideological doctrine and the "opium of the intellectuals," to use Raymond Aron's formula.[41] It was much less interesting in the United States, which had always been able to do without ideology, and in the face of which they had, indeed, always maintained an attitude of healthy distrust.

Distrust toward Ideology

The basis of North American culture is undoubtedly pragmatico-scientistic. Its characteristic exponents, from Charles Peirce to John Dewey, one way or another all show a clear tendency to consider an idea true when it works. Ideological partitions have no currency. What counts, and what can differentiate social groups and classes even markedly, is the (technical) way to realize on the practico-organizational level, common ideals—that is, the promises contained and assured to all in the Constitution.[42] The basic trauma of American social and political life in its two centuries of history, the Civil War between the North and a South reluctant to accept the emancipation of the slaves imposed by Lincoln, did not appear as an ideological war, played out on opposing fronts distinguished by a global, exclusive faith, expressed in rigorous and mutually incompatible terms.

Even the American Revolution of 1776, moreover, cannot be adequately expressed, still less understood, in ideological or essentially dogmatic terms with universal application. It should rather be linked to local needs and strongly distinguished and specific needs. Its motto could never have been confused with that of the French Revolution: "Liberty, equality, fraternity," typically doctrinaire and ideologically universalizing. America's was much more prosaic. It seems the decision of a diligent board of directors: "No taxation without representation."

To believe therefore that the Americans are the true, only "primitives" of the modern world—as Jean Baudrillard seems to think—means to see, superficially, as resolved the complex, cultural, and historical problem probably destined to have serious consequences. Given the hegemonic position of the U.S. on a world scale, the consequences will weigh on the whole of humanity for the next millennium. If we are dealing with "primitives," we shall need to agree that we face technically very advanced ones against whom nothing, or little, can be accomplished by French grandeur and Eurocentric prejudice.

I think it should be stressed, also as regards such a traumatic event as the Civil War, that there has been no true theoretical or ideological confrontation between North and South. Overall there emerged victorious a reasonable sense of compromise and an attitude of judicious minimalism. In this sense the American Civil War is not to be confused with European civil wars that were carried on on the basis of unyielding theoretical reasoning and that do not admit and, moreover, eliminate the space for any chance of compromise between the conflicting parties. The U.S. case seems quite different.

It has been subtly remarked:

> Whatever the crimes or sneseless bitterness perpetrated in the South, they were carried out in a vindictive and narrowly provincial spirit. The triumph of the national emphasis of the federal structure was not to bring with it the victory of a nationalist philosophy. In Lincoln's words, the Union—not a self-conscious national culture—was what must be preserved. This distinguished it markedly as regards its contemporaries, like Bismarck and Cavour. The remarkable reintegration of the South in our constitutional system is the best proof of our constitutional system and the best evidence of the community of certain assumptions. . . . Not least among the important characteristics of the Civil War . . . is to be seen in the fact that it was so unproductive from the viewpoint of political theory. This war, the bloodiest in the nineteenth century, was perhaps also the least theoretical. The sectional character of the conflict had tended to make sociology—the description of things as they are—take the place of the uncharted exploration of things as they ought to be.[43]

The underlying reason for the absence of political militancy, in an ideological and partisan sense, in the U.S. is to be sought in things not always explicit and often masked or obscured, in the persistence of religious elements (mixed with and working within projects for social action), and in political initiative. These religious elements still have a remarkable vigor, though they appear in disguise. This is a vitality that admits no challenges and watches over and confirms American life as a whole, like a *basso continuo* or the prayer every American politician feels pledged to when he speaks in public and greets the people with the inevitable "God bless you." It is therefore no surprise that values in the U.S. should be seen not as historical products but as "given," handed out from above, once for all. They are frozen values, immobile and astorical. In this sense they are "religious" values, but not in the sense of a sectarian religion, which would necessarily imply the implacable struggle of one religious group against another. The U.S. does not recognize wars of religion. They are religious values in that they

belong to a metapolitical religiosity that enfolds and involves everyone, which it is impossible to refuse to participate in without falling,
almost automatically, out of the life style or American system:
without, in other words, becoming un-American. Generally in the
U.S. the term "atheist" is not used. It is avoided, as one avoids
obscene language in high society or among respectable people. A
less drastic term is preferred, perhaps a less offensive one, where
the denial of the divine-religious is less cutting and less definitive:
such as "nonbeliever," which always leaves the hope that one day
in the future the person so designated can find the reasons for
believing.

If the values are given, the final ends of social action and political
initiative are already decided and the goals of the sociopolitical
project cannot be discussed and must be accepted for what they
are. Whoever addresses a doubt about them is ostracized. The
technical means of realizing them more effectively can, indeed
must, be discussed, so as to assure them to everyone, and make
them effective and spread them if possible throughout the world.
But their acquisition, their nature, the imperatives derived from
them, the rules of moral—individual and group—conduct that
spring from them are not discussed. They are not problematical
material; they can only be observed. Whoever does not come under
them, or identify with them, is a traitor to the covenant with the
community, as well as a breaker of the rules. He is no longer a
"regular fellow" and loses his good standing in the community. He
becomes an unreliable person, not to be fully trusted, and whose
word, however elegant and attractive, is really insidious and perhaps insincere.

In Mediterranean cultures, the lie is accepted as a venial sin.
Always and only telling the truth is regarded as a lack of imagination, a serious lack of invention. It is the virtue of the mule. In a
culture with the memory of the frontier and puritan militancy still
living in its flesh, where everything is based on one's word, the lie
is very far from making one think of the amusing trick and the
clever turn of cunning. It makes one think rather of the tragic
breaking of a basic contract, interpersonal and communitarian. The
puritan legacy is transparent here. The presidential or congressional
candidate who is caught in an adulterous relationship, even if

pardoned by his wife, seriously prejudices his political future and practically destroys it, for the simple reason that he is no longer reliable and probably not trustworthy even in the political sphere. There is no distinction between public and private. The politician, the public figure, is always, today as in the time of the original puritanism, a man and also a symbol.

Think of the shipwreck of Gary Hart's political hopes, Ted Kennedy's refusal to present himself for the presidency after the incident at Chappaquiddick, of the nonapproval by the Senate of John Tower, selected by President Bush as secretary of defense, only because, it was said, he drank and had had relations with women not his wife. The shadow of Calvin, his unbending rigor that embraces private and public life, is not just a metaphor here. In the American politician there is always the minister, the preacher. The political strength of Reagan lay in the parareligious sound of his slogans, intellectually empty but filled with "simple American virtues."

A Nondogmatic Religious Presence

There is thus a religious presence that permeates all American life. But it is not a militant presence, dogmatic. It is not based on theoretically worked-out theological truths. In the U.S. there is a multiplicity, one might say a nebula, of religions, sects, denominations, and congregations. At most, anyone can invent his religion, all the more since he pays no tax on it and no one can report even the most glaring abuses for fear of a juridical precedent dangerous for all. None of these religions has the exclusive claim, the monopoly, to truth. They are all true and to some degree false, but all are equally respectable.

William James expresses the point admirably: "Religion . . . cannot be a mere anachronism and survival, but must exercise a permanent function, whether or not it has intellectual content and, if it has one, whether this content is true or false. . . . [I]s there, under the differences in the various creeds, a common nucleus to which they unanimously bear witness?"[44] William James's reply, and with it all the American tradition, is affirmative. The reason for this affirmative reply, which sees in the religious phenomenon rather than in a specific religion a positive function both for individuals and the national community, must be stated in full. It summarizes the terms of the religious-political syncretism that is the peculiarity of the American social environment:

> The gods and the warring formulas of the various religions cancel each other out, but there is a certain common uniform deliverance in which all religions seem to meet. It has two parts: 1, an unease and 2, its solution. 1, The unease, reduced to its most simple elements is the sense that there is in us something wrong with our natural condition. 2, The solution, is the sense we are saved from the wrongness by establishing the right contact with the higher powers.[45]

Here lies the strength of American conservatism and the deep, innate root of anti-intellectualism. Religious values are removed from the changeable climate of historical movements, even in the sphere of the political. Hence arises the dull, conformist immobility of the political system, inclinded to the center, worried first of all with preserving the balance between social forces, with setting up a counterpower to any power that threatens a monopoly through the complex politico-institutional engineering of checks and balances. Behind all this surface mobility, the essential immovability of the ruling oligarchies is not surprising.

Their strength is not only political or economic. More exactly, their economic and political strength is consecrated by a powerful, if indirect, religious chrism. In American culture, powerful observation of political theory is lacking, just as there are no deep, radical struggles in the field of religious doctrine. The master stroke of the U.S. lies in having separated the churches from the state and at the same time consecrated and justified forever the authority of the state in religious terms beyond the sectarian divisions of the individual churches.[46] The Constitution in this sense is a religious text: the basic document of a civil religion or of a lay morality that requires an inner disposition to obedience of a religious kind, at the risk of expulsion from the American commonwealth, isolation and civic death, exclusion from the community. Saint Clement asked, "What country would ever welcome a deserter of God?" It is a question that describes the desert to which dissidents in the U.S. seem destined. Undoubtedly, as Daniel J. Boorstin has rightly stated, "givenness" is a gift, like grace, and is thus not an article to be exported wholesale.

Moreover, considering the original "givenness" as a grace, or, if you prefer, as the basis of a lay religion, one does not see why Europe should have had to import it from the U.S. A quick glance here is enough for the "morality of the positivist" and the "civil religion," which from the second half of the nineteenth century to the First World War is to be found fully expounded and subtly argued in the work of Auguste Comte and Roberto Ardigò, who as regards ancient Rome were said to be the "worms in the carcass." Later, Benedetto Croce appeared, according to Antonio Gramsci's happy but also despairing formula, as the "lay pope," the system-izer of Italian culture. But one had to ask oneself: How had this supposed systematization been achieved? With what instruments? What ideals? Is it possible to see Croce as the Italian champion of "lay morality," open to reality not only vitalistically but with means adequate from the analytical and critical viewpoint?

It is true that Croce had, at the time of the great national crisis of the Great War, loudly proclaimed, "We cannot fail to call ourselves Christians." It is also true that his support for European culture, apart from a vague "religion of freedom," has been sought by his most ardent supporters and disciples in that "reform" of the Hegelian dialectic that ended up as a real counterreform. Croce put judiciously alongside the "dialectic of opposites" the "dialectic of distinctions" and so changed tragedy into comedy. He lumped together everything and its opposite, cut up human experience according to the criteria of a game reserve and watertight compart-ments, which could not escape the lamentable result of a systematic historical and political justification, both opportunism and transfor-mism. It is hard to put all this in agreement with lay morality and civil religion.

At the end of the century, positivism as expounded by Roberto Ardigò seemed much more committed. From the start of the twentieth century, this had to endure, not always undeservedly, Croce's rough attentions. There is still a problem, historiographic and in the sociology of culture, to unravel, that of the slight or nonexistent resistance put up by the end-of-the-century Italian positivists to the neoidealist, destructive criticisms—especially if one thinks of the remarkable development of the social sciences and the luxuriant, rich spread of sociology in fin-de-siècle Italy.[56]

For the moment it seems to me well-grounded to believe that however great and generous on the part of the positivists their civic commitment was, so their methodological design and the theoretical, conceptual apparatus of their studies was in proportion uncertain, defective, and at times frankly erratic.

The ex-friar of Mantua's commitment, however, is unquestionable. Roberto Ardigò felt deeply the need that his philosophical system and sociology should not remain only academic exercises or dreams on paper. Bear in mind that the years 1860–1900, between the proclamation of the kingdom, the breaching of Porta Pia, and the assassination of King Umberto, were decisive for the formation of a unitary national consciousness that would not just resolve itself into a matter of superficial administrative policy but be consolidated into a genuine social cohesion. This was a difficult operation, that not even modern Italy can calmly say is completed. With great accuracy it has been remarked that

"The doings and thought of Roberto Ardigò should be inscribed in the movement of ideas committed to upholding cultural unity, social fusion, and the political cohesion of the Italian state that was being proclaimed as an independent and autonomous institution. For that purpose it is important, as Rousseau showed, that the state should count on a religion that educates the citizens to love their duties and be faithful subjects. And this was the historic mission of Roberto Ardigò's positivism.[48]

It is scarcely necessary to recall that, more urgently than the formation of "faithful subjects," from the beginning of Italy's political unity, it seemed, more important to obtain full citizenship for all Italians, in the north and south. It is an objective still far from effective achievement today, both on the economic and the practical, existential levels. However, it is nonetheless true that Giovanni Gentile himself referred to an "historic mission" to ascertain the function and social effects of Roberto Ardigò's positivism.[49] From the point of view of contemporary comment, it is also instructive to note the polemic set off by Ardigò's appointment as professor at Padua University, when the minister of education, Guido Baccelli, had to face the crusading uproar by asserting with conviction that "if from the age-old chair of St. Peter, surrounded in Rome by sovereign guarantees, the pope proclaims to the faithful the need for faith in the sphere of the incomprehensible, it is the task of the king's government, from its scientific safeguards, to spread the light of human knowledge and assert its inextinguishable acquisitions fearlessly."[50]

The minister's tone and content in this speech were of a pure Spencerian kind, and betray in the linear design of the symmetrical comparison between the papal see and the king's government, with its related "scientific guardians," the solution that was given by Spencer to the dispute between religion and science (a rather poor one conceptually): "If religion and science are to be reconciled, the basis of this reconciliation must be the deepest, most comprehensive and most certain of all facts, that the Power the Universe shows us is inscrutable."[51] This is in fact a reconciliation in the dark, and one can imagine the irony, at Spencer's expense, of the neoidealists, from Croce to Guido De Ruggiero, to whom in reality it seemed, not wholly erroneously, that as regards the famous "Unknowable" the positivists knew too much.[52]

Roberto Ardigò's Apple

The neoidealists' sarcasm, which was moreover at least partly favored by the Fascist dictatorship, to the point of becoming in some cases its servants and accomplices, cannot, however, allow us to forget the positivists' attempt not so much to liquidate traditional religion summarily, according to the outdated precepts of a largely unconscious scientism, but rather to reformulate religious sentiments of tradition into a new morality. This was the morality, in fact, of the positivists, "a more direct, more sincere, and more undiluted corollary than the gospels."[53] This attempt referred directly to the motto with which Comte began the first volume of his *Système de politique positive* or *Traité de sociologie instituant la religion de l'humanité*: "L'amour pour principe; L'ordre pour base, et le Progrès pour but."[54]

Ardigò's reference to the gospels in its most literal or purest form, not yet polluted by the self-interested comments of priests and pharisees, impressively recalls the current polemical demands of the "Catholics of dissent" and liberation theology; Ardigò counterposes the "morality of the positivists" to the "morality professed by the Roman church": "The Roman church, whose origins are owed to the strength of an ideal that produced an association, variously progressive, for the natural (more or less perfect) way of federation, *as, a little at a time, the legitimacy of that ideal decreased—an ideal that gave birth to it—this church still remains as the greatest, in the specific sense of the word, as the most striking negation of true ideality*: that is, of science, in its dogma; and so the most marked and most absolute negation of social right in that it is the most marked and most absolute negation of individual right and the federation derived from it."[55]

If Ardigò reminds us of today's criticisms of the communities and Christians of the base when he stresses the "degeneration" of the Church and its transformation into a power structure, the natural ally of the ruling social and economic potentates, his link with Comte's teaching is a direct one as regards "social idealities." He did not accept the precept of loving thy neighbor as thyself. To him, the genuine precept could only be that which enjoins loving others, seeing in others not rivals or enemies, real or potential, but neighbors, who let us recognize ourselves; as Plato in the Phaedrus observed, the friend can recognize himself only seeing himself reflected in the friend's eye. Ardigò's revision of the gospel text has the sharp, decisive tone of a teacher who does not spare the rod.

> There is only one command: that of loving one's neighbor, or social ideality. The order to love oneself is absurd, which certainly occurs without being ordered. If love of oneself is recalled by the command to love one's neighbor, that means there is already in man the lower stratum, common to all the beasts, of self-love, and that this does not diminish until his animality diminishes; and that, however, in man one must add to simple animality his distinctive character, or *humanity*, and that this depends on social ideality, expressed in the phrase love of one's neighbor. And that by this must be understood the labor and special, higher effort of man. The same content is then scientifically summed up in the word *justice*. They have the same meaning: justice and morality, just and good. And justice is absurd without reference of the individual to society, outside social ideality.[56]

Thus for Ardigò "social ideality" is not just the goal Comte summed up in his "vivre pour autrui": "It is the Law itself established in Society. . . . [T]he very attitudes of the individual are . . . to the largest extent directed in their *natural functioning* by the order of things in the Society in which he lives."[57] But where does this "individual" whose attitudes "function" in harmony with "social idealities," and which are thus the "laws" of "society," spring from? Ardigò's "naturalistic individualism," as it has been suitably defined by Eugenio Garin, emerges here in all its clarity, but also with some inescapable problems. If the attitudes of the individual fitted perfectly, or nearly so, with the laws of society, it is clear that the question of the tension between the individual and society would be resolved even before it appeared in all its significance, but only because it would be, as it were, suffocated in its cradle. Elsewhere, but especially in *La ragione* and more widely in *La morale dei positivisti* and *La sociologia*, Ardigò reflects on the process of the genesis of the individual's psyche, content, however, with assuring us that social ideality takes root in the individual through "the process of recognition of the distinct in the indistinct,"[58] whereas the source of higher moral obligation, that which makes the individual pass from the brute state of self-love to the higher one of "love for others and society" was to be sought in natural law. Ardigò asserts, this is "absolute law like the nature from which it emerges."

What a pity that this absolute law, historically speaking, does not exist. From the historical point of view (the only view that can interest positive scientific research), apart from of customary rights, one only has news of sanctioned, formally codified and juridically forceful rights. Ardigò's naturalism, whether derived from Spencer or from ingenuous materialism, or whether seen as, according to some, paradoxically "idealist," here shows its most serious deficiencies. The genesis of the individual remains nebulous.[59] The very functioning of perception does not move away from the mysterious as well as laborious mechanism of the passage from the indistinct to the distinct, on the basis of which it is not at all easy to account for the multiplicity of sensations, their ultimately contradictory nature, their internal organization—especially once the sole source of truth is seen, as Ardigò insists, in experience. Not only the unity of consciousness but the very genesis of a unitary, conscious interpretation of the flow of perceptions is seriously undermined or at any rate is apparently undercut from within by insoluble contradictions. Comte was probably better advised when he simply took for granted the problem of gnoseology—But not Ardigò, who returns to it and is long troubled by it. Fortunately, for him too there is a Newton's apple. His apple appears as a rose, or rather, the red of a rose:

> "One day I was reading, with my inevitable gnoseological concern, in Giovanni Müller's *Manuale di filosoifa dell'uomo*, and, reading and reflecting, I went to sit in the little garden of the canon's house where I was living, on a stone in front of a flowering rosebush. A rose at the full stretch of its petals particularly attracted my attention. And I exclaimed, Look what a beautiful *red!* And I pronounced the word out loud. And doing so, I suddenly began thinking that I had this word at my disposal, and with a meaning that shone in my mind: that is, with a related idea: indeed, with a *general* idea, which I could apply to that particular object that I qualified as red; to this, and to all the infinity of others that agreed with it: in the same way that one applies some other conception to a particular case, and which precisely because of this applicability I call general. And so, if this idea of the red, being so general, is a sense datum, why cannot all the others equally be a sense datum, which are said to belong to the intellect?"[60]

It seems Ardigò had taken a step forward as regards the rigorously naturalistic conception of perception that, in Bergson's terms, makes it "a photographic view of things." The knowing subject moves, is not a simple, passive "photographic plate." But his contribution is restricted to "applying" and stops there. He does not manage to understand perception as an opening of the subject with regard to reality and at the same time as a structure that unifies thought and existence. If the intellect and its functions are no longer reduced to the physical organ, we are nonetheless still far from the idea of an active subject, certainly included in nature but not thereby bound to a natural "virtuality," whereby all control escapes it, so as to reduce it ultimately to a mere "physiological organ," a thing among things, one among many. The subject as person is here endangered, and perhaps never born. Faced with the unopposed domination of the "circle of nature," we might say Ardigò would have no difficulty today in accepting Niklas Luhmann's definition of the individual when he rather brusquely and quite logically from his systemic, desubjectified viewpoint affirms that "the individual is nothing other than the environment of the system."

Once the conception of perception has been thus bleached out, naturalistic reductionism celebrates its victory. The physical organ prevails over the intellectual function—it not only helps it, it supports it. It ends by making it. The life of the spirit, wrongly considered by the idealists as self-sufficient and disembodied to the point of making it unreal, is here wholly absorbed in the "sensorial shocks" as a mere epiphenomenon of physiological processes. Ardigò provides us with another anecdote, not without its own attractive, ingenuous crudeness:

> "It happened to me once that, having an intestinal infection, and thus with my gut a bit swollen, and my clothes being tight over it, I experienced a very intense feeling of melancholy, which I naturally saw as a state of mind and dependent on precise moral reasons in it. And then I felt a very pronounced pessimistic humor, which drew from me a series of dispiriting reflections on the unhappy fate of man and the painful enigma of his Io, with no means of comfort. When suddenly it came into my mind to undo my belt round my belly, which was suffering from the constriction. After this, the sense of melancholy diminished and disappeared, and as if by magic the pessimistic outlook changed, as the sky lightens when the sun appears. So, the melancholy was simply a sensation, produced by my painfully squeezed intestines, and not the very entity of an individual and spiritual Io, which compelled me to that state. Not the soul, but a trouser button. Nothing more than a sensation produced by a bowel, which I did not refer it to, as I do that of feeling the cold when I put my hands in running water."[61]

It is not hard to understand how thus and similar "intestinal" theories of melancholy assisted the tough antipositivistic polemic in the first years of this century. Seeing that pessimism, melancholy, and a tight belt are equivalent, how could Ardigò ever have managed to distinguish the soul from a trouser button? And the "morality of the positivists," "civil religion" itself, how can it be guaranteed if the person, the subject, is not in turn guaranteed as autonomous consciousness, and thus responsible?

The weakness of the theoretical, conceptual apparatus of Italian positivism is obvious, but the difficulties for "civil religion" in Italy, as I remarked earlier, did not arise only from philosophical deficiencies. From its unification in 1860, Italy lacked a profound national experience, shared by all citizens, which would consolidate its basic cohesion. The process of unification through the Risorgimento remained an undertaking, all in all, of the dynasty of Savoy, which the spirit of Garibaldi did not manage to scratch, and which ended, with the law of 1859, by applying to the whole peninsula, with its variety of historical and anthropologico-cultural formations, the same photographically enlarged structure of old Piedmont. Nor is this just a repetition of Piero Gobetti's complaint that Italy had had neither a political revolution like France nor a religious reformation like Germany—a justified complaint. Certainly we can console ourselves with the Resistance to nazism and fascism. It is true the Republican constitution has in the Resistance its moral, legitimating foundation. But we must not be led away by celebratory rhetoric, at times tediously self-glorifying. The Resistance did not involve the whole of Italy. It did, at certain times and in some areas, deeply involve the center-north. The south was essentially kept out. The "Italian disease" has more distant origins. One must go back to Leopardi, to the antimodernity that covers, poorly, the absence of society, and reconsider critically Italian "familism." It is a fact that, among so many scandals, from the Mafia to terrorism, we have not even had a Dreyfus case!

In 1876, when the historic right that had "made Italy," fell, and the left came to power, and in the same years as Ardigò's preaching for "civil religion" and the "morality of the positivists" became more decided and loud, the disturbing phenomenon of "transformism" was making its first appearance, making its first moves. This was destined to color all Italian life, from the betrayals by intellectuals to systematic confusion and endemic corruption among politicians. I have recalled above, Rousseau's social contract and its nucleus of ideas from which, historically, "civil religion" and also the idea of "social covenant," arise. These notions lie at the basis of modern democracies, clearly defining the frontiers between democratic opposition and total, violent subversion. Rousseau's text is well-known: "Without being able to oblige anyone to believe in them (the rules of the covenant), (the sovereign power) can ban from the State anyone who does not believe in them: it can ban them not because they are impious, but because they are unsociable, as unable to love the laws sincerely, to love justice, and in case of necessity to sacrifice their life to their own duty." Rousseau, though he has a clear idea of "sociability," still speaks of the state as though in fact this coincided with and in fact absorbed, without leaving anything behind, the whole of civil society. In the Italian experience, at any rate, the state seems fragile, uncertain, the base and forum more for mutual blackmail and stalemates than of "general will" in Rousseau's sense: that is, the will and judgement of the community. In this situation, "civil religion" seems destined to have a difficult life and little capacity for obtaining that "interior disposition" to service for the common good that today seems to present itself as a basic precondition for the orderly progress of civil society.

Notes

1. Henri Bergson, *La pensée et le mouvant* (Paris: Alcan, 1946), 47ff., passim.
2. H. Bergson, *Les deux sources de la morale et de la religion*, (Paris: Alcan, 1961), 274.
3. See Robert N. Bellah, "Civil Religion in America," *Daedalus*, Winter 1967, 1–21; reprinted, with comments by others, in Donald R. Cutler, ed., *The Religious Situation: 1968* (Boston: Beacon Press, 1968).
4. Bellah, *Al di là della fede*, 185.
5. See B. Franklin, *Autobiografia, lettere, scritti vari* (Turin: Utet, 1964).
6. Bellah, *Al di là delle fedi*, 195.
7. R. N. Bellah, *Apache Kinship Systems*, (Cambridge: Harvard University Press, 1952).
8. R. N. Bellah, *Tokugawa religion* (Glencoe: Free Press, 1957).
9. R. N. Bellah, "Religious Aspects of Modernization in Turkey and Japan," *American Journal of Sociology* 64 (1958), 1–5, and *Al di là delle fedi*, 159–183.
10. Bellah, *Al di là delle fedi*, 208–209.
11. Bellah, 271–290.
12. Ibid., 273.
13. Ibid., 274.
14. Ibid., 277.
15. Ibid., 288.
16. Ibid.
17. Rocco Caporale and Antonio Grumelli, eds., *Religione e ateismo nelle società secolarizzate* (Bologna: Il Mulino, 1972): Martin's intervention on Bellah's paper.
18. Rocco Caporale & Antonio Grumelli, *cit.*, 308 (Parson's intervention, "Belief, Nonbelief, and misbelief").
19. Ibid., 207.
20. Ibid., 122 (Bellah, "Religion and Polity in America, *cit.*, p. 122).
21. Ibid., 124.
22. Roland Robertson, *The Sociological Interpretation of Religion* (Oxford: Blackwell, 1972), 40.
23. Thomas J. J. Altizer, "Theology and Contemporary Sensibility," in W. A. Beardsloc, ed., *America and the Future of Theology*, (Philadelphia, 1967), 155: quoted in Robertson.
24. Charles H. Long, "The Ambiguities of Innocence," in Bearsles, 42.

25. In fact, there is no shortage of Bellah's interventions in the theological sector: see "Words for Paul Tillich," *Harvard Divinity School Bulletin* 30 (1966): 15–16, and his contribution to "Toward an American Theology" by H. W. Richardson, in *Harvard Divinity School Bulletin* 1 (1968): 18–19. He also took a position on *Honest to God* by J.A.T. Robinson: "It Doesn't Go Far Enough," *Christianity and Crisis* 23 (1963): 200–201.

26. Susan Budd, *Sociologists and Religion* (London: Collier-Macmillan, 1973), 96–97. I cite also a study on the role of civic religion in a small American town: A. Vidich and J. Bensman, *Small Town in Mass Society* (Princeton: Princeton University Press, 1958); see especially part 4.

27. See Robert N. Bellah and William G. McLoughlin, eds., *Religion in America* (Boston: Houghton Mifflin, 1968).

28. Robert N. Bellah, "Il nuovo senso religioso e la crisi del moderno," in Rocco Caporale, ed., *Vecchi e nuovi dei* (Turin: Valentino, 1975), 499–519.

29. See Robert N. Bellah, *The Broken Covenant* (New York: Seabury Press, 1975). See also "Religion and Polity in America," *Andover Newton quarterly* 2 (1974), and "Reflections on Reality in America," *Radical Religion* 3 (1974).

30. Bellah, *Broken Covenant*, xii.

31. Ibid., xiii.

32. Ibid., 3.

33. Ibid., 153. Compare Jonathan Edwards, *The Nature of True Virtue* (Ann Arbor, University of Michigan, 1960), quoted by Bellah. For a balanced appraisal of the whole question, see Michael W. Hughey, *Civil Religion and Moral Order,* (Westport & London: Greenwood Press, 1983), as regards the millenaristic and soteriological vocation of the United States see Eduard C. Tuveson, *Redeemer Nation: The Idea of America's Millennial Role* (Chicago, University of Chicago Press, 1968).

34. For a detailed analysis of Parsons's attempt, see Federico d'Agostino *Immaginazione simbolica e struttura sociale* (Bologna: Il Mulino, 1977), especially pp. 69–93. By Parsons, see "The Pattern of Religious Organization in the United States," *Daedalus* 87 (1958). By Guy Swanson, see "Modern Secularity," in Custler. For Willy Herberg, see *Protestant-Catholic-Jew* (New York: Doubleday, 1955).

35. Glasner, *Sociology of Secularization* 36–38.

36. Robin M. Williams, *American Society: A Sociological Interpretation* (New York: Knopf, 1951).

37. Robert Towler, *Homo Religiosus: Sociological Problems in the Study of Religion* (London: Constable, 1974), 148.

38. Daniel J. Boorstin, *The Genius of American Politics* (Chicago: University of Chicago Press, 1953).

39. Charles A. Beard, *An Economic Interpretation of the Constitution of the United States* (New York: Free Press, 1965).

40. See Daniel Bell, *The End of Ideology* (New York, Free Press, 1960).

41. See Raymond Aron, *L'opium des intellectuels* (Paris: Calman-Lévy, 1955).

42. See Hence the sense, indeed the fashion, of what I call the "organizational myth," of faith in being able to resolve all the social and political problems of our time in purely organizational terms and technological know-how; see my *Il dilemma dei sindacati americani* (Milan: Comunità, 1954).

43. Boorstin, The Genius of American Politics, 131–132.

44. William James, *The Varieties of Religious Experience* (New York: Modern Library, 1948), 498.
45. Ibid. See too the edition edited by John J. McDermot, *The Writings of William James* (Chicago: University of Chicago Press, 774; earlier in the book (p. 459), James had described the characteristics of religious life, which in his view include the following beliefs:

> 1, that the visible world is part of a more spiritual universe from which it draws its chief significance; 2, that union or ceremonial relation with this higher universe is our true end; 3, that prayer and inner communion with the spirit, be it "God or the law" is a process in which work is really done and spiritual energy flourishes and produces its psychological or material effects within the phenomenal world; religion then contains the following psychological characteristics: 4, a zest which is added as a gift to life and takes on the form of a lyrical enchantment or an appeal to heroism and seriousness; 5, a sense of security and a temper of peace, and, in the relation with others, the prevalence of loving affections.

46. It is worth noting that sociology and the social sciences in general in the U.S. show a clear religious stamp, never totally canceled by the process of laicization that at the start of the century had turned the old divinity schools into universities; see the basic work by Stanford M. Lyman and Arthur J. Vidich; *American Sociology—Worldly Rejections of Religion and their Directions* (Princeton: Princeton University Press, Princeton 1987).
47. The only important exception was the polemical exchange between Croce and Pareto in 1900–1901, for which see my *La sociologia alla riscoperta della qualita* (Rome-Bari: Laterza, 1989).
48. Cf. Anna Luisa Gentile, *La religione civile—del positivismo di Roberto Ardigà* (Naples: Edizioni Scientifiche Italiane, 1988), 9. Though insufficiently critical, this is a noteworthy contribution of a descriptive kind, which does justice to writers and books that the "Crocean season" unwarrantedly consigned to oblivion.
49. G. Gentile *Storia della filosofia italiana*, vol. 2 (Florence: Sansoni, 1969), 388.
50. Roberto Ardigò, "Il mio insegnamento della filosofia nel Regio Liceo di Mantova," in *Opere filosofiche*, vol. 6 (Padua: Draghi, 1894), 405.
51. H. Spencer, *First Principles* (London: Williams and Norgate, 1918), 34.
52. See my *Trattato di sociologia* (Turin: UTET, 1983), chap. 3, "La sociologia evoluzionistica di Herbert Spencer."
53. Cf. Roberto Ardigò, *La morale dei positivisti*, 133.
54. Auguste Comte, *Système de politique positive* (Paris: rue M. le Prince, 1890).
55. Roberto Ardigò, *La Morale dei positivisti*, 175; my emphasis.
56. Ibid.
57. Roberto Ardigò, *Sociologia* (Milan: Marjorah; 1973) (orig. ed. 1986), 50–51; my emphasis.
58. The formula fashionable among all the Italian positivists of the time marks once again their dependence on Herbert Spencer, too hurriedly put in company with Darwin and Marx, completely ignoring the antinaturalist, historicist orientation of the latter; for Ardigò's philosophical defects, see the brilliant critical comment by G. Papini,

> In Ardigò, therefore, the fact and the Indistinct both compete for the *role* of divinity,

and their claim is of almost equal value, in that the Indistinct has one that could give it primacy—creative power. To Ardigò, things exist insofar as they are distinct, or rather, distinction is the sole symptom of existence. The Indistinct, which is the opposite, it seems, of the distinct, is thus the inexistent *par* excellence. Now, since Ardigò tells us the distinct is born of the indistinct, we can substitute equivalent terms and say being is produced from nonbeing, that is, everything came out of nothing. We thus have a creation *ex nihilo* fully in order: Genesis is vindicated. (G. Papini, *Stroncature* (Florence: Vallechi, 1942, 41).

59. See, among others, G. Marchesini, "L'idealismo di Roberto Ardigò", *Rivista di filosofia* (Milan, 1928), *passim*; it seems clear that the term "idealism" used here bears the current meaning of "faith generous to ideals," and not the rigorous philosophical sense.
60. Roberto Ardigò, "Guardando il rosso di una rosa," *Opere filosofiche*, vol. 10 (Padua: Draghi, 1907), 242.
61. Roberto Ardigò, *Il Vero* (Padova: Draghi, 1891), 379–380.

6

The Satanic Ambiguity of the Sacred

Unkept Promises

How the spirit of the times changes! How, in the course of three or four generations, the prevailing mental climate changes and is transformed! At the end of the nineteenth century, and up to the start of the First World War, it was hard to escape the atmosphere of general euphoria and optimistic enthusiasm with which humanity—or, to be precise, the accredited representatives of western European culture—was preparing to enter the new century. In order not to be thus infected, one had to be able to rely on the acute, painful farsightedness of genius—as in the case of Friedrich Nietzsche. But then there was already Sigmund Freud, who at the end of 1899 had his manuscript *The Interpretation of Dreams* ready for publication in Vienna, keeping it timorously in a drawer, to be published only at the start of the new century: the century, the great, mythical twentieth century, which was to have inaugurated the new golden age, the *saturnia aetas* linked to industrialism and science, and consecrated to the new lay religion of progress.

These splendid promises were not kept. The twentieth century draws to its close in an inglorious atmosphere pregnant with uncertainties, laden with tormenting questions. The very physical survival of humanity and of the planet earth are today in question. Humans as we have known them from classical antiquity to today, from Homer and Dante to Shakespeare and T. S. Eliot, appears a species running the risk of extinction. The fine certainties of the past are dissolved like dreams at dawn: not with a bang but with a whimper. Omnicalculability and omnipotence, which seemed achieved, are shown to be childhood fantasies of someone without experience of the complexity of history and the crude facts of life.

And yet, this century has known two disastrous world wars and with science applied to industry has polluted the very roots of existence—thereby endangering the real possibilities of humanity's perpetuation through time. But it does not resign itself, it does not manage to become aware of its condition, or able to escape from itself and its own formulations so as to transcend itself and evaluate on a world scale the nature and extent of its deformations. In other words, humanity is unable to recognize the underlying nature of its limits and the deeply amoral character of its technical progress. Rather, it goes on deluding itself about being able to ward off the mortal dangers threatening it, which undermine it from within, by resorting to measures of socio-political engineering, institutional patching, and technological specializations.

The experiences of this century have shown that it is not enough to go forward in order to go well. Novelties are not necessarily best. The modern needs the ancient. For this reason, the term "post-modern" is linguistically and conceptually unfortunate. The ultimate solution of the problems of the modern is to be found not *post* but *before* the modern. In the tradition from which we have so hastily liberated ourselves, there were seeds of the future that have been forgotten and that should be rediscovered, reconsidered, and recaptured.[1] One day, we left the old home full of hope and enthusiasm as vainglorious as it was rash. But now, we must go back, because we have seen that in the rush to leave something important was forgotten.

Progress is not a chronological inevitability: it is not a necessary outlet. Progress has become a problem. Technical progress guarantees nothing about moral progress. The minimum conditions of human coexistence are in danger. Technical progress has borne us to the edge of the precipice. Clean air has become a scarce resource.[2]

The Negation of Evil

Years ago, the lack of a "sociology of evil"[3] was learnedly documented and duly deplored. The reason for this lack was sought in the history of the Western conception of evil.

This conception in the first place has been marked by the Judeo-Christian tradition, especially its Christian component. . . . The Western conception of evil would thus dissolve with the diminution of this tradition, especially with the decline of Christianity itself. . . . [B]ecause of its "particularism," it appears hard to reconcile Christianity with "universalism" (both terms in Talcott Parsons's sense) that characterizes industrial, technological, and bureaucratic society, both capitalist and socialist. . . . This difficulty explains much of the controversy and the disturbances that have for some time upset many churches, especially the Catholic church, since the pontificate of John XXIII. . . . God has been replaced by other absolutes—State, race, the Future of a given people, if not the human species, to which the current generation must be sacrificed. . . . Modern social control is thus much more total and cruel, and at the same time more efficient than previously, when crimes against humanity were not yet recognized as such."4

Despite this last recognition, evil as such is not, however, comprehensible in the framework and logic of development of industrial society. At most, it may be thought of as a parenthesis, a brief, casual deviation. Industrial society, as a society that believes itself and thinks of itself as one intrinsically rational, is a society that does not know evil, just as it does not recognize death. It is not enough for this society to have the banality of evil revealed, as Hanna Arendt did so admirably in the Eichmann case. It simply does not recognize the existence of evil and reduces it to a mere consequence of ignorance. It is a society proposing to free itself from the past, which does not even want to hear evil mentioned, and which appears irritated and intolerant, rather than incredulous, when the Fall is mentioned. Technically advanced, rationalized, contractual, calculating, and utilitarian industrial society, forgetful of the past and spasmodically intent on the future, has one insurmountable limit. This society closes its eyes in the face of death, just as it persists in denying the existence of evil.

If I may be allowed a quite innocent play on words, one could say that its limit lies in not knowing the meaning of limit. It reduces evil to an organizational dysfunction. In this perspective and viewpoint, evil for this society is a scandalous fact, to be blanked out, forgotten as soon as possible, and buried without formalities. Greco-Roman civilization and the Christian world are marked by a sense of limit, by the attention with which they keep a safe distance from Bacchic possession and the paroxysmic hubris that defines the demoniac.

Thus one explains how the presence of the Evil One in "advanced" industrial societies, as they are usually called ("technically advanced" seems a more accurate description), is a disquieting fact. It is disturbing because it is perceived as an unexpected return. At least from the Enlightenment onward it was supposed that philosophical, technical progress, along with both political and social progress, would gradually but inexorably have "swept away not only the "idiocies of rural life"—as Marx and Engels generously but rashly assured us in the 1848 *Manifesto*—but also, and still more radically, the superstitions, devils, witches, the false beliefs of a prescientific world, the whole religious and parareligious armory that accompanied tradition.

Even on a superficial appraisal, things today are different. Tradition has not yielded at all. The need for the "totally other" seems stronger than ever. Not only is there no eclipse of the sacred and supramundane values, but rather, the latter assert themselves and root themselves in the recesses of the everyday of individuals and of groups and social classes. The "paradox of the sacred" seems indeed to lie in the empirically ascertainable fact that the more a society is rationalized, the more the hunger for the supramundane and the invisible grows.

The Ambiguity of the 'Prince of This World'

In this framework, the devil has an ambiguous, "transverse" position,[5] crosswise, or one of essential obliqueness. It is possibly not by chance that John Paul II in Turin itself, the city of industrial efficiency and architectonic and political rationalism, went back to speaking explicitly about Satan. Moreover, recent news is full of peculiarly interesting evidence of Satan and "Satanic rites." The papers report that in September 1988 the pope spoke, on the occasion of a lunch with the 18 Piedmontese bishops, about the "demon," presented as "prince of this world." He especially emphasized the ability of Satan to camouflage himself so as to surprise and more easily outwit his victims. John Paul II confessed, "Turin was an enigma to me, but from the story of salvation, we know that where there are saints there comes in another as well, who appears not under his name, but under other names. He is called the prince of this world, the devil. What party, what ideology, does not wish to be the prince of this world? This is a matter I leave to you bishops, the pastors of this region. . . . , I know that religious observance is low. There is a challenge to Turin and for all Piedmont, but especially for this city."[6]

The pope's statements belong in the tracks of a rich literature on demonic polymorphism, which runs from the biblical serpent (only later coinciding with the Evil One) to provocative feminine nudity, the temptation and torment of the Anchorites and Eremites, and on to the medieval and postmedieval witches who, according to the calculations of the theologian Hans Küng were put to death in numbers approaching nine million,[7] a genuine foretaste of the holocaust. John Paul II seems to point in the current political parties to a devilish operation, at least in the sense that this involves instruments for the conquest of power in this world. It seems to me a more precarious judgement, that of the political party as instrument of the devil in that as *pars* it is said to put itself on the political and social plane as the occasion and instrument of division of the community of the faithful and the "People of God itself.[8]

In the same period of time, again in Turin, the city that with Prague and Lyons forms the diabolical triangle in Europe, the papers reported a "massacre in the name of Satan" in a modest apartment on the outskirts. Here, the police came in response to the alarmed neighbors and surprised two men "dancing" on the naked body of a young woman, still alive, but with her ribcage almost smashed, who were shouting: "The devil's in us; he is God; I am the devil, and she has him too. . . . We must smash her to get him out. . . ." While similar episodes, though less turbulent and with no deaths, were recorded in Treviso and Bologna (see the papers for 15 April 1989), in northern Mexico a band of drug dealers killed and ate fourteen people, mixing satanism, black magic, and cannibalism.

This recalls to mind the collective suicide of the Reverend Jim Jones's sect, the People's Temple." But they should clearly be carefully analyzed, these similar cases where the variable of history is so dominant, and whose different cultural and anthropological backgrounds should be examined to bring out possible points of similarity.[9]

Alfonso M. Di Nola has remarked,

> In the current important debate on satanisms in Europe and the United States, there emerges a constant attempt to define more or less fluid connections with the different cultural backgrounds, almost to the point of implying a search for roots that might justify the cruel rituals and ceremonial murder. The phantasmagoria of black masses, with rare cases of the murder or mutilation of the victims, has in Europe sought its historical precedents in a long Western tradition rotating around the figure of the Christian devil and the witches. . . . It is not thus unlikely that the data arriving from Mexico and the nearest area of Mexican population settled in the southern United States reflect a syncretism of satanic themes with ancient beliefs belonging to the archaic pre-Columbian peoples, more especially the Aztecs. . . . Drugs and sacrificial death belong . . . to the ancient Aztec tradition, documented in the sixteenth century by the Franciscan missionary Bernardin de Sahagun, and penetratingly studied in the last decades by the most committed specialist in the field, Father Garibay. In pre-Columbian Mexico, among the forms of human offering, the most impressive was the so-called "sacrifical death," consisting of the excision of the heart, still beating, from the victim, then offered to the sun so that it should not fall into growing decline—to the point of causing the end of the universe and time.[10]

Hell Exists, but It Is Empty

This fear of an unstoppable and progressive decline toward the void recalls a conception of hell as a void, not lacking in refernces outside Western culture. It is a kind of "fear of the void" opening up at the heart of everyday life. One of Yasunari Kawabati's first books, *The Story of Asakusa*, seems to bring out strongly the stifling, despairing grayness in the everyday life of a district of Tokyo half-destroyed in the 1923 earthquake.[11] Hell as a void and the devil as metaphor have latterly, and in a modernizing sense, been taken up by some Catholic theologians. Hans Urs von Balthasar stands out, having worked out an interesting theory of hell as void, not so much a place of positive punishment as of privation and distancing. According to von Balthasar, two positions can be distinguished in the Holy Scriptures regarding damnation, hell, and God's judgement. The first stresses and rests on the fear that humanity may be lost definitively. The other expresses the hope, never the certainty, that salvation is not lost. However, there is a supreme uncertainty reigning over both positions, deriving from the simple consideration that no theologian or minister can ever literally foresee and discount God's judgement. Von Balthasar argues: I do not judge myself alone, Christ judges me, and it would be useless if not sacrilegious to set out theories on how it will be done and on the basis of what criteria. What Christian theology can establish for certain is that the rejection of Christ's love ends up becoming a self-condemnation for humankind, transported into the eternal fire and destined to burn forever.

One might say we are stuck in a somewhat anthropomorphic conception of divine judgement, supposedly not seeing any other punishment possible for disrespectful, rebellious humans except the precise application of a kind of harsh law of retaliation. Whoever does not wish to accept the offer of divine love will be condemned to burn for ever.

However, the Christian could not be expressed in terms of a law of retribution so schematic and simplistic. In reality, the evolution of the concept of evil and the figure of Satan in the Judeo-Christian tradition is much more complex. The amazement raised in averagely educated circles by John Paul II's recent statements does not seem justified. The polemic about Satan, for example, managed to split the people of Turin as if it were a matter of a sporting derby, or the defense of the city's good name.

It is forgotten that Paul VI, to cite another recent case, noting one day that the work of Vatican Council II was not proceeding with the anticipated expediteness, had already discovered in Satan the reason for the delays and misunderstandings: "From some crack there has entered smoke from Satan into the temple of God. We believe something preternatural has come into the world just to upset the product of the Ecumenical Council. . . . Evil is no more a deficiency only, but an efficiency, a living being, spiritual, perverted and perverting; a terrible reality, mysterious and fearful."[12]

A Cultivated Literary Satanism for the Elites

The idea that the notion of Satan and evil have progressively developed in the Christian tradition and, gradually, increasingly spiritualized themselves, have drifted away from the cruder conceptions typical of a crude peasant world, so as finally to arrive at the refined doctrine of St. Ambrose, does not seem tenable. The saint argued that Satan is no longer to be seen as a being outside people, but rather as the expression of the freedom of human beings able to choose the high road of evil or the rather narrower one of virtue and thence of beatitude in eternity. This reflects a view of human history as a progressive and unstoppable journey toward a higher spirituality that appears as the counterpart to the lay idea of progress. No doubt the existence of evil in the world was an open problem for ancient as well as modern consciences.

Perhaps the most dramatic record of this awareness is to be found in St. Augustine's *Confessions,* in book 7, chapter 5; the author asks:

> So where does the approval I give to evil and deny to good come from? . . . [W]ho has sown and awakened in me this shoot of unhappiness, if I am the creation of my God, full of good will? What then if I were instead the creation of the devil, wherever then would the devil in turn come from? If the devil, on the other hand, became such from being the good angel he was, through an act of ill will—this perverse will that made him the devil, whence did it penetrate into he that was created wholly angel by a good creator?"

The perceptive orator does not contradict himself and moved from the particular to the general:

> "Whence did evil come? Or perhaps there was an element of evil in the material of creation, and God gave it form and substance, and anyway left in it something not transmuted into good? Why, then? Though omnipotent, did he perhaps lack the power to change and transform everything in such a way that no trace of evil remained? Indeed, but why should he choose such material to make anything? Could he not rather, with his omnipotence, just produce its nonexistence? Could this matter perhaps exist contrary to his will?"

These are lacerating questions for the believer, which it would be the turn of the prudent Aristotelian St. Thomas Aquinas to resolve by criteria of cautious reasonableness. Since there is no cause that does not produce a positive reality, evil is an "accidental" product, caused by a triple order of factors: *ex virtute agentis; ex defectu agentis; ex defectu materiae.* But none of these cases is applicable to God, who is the cause without a cause, the first cause, perfect and so incapable of error. Evil, therefore, created by God, must correspond to the designs of a supramundane plan, transcending the individuals active on an historical level, and which has its divine logic in terms of cosmic balance and order. In God's plans—and here Augustine's Platonism and Aquinas's Aristotelianism converge—evil in the world has the great if hidden or scandalous function of testing man, or allowing him a margin of choice between good and evil. In this perspective one sees clearly the tension between the conception of Satan in the books of the Old Testament, where the devil is still part of God's court and mostly comes out as a kind of prosecutor of man, and the conception of the devil in the Christian tradition of the New Testament, where the devil plays the part of tempter and "enchanter," seducing the soul and then dragging it down the road to perdition.

Recent news stories that describe satanic rites in various parts of the world, including those of the world that thinks itself civil and technically and politically advanced, do summary justice to the distinctions between a crude satanism, characteristic of underdeveloped cultures and countries, and an intellectually more evolved satanism.

It has been said: "Human sacrifice and the sacred banquet, particular inversions of the eucharistic supper, are novelties even for traditional European Satanism, which confined itself to internal, symbolic acts, and a gift to Satan of one's own soul. The myth of Faust shows the internal and intellectual character of European Satanism, literary and cultivated. What is offered to the devil is not the body but the soul of the person who turns to Satan."[13]

It is true that the myth of Faust, at least since 1500, passing by way of Christopher Marlowe and Goethe to Thomas Mann, is one of the foundations of European culture. But it would be a mistake to disembody it, counterposing it to satanic rites pervaded by a painful, massive corporeality, which cannot be said to be alien to it. It is not by chance that the protagonist of Mann's *Doktor Faustus*, the musician Adrian Leverkuhn, treats with the devil over the achievement of an artistic, musical perspective, revolutionary and liberating, not restricting himself to giving up his soul, but also yielding up as a bonus his physical health. Hence arises the romantic relation of illness-genius, the possibility of loving, whence derives the condemnation of love to bring death to the one who is loved, according to the "grand synthesis" of love and death, the inexorable decline of genius into madness, whence inevitably derives the loneliness engulfing he who has denied the past.

The connection between Mann's character and Goethe's Faust is clear. In both works the pact Faust makes with the devil, or Mephistofeles, is central. Then, still more impressive is the result Faust encounters in Goethe: tired, if not yet completely exhausted, having gone through extraordinary adventures and experiences, the one-time *clericus vagans*, cured from the excesses of *libido sciendi*, finds again the path of faith and true life against the wiles of Mephistofeles as genius of evil who denies, vainly protests against, and finally blocks the natural growth of things.[14]

Here we have collected and admirably synthesized, beyond the crude anthropomorphic personifications of Satan, the universal reasons for the struggle against Satan. "Hell exists, but it is empty," it has been said. We must understand what hell is today. With an emphasis that necessarily runs the risk of being a summary judgement, it has been noted that "today, the workshops of the Great Satan are the arms market, nuclear weapons, drugs, betrayal of justice, world hunger, planetary pollution, ideological, political, scientific, and cultural 'golden calves'; it is the indifference and sleep of reason that produces monsters. All is the work of that part of man we may call Satan, the part that rejects love and plans death, even when it is no longer aware of it."[15]

The Demonization of a Political Leader

A specific case of demonization, or personification of evil with reference to a person, was provided by Friedrich Tenbruck (during the Conference on the Devil, Turin, October 1988): he studied the attitude of Stalinism with regard to Leon Trotsky from this angle. According to Tenbruck, the great revolutionary became, in the 1930s—by then a private citizen without authority, living in exile—demonized by the party to an increasing degree, as symbol and forger of universal evil.

Tenbruck remarked that the evident demonization of Trotsky could not be explained by the power struggles and usual suspicions among the Bolsheviks. Nor was it produced by the fact that a revolutionary community, such as communism, claims from its own members public confessions of guilt and repentance inside the party and has always staged these confessions, not only within Bolshevism. This differs from the nonpublic confession and examination of conscience known to Christianity. However, trials that have now become public, no longer taking place only within the party, show that this was not simply a matter of an internal self-review, but the justification by an omnipotent party of its own failures. Those responsible must be sought in its own ranks, that is, at the summit, after the objective defeat of the class enemy. Thus, the party kept its orthodox explanation ready, that Trotsky like all his comrades was the agent of the reactionary powers of the class enemy, as the classic party history never tired of repeating. But behind these formulas a disturbing experience was concealed, one inconceivable in communism, since in it was announced the return of evil in its ineffableness.

In Marxism, Tenbruck states, evil makes no appearance as a moral problem since class relations objectively push history forward, so that even capitalism has historically a reason, and its advantage. There remains almost no room for moral accusation and blame, despite making assiduous use of this in the struggle. However, objectively what is interesting is the elimination of the capitalist class, which precisely for this reason can be simply liquidated without personal demonstration of guilt. The working class, on the contrary, cannot be implicated in evil. This faith in the objective certainty of a "good" and a "bad" class must, however, start to tremble the moment growing, novel elements of disturbance and heresies are discovered in the leadership of the party. Despite and because of the monotonous unmasking of "agents," the disconcerting conviction was to arise that objective membership of a class and class condition did not have the power to give birth to a common stance, or if this were decided by the party, they did not have the power to guarantee either the expected consensus or even a readiness for its active realization. In distinction with the teaching of communism, it became clear that differences of opinion could not be overcome by objective analyses of situations, because these were based on personal feelings and convictions and thus implied decisions for which one must respond morally. In turn, the accused were confused because it was impossible to believe any longer that they were able themselves to find the right political position, or to approve the party line with the conviction of their own feelings.

Tenbruck concluded that it was in these phenomena that evil, already declared defunct, reappeared, taking on its primordial forms. The doctrine that had replaced individual conscience with the logic of classes became fragile, since its believers returned to discovering that behind the multiple varieties of their own opinions there were in the last analysis decisions of conscience, which were to be taken by each individual. Since for their own rules this was impossible, the followers found themselves placed before the temptation of doing evil unawares. Faced with this situation, the party was bound to rediscover evil in its lay form: that is, in the demonization of Trotsky, the exorcisms of the Moscow show trials, and the party purges.

The Catholic Church against the Metaphoric Conception of the Devil

The devil is thus not a personal reality. It is not Satan, or Beelzelbub, or Mephistofeles, wandering through the world, like a "raging lion, seeking whom he must devour." Rather, he is a picturesque metaphor. This interpretation of the devil is clearly rejected by the official doctrine of the Catholic church.

John Paul II's statement leaves no doubt:

> The sin [of Satan] has been greater as spiritual perfection and the cognitive farsightedness of the angelical intellect were greater, and the greater the latter's freedom and closeness to God. By rejecting the known truth about God through an act of his own free will, Satan became a cosmic "deceiver" and "father of lies." He thus lives in the radical, irreversible negation of God and tries to impose on creation and on other beings created in the image of God, especially men, his tragic "lie about the good," which is God. In the Book of Genesis we find a precise description of that lie and falsification of the truth about God. . . . In this condition of existential lie, Satan, according to St. John, becomes a "murderer" as well, destroyer of the supernatural life God had placed in him and his creations. . . . As an effect of original sin, this fallen angel has conquered to some extent the dominion over man. This is the doctrine constantly professed and proclaimed by the Church and that the Council of Trent confirmed in its tractatus on original sin. It finds dramatic expression in the liturgy of baptism, when the initiate is required to renounce the devil and all his works. . . . It is not impossible that in some cases the evil spirit also presses to influence not only material things but also the body of man, whereby one speaks of "possessions by the devil." . . . The skill of Satan in the world is that of inducing men to deny his existence in the name of rationalism and every other system of thought that seeks every pretext so as not to admit his works. However, this

does not mean the elimination of free will and the responsibility of man, nor yet the thwarting of Christ's action of salvation.[16]

The clear restatement of the devil as a person should not, however, be understood as a justification of attitudes of diabolic "obsession" that have in specific epochs characterized the Christians.

It has been authoritatively proposed that

we must observe that the "obsession" with the devil and his malign power over man and the world, which has existed in certain periods of Christian history— one thinks of the fifteenth to the seventeenth centuries with their witch-hunts— and which one sees still today in some Christians . . . is not not only psychologically unhealthy, but, more important, is not "Christian." We are not under the sway and power of Satan, but under the paternal and benign omnipotence of God, our Father, and under the overlordship of love and salvation of Jesus Christ, conqueror of Satan and Lord of history."[17]

The teaching of Christ is explicitly recalled in the light of the Gospels, though it is known that there is most talk of Satan and evil spirits in the extrabiblical texts such as the First and Second Books of Enoch, the Book of Jubilees, the Life of Adam and Eve, the Testament of the Twelve Patriarchs, and so on. First, Jesus taught that the devil existed as a person, against whom he fought with the preaching of the gospel, and with the liberation of the possessed. This struggle began with the temptation in the desert and carried on until his death on the cross at Golgotha. Second, Jesus brought out the various activities of the devil and his essentially spiritual character as "tempter," trying to lead man into evil and turn him away from the faith. In this regard, the Church's teaching has undergone noteworthy changes and internal transformations.

We can say that until the ninth century, the Church tended to deny the existence of witches, for example, as part of its struggle against pagan superstitions, in order that new converts should not revert to believing in demons or fall into forms of polytheism—a far from unlikely danger. Moreover, St. Augustine still believed in the possibility of intercourse between women and the devil, while St. Thomas decisively denied the corporeal nature of the devil. Later a whole school of thought and doctrine emerged, which led to the bull of John XXII (1316–1334) *Super illius specula*, and Innocent

VIII's "witches' bull." This, though not a true dogmatic definition, inaugurated the witch hunts in grand style. Indeed, it seems clear from the witch trials and the variously extorted confessions that "with women, the devil plays the part of the man who appears as incubus; with men—a rarer occurrence moreover—he takes the role of the woman who appears as succubus."[18]

The Dialectic of Salvation through the Fall in Christianity

Generally we may say that there is a close connection between belief in demons and the depreciation of sexuality, and that it is not rare for social evils and crises to be transcribed and translated into intimate diabolic terms. However, official Christian doctrine does not recognize the autonomy of Satan as prince of evil. "It rejects all dualism, stating that Satan and the devils are beings created by God and thus have no absolute autonomy, nor are placed on the same level as God. That is, the idea that evil is an autonomous principle that confronts Good, that there is a God of Evil confronting the God of Goodness, is rejected."[19]

Here, there clearly emerge the outlines of a complex dialectic of salvation that upholds the dogmatic theology of Christianity. Though a creation of God, and hence under divine power, Satan acts against divine will and tries to involve human beings in his revolt. These, hanging between faith and damnation, may in turn choose between God and rebellion against God, and live to the full their dramatic destiny, since they can, for all their lives, at any moment, make a gesture that saves or damns them. In the dialectic of salvation, temptation and sin are an essential negative term.

It suffices here to say that, though rebelling against God and setting himself up as instrument and personification of evil, Satan ends up in the general plan that God sets up as regards humans, and their history as instruments of God—by becoming again his unconscious servant. Hence perhaps arises the characteristic polymorphism of Satan, dictated not only by the needs of the great seducer who has to disguise himself according to the circumstances in which he has to perform, but also by the different trades he has to tackle in a divine design that transcends him and whose scope and global outlines inevitably escape him.[20]

The Champion of the Rebels without Hope

In this final, necessary failure it is perhaps possible to see in the devil the prince and champion of the rebels without hope, and thus also the representative of "free thought." I wonder if the Evil One cannot also be identified as the champion of modernity. When, in the 1950s, at the University of Chicago, Leo Strauss commented on Machiavelli's thought, at times using some of my literal translations of passages from *The Prince* and *The Discourses*, and did not hesitate to point out in the Florentine secretary a diabolic "teacher of evil," I confess I was not always able to hold back a tremor of admiration for the fallen angel. I feel there is no trace of Carducci in this, as the Hymn to Satan seems too linear and simplistic. The fervent eulogies of the locomotive as the beautiful monster who "jumps the track" at top speed and conquers the whole world according to a model of emancipation that smelled too much of localism and the "branch line" was not convincing to me. Nor did the quiet, even gentle submissiveness of another who hymned progress, the spiritual, mild abbot Giacomo Zanella, seem quite "diabolic." He was absorbed in an evolutionary, scientistic meditation in the face of the "fossil shell," used as a paperweight on his desk in a study one guessed was furnished with massive black, vaguely Giolittian, ministerial furniture, poorly lit by the yellowish light of the lampshade that had the capacity to enrage Filippo Tommaso Marinetti.[21]

If I really had to choose a guide in the forest of books and studies that reach the First World War by way of the last quarter of the nineteenth century—a time when shortly they were to be silenced, not only or mainly by the "clarification" of Benedetto Croce so much as by the authoritarian, ready rod of fascism—I should trust myself to a lesser figure. I should entrust myself, for example, to a polygraph such as Arturo Graf, and above all to some of his articles full of critical insight regarding Lombroso's and other scientists' excesses, and those of the paleo-positivists that the iron tines of Croce's pitiless criticism were about to destroy summarily.[22]

It is strange that in order to gather incisive aspects of a positive conception of the devil, one should need to turn to a poet, John Milton. Not even the most eloquent of recent and contemporary writers seems as capable as the author of *Paradise Lost* of giving the sense of a lost power and majesty. Not by chance did William Blake suspect that Milton "was of the devil's party without knowing it." It is too easy to think that all the evil in the world is due to the devil. The Book of Job is at once instructive and scandalous in this regard. God is called to respond; he has to rid himself of blame. No theodicy could send him away free from blame. Satan's rebellion is evidence of heroic energy, an unprotected offering to the unknown, and also the extraordinary presumption of claiming to create from himself, from within, purely and exclusively by immanence, his own values. It is this devilish presumption that defines modern societies. They have rejected the traditions of the fathers and the supramundane wisdom of God the Father as guide and source of legitimacy in favor of rational criteria. Certainly the sin is of pride—but perhaps one should examine the role and function of sin in human history. The scholastic definitions of traditional dogmatic theology no longer seem adequate. Original sin is a necessary sin, opening the way for "free thought," the precondition for every act of human freedom, and thus of every humanly meaningful ethic. And it is at the same time the gesture that opens the door of suffering.

One now understands why the Evil One takes on in Milton the "aspect of a fallen beauty, splendor clouded by melancholy and death . . . all the fascination of the unbroken rebel that once belonged to the figures of Aeschylus's Prometheus and Dante's Capaneo."[23]

Anyone who has studied or indeed experienced a crime, from Machiavelli to Dostoevsky to Genet, knows there is an autopoietic divine or diabolic character in sin. He understands that there is an intrinsic violence to it, not far from the manic fury of the Homeric heroes. When Leo Strauss said he saw in Machiavelli the "teacher of evil,"[24] he knew and had indeed scientifically shown, that it was to Machiavelli, even before Hobbes, that the merit, however dubious from Strauss's viewpoint, of having opened the age of modernity belonged, by drastically separating ethical happiness from practical political success. Sin, in other words, "the devil's work," is not necessarily a lack, a void. It may be excess of life, impatience, expectation, a drive to plan. I reiterate an earlier statement:

"Rather than the scholastic, static counterposing of good to evil, sin *makes one think, or at least glimpse the possibility, of an order beyond the constituted one.*"[25]

Perhaps the parable of the prodigal son should be interpreted in this sense—the penitent sinner whom one does not ask to account for the sin committed with the shortsighted meticulousness of the shopkeeper concerned over the accounts as though there was a case of a double order. In sin there is the possibility of enrichment fated to escape the literal, pharisaic interpretation of the moral law. The reason that drove the late Max Horkheimer to maintain that theology is not the science of God but only the expression of nostalgia becomes He had written, "The last strategic withdrawal of Protestant theology tries to save the idea that individual life has a meaning peculiar only to itself. In life-in-the-world the important thing would be to intend something more than the mundane."[26] He saw in this a kind of diabolic tendency. The theology that tends to modernize so as to keep in tune with science and generally with a world dominated by technical rationality is really the instrument whereby God is canceled from the field of practical human experience. His pact with the world corresponds to the diminution of ecclesiastical space, the end of religion. Horkheimer does not specify if this concerns church religion understood as religiosity or as profound personal experience.

In fact, sin, or the breaking of the rules, its conscious transgression, seems to present itself as the sign of modernity. Crime has its "beauty," exercises a Medusa-like power that it seems right to describe as diabolic. At the same time, this enchantment is at the root of the modern age and seems the price to be paid for emancipation.[27] What seemed to Weber the "world of disenchantment," the contradictory effect of an historic break and *Entzauberung*, is in reality a self-enchanting world, presuming to express its basic, legitimating values by itself. The biblical disobedience of Satan here appears in the guise of presumption or the request for absolute autonomy.

The Satanic face of modernity is to be sought in this dream of total, indeterminate freedom. From the lay side too, the false prophets in this regard have not been lacking. Cioran's warning has not passed in vain: "Relieved of the burden of history, man, arriving at the limit of exhaustion, once he has abdicated from his own peculiarity, will possess only an empty conscience, with nothing that can fill it; a disappointed troglodyte, a troglodyte tired of everything.''

Tired, maybe, but like Abraham, never sated. It is in this never satisfied appetite, this perennially unsatisfied search, that one should recognize the satanic face of modernity. This has been grasped again recently with great acuteness. André Neher in his *L'esilio della parola*,[28] tries to establish a dialectical relation, at once contradictory and inseparable, between Faust, the typical representative of the modern age with his tormented and superhuman activism, and the Golem, here called on to represent the fall of orders and ideas, and a sharp nostalgia for the cosmos of abandoned tradition, which are the essence of the current historical era, in default of a better-defined "postmodernism." In Neher's view, these twin myths, both born in the sixteenth century, cross history and intersect variously, unexpectedly, and at times tragically, through the development of modern man: from the Renaissance to Auschwitz, from Goethe to Hiroshima, finally arriving at the imminent ecological disaster where the very survival of the planet is now at stake. The Faustian pact of modern humans with the devil is at the origin of this epoch, so trusting in itself and presumptuous as to try again the fatal adventures of Icarus and Prometheus, and both so attracted by the secrets of the world as to risk everything on the altar of knowledge and experience. And these aspire not only to imitate or know, but also to attack, transform, and even create anew society and nature.

Satan, Son of God, and the Ambiguity of the Sacred

Perhaps the most important lesson Satan offers humanity—temptations, diversions, and pain apart—is the reminder that the divine and the diabolical have a common source. Beyond questions of interpreting the Scriptures, the fact remains that Satan, not only Christ, is the son of God. In the Book of Job, Satan is presented as one of the "sons of God." From the start of time, the forces of good and evil seem inextricably linked. It has been said, "The Iranian term *daiva*, which linguistically corresponds to the Indian *deva* and the Latin *deus*, does not in Iran indicate, as it does in Sanskrit and Latin, a divine figure, but on the contrary a demonic one, to the point that the name *Indra*, a *deva* and one of the greatest divinities of the Vedas, came to signify an arch-demon in Iran."[29] From this viewpoint, the hypothesis of a radical separation and difference between Satan in the Old Testament and the figure of the devil or "foul spirit" as we know in in the New, seems plausible. Here, the devil seems to have lost any function of service to the divine: I mean, any function immediately positive, wished by God, save for the great function, definitively one of salvation, which temptation, sin, and forgiveness play in the great soteriological project set out in Christianity.

In the New Testament, the devil emerges not as accuser on God's account, but simply as tempter. More generally, he is the object of the act of exorcism of Christ or his disciples. It is the evil from which we must be gratuitously liberated. "And as ye go, preach, saying, The kingdom of heaven is at hand. Heal the sick, cleanse the lepers, raise the dead, *cast out devils*: freely ye have received, freely give." (Matt. 10:7-8; my emphasis). Dietrich Bonhoeffer is very clear in this regard: "The kingdom of God, Jesus Christ, the forgiveness of sins, the salvation of the sinner through faith, all this coincides *with the destruction of the power of the devil*."[30]

When Jesus calls his twelve apostles and sends them to reap the harvest, he does not confine himself to giving them a doctrine. Bonhoeffer's comment here too should be borne in mind: "What they receive is not a word or doctrine, but a real power, without which the work cannot be completed. They need a power stronger than that of the prince of this world, the devil. The disciples know quite well the power of the devil, though his cleverest trick lies in denying this power and making believe it does not exist."[31] Satan is thus the great enemy in Christianity. In his presence the struggle can know no rest. It is a battle of mutual destruction that allows no pauses or treaties, since it concerns a faithless enemy, a master of disguise who can present himself in false appearances. The false prophet is in this regard his favorite mask: "He hides his dark purposes beneath the cloak of Christian piety, hoping his harmless mask with prevent his discovery."[32]

In the Old Testament, Satan is not against God. He is part of his

court. He also has an important function—he is the accuser of
God's enemies. He contains all the tasks of the investigator and the
accuser. He is not an insidious tempter, as in the Christian world,
but rather a provocateur, in the sense that he suspends doubts and
clouds certainties regarding God's faithfulness to Job, for example.
Christianity, on the other hand, sees in Satan essentially the personification of the Fall, through his own fault, through pride and
rebellion against God, and thus the example of an eternal condemnation with the consequent institution of hell as a place where the
sentence is eternally served.

Satan's challenge to God is thus his sin and blasphemy. It is a
challenge in terms of cognition—a functioning, infinite knowledge
that in an instant knows, creates, and combines past, present, and
future on a world scale, canceling out time spans and the breaks
that appear to human intelligence as insurmountable barriers. In
this sense the biblical serpent is not Satan. He is only the "cleverest
animal." In this sense again there is a satanic element in all the
highest and most noble human enterprises, those in which the
instant of heroism shines out when the hero forgets himself in favor
of the ideal he represents: from the hunting of the white whale by
Captain Ahab in Melville to the unattainable artistic ideal of Adrian
Leverkühn in Thomas Mann. As the Old-Testament God needs the
Satan-accuser to flush out his enemies and make them come out
into the open, so Mann's protagonist needs the devil to conquer
creative paralysis and the psychological block imposed by his own
thirst for perfection.

One can grasp a last lesson from Satan in the necessary distinction between sacred and religious. I have remarked elsewhere that
reduced to its nub, the sacred is ineffable, that is, unsayable.[33] One
must ask how one may speak of it. The only logical attitude to it
would be silence, and in this Wittgenstein is certainly correct.
However, the need to speak of it is obvious. This need does not
correspond only to an internal urgency of a psychological kind. The
sacred points to and presupposes a community link. In its external,
ritualistic aspect, this link is the religious bond, the community of
the faithful, the Church. But precisely for this reason, sacred and
religious must not be confused. They are two realities that should
not be hastily conjoined, even if in everyday language they are

often used as synonyms. The fact is that the idea of the sacred precedes the very idea of God, and that the religious is probably none other than the administrative arm of the sacred, a power structure that continually runs the risk—diabolically—of replacing the sacred while proclaiming itself at its service.

Notes

1. See my *Ricordo e la temporalita*, passim.
2. For a full analysis, see L. Strauss, *The Rebirth of Classical Political Rationalism*ed. T. L. Pangle, (Chicago: University of Chicago, 1989), especially pp. 227–270.
3. See K. H. Wolff, "For a Sociology of Evil," *Journal of Social Issues* 1, 25 (1969).
4. Ibid., 113–114; but see also M. Coleman Nelson and M. Eigen, eds., *Evil, Self, and Culture* (New York: Human Sciences Press, 1984), especially M. Eigen's "On Demonized Aspects of the Self," pp. 91–123.
5. For a general overview of the demonological problematic, see Alfonso M. Di Nola, *Il diavolo: Le forme, la storia, le vicende di Satana e la sua universale e malefica presenza presso tutti i popoli* (Rome: Newton-Compton, 1987) and *Il diavolo: La sindrome demoniaca sovrasta l'umanità*, (Rome: Scipioni, 1980); see also J. B. Russel, *Satana, il diavolo e l'inferno tra il primo e il quinto secolo* (Milan: Mondadori, 1986), *Il diavolo nel mondo antico* (Rome-Bari: Laterza, 1988), and *Il diavolo nel Medioevo* (Rome-Bari: Laterza, 1987); and R. Villeneuve, *La beauté du diable*, (Paris: Berger-Levrault, 1983).
6. S. Giacomoni, "Un pranzo col diavolo . . . ," *La Repubblica* 6 (September 1988), 18. But even earlier (see ADISTA, no. 62 and no. 66, 13–15 August 1986), Pope Wojtyla had made broad statements about the devil. A revival of attention to the devil had been observed with Paul VI; in October 1986, Corrado Balducci, a well-known monsignor, expert in the problem, said in a contribution at the Rome Circolo Montevecchio: "There is a clear increase in possessions by the devil as compared to thirty years ago; out of five thousand claimed cases, only two or three are real; currently those really possessed in Italy are said to be about twenty; the pope is more cognisant of this than his predecessors, in his view, since he knows the third secret of Fatima" (C. Balducci, *Gli indemoniati*, [Rome: Coletti, 1959], and *Il diavolo esiste e lo si puo riconoscere*, [Casale Monferrato: Piemme, 1988]).
7. See, for example, B. P. Levack, *La caccia alle streghe* (Rome-Bari: Laterza, 1988), according to whom just between 1450 and 1750 a large number of women were tried and executed for witchcraft in Europe; at least 110,000 people were dragged before ecclesiastical courts and secular ones. It was believed that Satan, in the form of an elegant, beautiful young man, lured the witch with promises of material and above all sexual gratification. To seal the "pact with the devil," the woman trampled on the crucifix and agreed to being rebaptized by Satan, who marked her on a secret part of her body with a stamp, thereafter summoning her with other witches for orgies, which included infanticide and cannibalism and were a serious threat for the whole social order. For a

historically-relevant instance, see P. Boyer and S. Nissenbaum, *Salem Possessed: The Social Origins of Witchcraft* (Cambridge: Harvard University Press, 1974).

8. An analogous interpretation of the political party of the Jacobin type can be found in S. Weil, *Note sur la suppression générale des partis politiques*, in *Communità* (1949), with my introduction, and in *Diario* (1988; ed. A. Belardinelli and G. Bellocchio).

9. See a (sociological) suggestion in my *Paradosso del sacro*.

10. See A. M. Di Nola, "Se Satana risale agli Aztechi," *Corriere della Sera*, See 13 April 1989. But it would be a serious mistake, probably caused by unconscious ethnocentrism, to believe that magic, witchcraft, and satanic rites are sole preroratives of backward peoples. See the recent book by T. M. Luckmann, *Persuasions of the Witch's Craft: Ritual Magic in Contemporary England* (Cambridge: Harvard University Press, 1989), where the American anthropologist explores and analyzes through participant observation some strata of the London population, concluding that magical practices and satanic rites exist even in London today and are a syncretic whole of not-necessarily-coherent procedures and concepts, in which the middle strata of society in particular seem to indulge—people at times educated, even intellectually refined, avid readers of J.R.R. Tolkien and Ursula K. Le Guin. See also M. I. Macioti et al., "Caratteri del magico fra regressione e nuova razionalità," *La critica sociologica* 86–87, (Summer–Autumn 1988); and A. M. Di Nola, *Inchiesta sul diavolo* (Rome-Bari: Laterza: 1979).

11. See Y. Kawabata, *Chronique d'Asakusa* (Paris: Albin Michel, 1988).

12. This and other statements was collected by D. Del Rio, "Wojtyla contra Lucifero nella citta delle messe nere," *La Repubblica*, supp., October 1988; an interdisciplinary conference, organized by Professor F. Barbano in Turin, 17–21 October 1988, was titled "Diabolos, dialogos, daimon"; see below. On the presence of evil in the world, see, from the socioanthropological viewpoint, S. M. Lyman, *The Seven Deadly Sins: Society and Evil* (New York: St. Martin's Press, 1978); G. Filoramo, et al., "Il Male," *Leggere* 10 (April 1989):18–27.

13. See G. Baget Bozzo, "Ai confini di Satana," *La Repubblica*, 20 April 1989; I cite this piece for its emblematic quality, representative of a mentality widespread among the European educated middle strata in particular.

14. For a case of possession at a very low social level, see L. Borello, "Maggio 1850: Due indemoniati nel Santuario della Consolata a Torino," *Bollettino storico-bibliografico subalpino* 86, no. 1 (January–June 1988): 271–305.

15. See N. Fabbretti, "Satana é nell'uomo; non e' una maschera," *Stamp Sera*, 12 September 1988; this is interesting because it is part of the polemic on interpreting the satanic rites and black masses, which in those days, especially in Turin, the press was concerned with.

16. See *Catechesi* Bulletin no. 299 (13 August 1986).

17. "La fede cristiana e il diavolo," *La civilàta cattolica* 137 (20 September 1986): 450.

18. See H. Haag, *Teufelsgabe* (Tübingen: Katzmann 1974).

19. *Catechesi*, 457.

20. A little work of extraordinary interest, aiming at bringing order among the devils by classifying their aspects, levels of intelligence, and power, their various jurisdictions and thus their overall hierarchy, is the one attributed to

the Byzantine courtier Michele Psello (1018–1078?), *De Operatione Daemonium (Le opere dei demoni* [Palermo: Sallerio, 1989]). The author, in a dialogue between three characters, the Thracian, Marcus, and Timothy, distinguishes the devils into fiery, airy, earthly, watery, subterranean, and light avoiding. Without removing himself from experience and popular myths, and indeed using these widely, Psello more or less consciously tried to set out a critical demonology from the often formless empirical knowledge and beliefs that were especially widespread among the lower, weaker strata of society.

The first, "incandescent" kind of devil, floats in the ether; the second, the airy one, is closer to us, though "on high"; the third is among us, on this earth; the fourth is the "marine and aquatic" kind; the fifth resides permanently underground; and finally, there are devils who prefer the darkest depths, the most inaccessible on earth. According to Psello, one may say that the devils live and act around humankind, from the highest circles of the sky to the deep darkness of the earth (here, it does not concern us to establish how much he owes to earlier schemas like that of Proclus or other neo-Platonists). Their presence can be noted everywhere, and one cannot escape them. Diabolic omnipresence, a permanent feature of the scriptures as of all hagiography, is accurately described here and was to be followed both through classifications (from Giordano Bruno to Swedenborg) and the condemnations of "experimental science," which paradoxically recognizes the demonic in the witch trials, as Rosita Copioli has noted (*Mercurio*, 29 April 1989).

21. For a call to the critical reevaluation of late nineteenth-century positivism, see pp. 3–5 of my *Sociologia alla riscoperta*.

22. For a well-documented overview, see G. De Liguori, *Materialismo inquieto* (Rome-Bari: Laterza, 1988). For the link between demiurgic function and Satan, especially in Islam, see H. Corbin, *Le paradoxe du monothéisme*, (Paris: Editions de l'Herne, 1981).

23. M. Praz, *La carne, la morte, e il diavolo nella letteratura romantica* (Turin: Einaudi, 1942) 59. For some neoromantic views in some contemporary authors, though classically set out, see the following. A. Camus, *Noces* (Paris: Gallimard, 1950): "Il y a des mots que je n'ai jamais bien compris, comme celui de péché." M. Yourcenar, *Sur quelques thèmes érotiques et mystiques de la Gita-Govinda et l'Andalousie ou les Hesperi des* (Marseille: Rivages, 1982): "Que le Christianisme . . . ait voulu, e en grande partie accompli une désacralisation du sensuel . . . pour n'y pas installer à perpetuité la notion de péché, cela n'est quère douteux."

24. L. Strauss, *Thoughts on Machiavelli* (New York: Free Press, 1958), passim.

25. Ferrarotti, *Una teologia per atei*, 183–184.

26. M. Horkheimer, *Zur Kritik der instrumentellen Vernunft* (Frankfurt: Suhrkaning, 1970), 227.

27. For an approach that puts the question in direct touch with the everyday, see J. Vergès, *Beauté du crime* (Paris: Plon, 1988).

28. André Neher, *L'esilia della parola* (Genoa: Marietti, 1989).

29. U. Bianchi, "L'antica radice di dio e demonio," *Sole 24 ore*, 14 May 1989. But for deeper analysis see this author's "Alcuni aspetti abnormi del dualismo persiano," in *Selected Essays on Gnosticism, Dualism, and Mysterosophy*, ed. E. G. Brill (Leiden, 1978), 390–405.

30. D. Bonhoeffer, *The Cost of Discipleship* (New York: Macmillan, 1963), 230: my emphasis.

31. Ibid., 226.
32. Ibid., 213.
33. See my "La transcription rationnelle du sacré et du religieux," in *Langages et déplacements du religieux* (Paris: Cerf, 1987); this contains my reply to D. Grasso, S.J, "Una teologia insufficiente," (*La civiltà cattolica* no. 3200), where there is a careful critique of the first of this trilogy, my book *Una teologia per atei*, as regards the satanic ambiguity of the sacred, see C. Kerény, *La religion antique* (Geneva: Georg, 1957), 81–82: "Les concepts antiques de pureté religieuse et, en général ceux qui se rapprochent le plus du sacré—comme les concepts latins de *sanctitas* et de *sacrum*ne présupposent d'ordinaire jamais le divin . . . ce qui est *sacer* est déjà propriété des dieux, originairement et en particulier propriété des dieux inférieurs."

7

Ecumenical Prayer

The Wonderful Play of Forces

The religious act *par excellence* is prayer. We are far from a potential universal religion and a faith without dogmas because every religion jealously continues praying in its own way. This is an exclusive and dogmatically defined way, amounting to a closure toward others and the world, a clumsy attempt to privatize God. In Assisi, during the great interreligious gathering of a few years back, each prayed on his own behalf, separately—a serious limitation. It is of no avail to console oneself in the spirit of that laicism that is a child of the ideology of progress as chronologically inevitable by saying that the prayer of modern society is the reading of the morning papers. The day's news, with its daily ration of poison and untruths, may well deaden in busy people the sense of history. It cannot placate, still less replace, their need for the absolute.

Niklas Berdyaev found prayer natural since it was in human beings' nature to kneel before the prince. It is not just this. It is not necessarily a homage to an outside power. In prayer there is a moment of intimacy that involves the universe. The inside opens to the outside so as to make the inside-outside dichotomy meaningless. Only a few great poets have been able to intuit this. Mostly, the intuition was paid for with amazement and stammering, if not with absorbed dumbness and silence. There is a reality that stands above me. I recognize it and beseech it. Not through cowardice, but so as not to disturb the cosmic order of which in that state I feel part.

> I find you in all these things,
> to which I am good and like a brother;
> like a seed you sleep in humble things
> and in the big ones, there you are big.
> This is the wonderful play of forces
> that so serving they pass through things:
> growing in the root, dwindling in the trunks,
> and in the treetops, like a resurrection.

The wonderful play of forces:[1] it is in this wonderful game that prayer is inserted. The limitation not transcended remains as a reproach. Prayer is born in the awareness of guilt, a distance to heal—a debt to pay? First of all, it signifies the inadequacy and finitude of the person praying. In addition, this marks the need to cross the boundary, to transcend it. The Confession is very clear on this: "Mea culpa, mea culpa, mea maxima culpa. . . . Ideo praecor beatae Mariae semper virgini, beato Michaeli Archangelo . . ." That *"ideo"* is the key. Once the sin has been admitted and confessed, one prays, to reestablish the disturbed order, to escape the cone of shade. It is not thus only an individual need. It is not just a sin to remove on the subjective level. The whole cosmos is called to account, in that the sinner is at once hunter and quarry, butcher and victim. In particular, it embodies both transgression and a supreme sacrificial moment. This ambivalence has also been exactly recorded in the extra-Christian world:

> The value of the Vedic sacrifice, which does not aim at setting up man in his little space, but at ensuring the perpetuity of the universal order, the regular functioning of the cosmos, finds its correlation in the cosmogonic myth of the Purusa, the primordial man who is at the same time the first sacrifice, the dismembered sacrificial victim, and the product of sacrifice, that is, the totality of the world—heaven, earth, air—gods, animals, men, born of the different parts of the body of the immolated Purusa.[2]

The Indefinite as a Consequence of the Loss of the Infinite

It is perhaps in this perspective that one may grasp the ambiguous role of sin and the related sense of an original guilt, of a primordial fall, in the mysterious economy of the divine government of the world, from which prayer springs. In fact, the "wages of sin" is death, but precisely for this reason sin is important and probably necessary, since it is death that shows peremptorily the boundary, the grounding finiteness of human experience. In this context it is interesting to note that technically advanced societies, which seem open to the *indefinite*, having renounced or lost the *infinite*, cannot accept this. Indeed, they cannot even understand it. They cancel it. They do not mention it, as one does not mention a dirty word or a scandalous reality.[3] In this aspect, contemporary industrial societies are the negation of classical antiquity, based on the sense of measure against any flight into irrationality of the unmeasured— μεσε`ν 'αγαν-*ne quid nimis*.[4]

In its true meaning, as recognition of the limit, prayer thus goes beyond prayer: not necessarily in the sense of the *esprits forts* of Charles Baudelaire, for ecample. This son of a priest, in *Mon coeur mis à nu*, writes, "What is not priesthood today? Youth itself is a priesthood, according to what the young say. And what is not a prayer? Shitting is a prayer, according to the democrats when they shit"—but in the sense that prayer is not only a demand to be formulated, as the mild Abbot Giacomo Zanella suggested, "when the need spurs." It is essentially dialogue, made up of words but also silence. The meditation of the Quakers restores the music of silence: it is silent prayer. The atmosphere of monastic prayer, it has been remarked, is that of the desert, where daily habits, almost automatic, of normal life are not present to give support. Even if he lives in a community, the monk is forced to explore the "internal waste," his disintegration as socially useful being, in his solitude. He has no other way of salvation but dialogue with God.[5]

Prayer is also a reminder of God, a moment of negotiation with God, a pact, an invocation that does not exclude the imperative. For this reason prayer is also an accusation of God, a calling to account for the evil in the world. At the origins of theodicy there is the scandal of an unanswered prayer, the shadow of an inexplicable injustice that certainly weighs on humanity, but for which God is bound to give account. It is such a generalized need it spills into literature from theology and philosophy:

It is a very poor reading of Kafka that sees in it only the cypher of man guilty in the face of the inscrutable power of a God who has become alien and remote. On the contrary, here it is God himself who needs to be saved, and the only possible happy ending we can imagine for his novels is Klamm's redemption of the Count, of the anonymous theological crowd of judges, chancellors and guards pressed hugger-mugger in dusty passages, or with head bowed under the too-low ceilings. Kifka's genius lies in having placed God in a closet, of having made the box room and the basement the theological place *par excellence*.[6]

Job Accuses God

God among the garbage recalls the man sitting on the manure heap. One cannot pass over Job in silence. His complaints have nothing complaining about them. It is a lament transformed into an accusation: "God does not listen to prayer" or "Useless is prayer when the hand of God strikes." Then, the cry of those praying becomes a protest against God. Traditionally, the appearance of God is enough to calm and resolve the conflict *("Sic ait et dicto citius tumida aequora placat")*. No. For Job, God is bound to excuse himself. We need God, but Job's prayer seems to show that God also needs us. The notion of prayer, from this viewpoint, appears rather obscure in recent currents of the sociology of religion. In Marcel Mauss it is schematic and sociologistic and excessively stresses the purely ritualistic aspects.[7] And yet the paradox of prayer lies precisely in the defeat of stereotyped formulas.

In this sense it is reasonable to speak of a *deep prayer*. Commenting on the massacre in the synagogue in Istanbul of defenseless Jews at prayer (October 1986), the *Osservatore Romano* denied the terrorists the right to appeal to the Islamic faith since this would never have tolerated the killing of people at prayer, still less would the great mystical tradition of Sufism have tolerated it. In reality, there is a prayer of the depths on which all positive historical faiths converge and which should be recovered as internal dialogue of universal significance.

De profundis clamavi ad Te, Domine. There is a prayer *of* and *from* the deep that crosses over the dogmatic partitions of the positive religions so as to reach and express the essence of *homo religiosus*. This deep prayer is ecumenical and expresses in its silence or in speech, beyond ritual formula, essential religiosity, overcoming the sacred-religious dichotomy. It helps us understand the internal constitution of *homo religiosus*: humility; the sense of a supreme cosmic order, not necessarily personalized and embodied in a single being as pantocrator; and an attitude of acceptance, not passive but waiting and attentive. The prayer of the deep arises and develops on the basis of an attitude that is a *giving beyond receiving*. Thus, it is placed outside the logic of commodification and brings out fully the paradox of the sacred: the metahuman as more necessary than the human. The act of prayer is the act of its recognition, even when it appears in disguise, since it is well known that what is deep loves a mask.

At this point it should not be a surprise that, regarding prayer more than other subjects, sociological arrogance, like the presumption of classifying that is the necessary condition for any scientific analysis, comes in contact with a peculiarly hard lesson of modesty. Dealing with prayer, a universal phenomenon, present in all human cultures, the social analyst asks: Is it ever possible to construct a typology? I believe the reply can be affirmative, but with a basic reservation. The various types, useful from a descriptive and, in an intercultural sense, comparative viewpoint, do not exhaust the phenomenon. Among students of the history of religions, Alfonso M. Di Nola seems interested above all in exploring and explaining the process of transforming individual personal prayer into liturgical prayer: that is, how one "passes from an absolutely free form of prayer marked by the characteristics of the great religious personality to the form that belongs exclusively to the life of historical religious collectivities."[8]

Perhaps the process might also be inverted, and then attention would focus on the techniques and ways through which prayer has passed, realizing itself in different types: a) magic-fetishistic prayer; b) formal, or liturgico-repetitive prayer; c) supplicatory, or contestatory prayer; d) prayer from the deep, already mentioned; and e) silent prayer, that in which the supplicant accepts state of quiet or abandonment, living to the full the experience of silence expecting revelation, the unveiling of the divine, according to the nonformally codifiable model of a rigorously aliturgical personal religiosity. This latter type of prayer, as I have made clear, lies beyond the historically prevalent types, linked variously to the five universal religions of the *Weltreligionen*, for whose study Max Weber's research is still, in a sociological perspective, useful.[9] If we isolate in these religions the concept of God, we find essentially three conceptions: a) God as absolutely transcendant and totally other being as regards man; b) the negation of God as person, and his assertion as presence, as it were, "disseminated" over everything; and c) God as *personal, transcendent being*, but not completely *alienated* from humans, with whom he communicates and for whose salvation he provides through the "go-between" of the son historically incarnated for this purpose.

Thinking as Praying

If I may put it rather schematically, one can say that three different types of prayer correspond to these three different conceptions of God:

1. Prayer is a homage to the Supreme Being, dominant and immensely powerful as regards the person praying, to the extent that one can only direct to him established, repeated formulas in modes, gestures, and times established on the basis of the authority of tradition, according to a rigorous liturgy.
2. Prayer and any act of prayer are mingled with the modes of daily living and tend to break down its limits by meditation and concentration, but without externalization from the everyday.
3. Prayer acquires the modes and substance of an exchange between the individual and God, and so takes various forms, from the exaltation of the divinity to the specific request in case of need.

One may say that the first type is clearly predominant in Judaism and Islam, the second is quite common in Hinduism and Buddhism, and the third type seems characteristic of Christian doctrine and practice.

The problem of the "scandalous," contestatory prayer of Job remains an open one. This, at least according to current logic, involves the distinction between the punishment of humans as such and humans as innocent victims. Again a poet provides a deeper interpretation than the one permitted by the logic of good sense and shows how the dissociation between the whole human being and the innocent human is a psychological error ends up at least partly obscuring the meaning of Job's rebellion against God. The downtrodden yields before God less through conviction than tiredness. In fact, "nothing allows us to consider goodness as the principal attribute of divinity. Joseph de Maistre himself at times seems tempted to think so. . . . The more terrible God appears to us the more we have to increase religious fear in his regard, and *our prayers must be fervent and tireless.* . . . There is no better side to take than that of resignation and respect, I should say even of love."[10] The old Savoyard reactionary is here unexpectedly, and certainly as far as he is concerned unknowingly, linked with the last pages of Plato's *Symposium*, where Alcibiades ultimately exalts Socrates as a lover and philosopher, revealing the common source and essential convergence of *studium* and *amor*, of knowledge as desire for wisdom, pleading, and internal dialogue: an Augustinian confrontation between *ego superior* and *ego inferior*. Is it not moreover true that throughout the Middle Ages, philosophical study was still very close to a ceaseless prayer, a nonformal one, not to be seen as ritualistic procedure but rather as tacit meditation, like a silent internal discourse, between self and self?

This silent prayer, not repeated and asking no help from stereotyped liturgical formulas, is made precisely between self and self. It goes beyond classificatory typologies and helps make us see the real meaning of prayer as *abandonment*. It is a moment of stasis that at times can be prepared and resolved into ecstasy. It is the quietness of the person who distances himself from the competitive tension of the market—the distance and submissiveness, in the sense of nonwill, that rejects representation so as to open completely, unprotectedly, to experience in all its indeterminacy. Praying, therefore, should be like thinking, not as project or proposal, but by letting oneself be, thought by thought, accepting being transcended by it, beyond any narcissistic presumption: discovering in it the meaning of self, the possibility of a meaningful relation with the other, or one's own place in the universe.

Notes

1. Rainer Maria Rilke, from the *Book of Hours*:
   Ich finde dich in allen diesen Dingen,
   denen ich gut und wie ein Bruder bin;
   als Samen sonnst du dich in den geringen

und in den grossen giebst du gross dich hin,
Das ist das wundersame Spiel der Kräfte,
das sie so dienend durch die Dinge gehn;
in Wurzel wachsend, schwindend in die Schäfte
und in den Wipfeln wie ein Auferstehn.

2. Jean-Paul Vernant, *Religions, histoires, raison* (Paris: Maspero, 1979), 24.

3. Ferrarotti, *Una teologia per atei*, 181–184. See also, in addition to the classical studies by Philippe Ariès, D. E. Stannard, *The Puritan Way of Death* (New York: Oxford University Press, 1977), especially pp. 188–196.

4. One of the most thorough treatments of this aspect is in O. Spengler, *Der Untergang des Abendlandes*, especially vol. 1, where, following the concept of *àpeiron* in Anaxamander, he examines closely the limits of classical mathematics, which could not find possible or plausible the conceptualization of negative numbers or imaginary ones, since the idea of "irrational" numbers ended by leading to absurdity, according to the classics, in separating the notion of number from that of size. But for a broader perspective on the Greeks' attitude to the irrational, see E. R. Dodds, *The Greeks and the Irrational* (Berkeley: University of California, 1951).

5. See T. Merton, *The Climate of Monastic Prayer* (Kalamazoo: Cistercian, 1981), passim, especially p. 39.

6. G. Agamben, *Idea della prosa* (Milan: Feltrinelli, 1985), 57.

7. M. Mauss, *Les fonctions sociales du sacré*, vol. 1 of *Oeuvres*, (Paris: Minuit, 1968), 355–477.

8. A. M. Di Nola, *La preghiera dell'uomo* (Rome: Newton Compton, 1988), 12.

9. See M. Weber, *Sociologia delle religioni*, 2 vols. (Turin: UTET, 1988), passim. Regarding the "feeling of the whole," see (as the expression of romantic intimism at the limit of Catholic orthodoxy, relived with the enthusiasm of the new convert) J. Langbehn, *Der Geist des Ganzen* (*Lo spirito del tutto*) (Brescia: Morcelliana, 1939). There is no shortage of testimony, apparently more modest but still meaningful: See R. T. Flewelling, *Conflict and Conciliation of Cultures*, (Stockton: College of the Pacific Press 1951), especially "Aspects of a Universal Religion," pp. 74–96; the Bahài's ecumenical position is well known—See S. Effendi, *L'ordine mondiale di Baha'u'llah*, (Rome: Baha'i, 1982).

10. E. M. Cioran, *Esercizi di ammirazione* (Milan: Adelphi, 1988), 30–31; my emphasis.

Postscript

Notes for a Discussion*

When the body of this book was set up and ready for printing, some contributions appeared in Italy that require at least a fleeting glance here, if not the deeper examination they deserve. I do not refer to the critical note Silvio Burgalassi insists on keeping ready for me in various places—perhaps unconsciously drawn to confirming the old adage, "No good deed goes unpunished."[1] I am thinking rather of the book *Fine di un'ideologia: La secolarizzazione*,[2] by S. Acquaviva and R. Stella, which appears with a rich bibliographic escort, and moreover does not spare the reader, however sympathetic, from the impression of being an odd mixture of sociobiology and quantitativism.

According to the authors, the religious fact is basically determined by a series of biological factors. Unfortunately, the positions of sociobiologists in this regard have not been very convincing.[3] Acquaviva's new formulations seem to me reduced to an attempt at a critical review, and actually a self-critical one, of the thesis of the "eclipse of the sacred in industrial civilization," this time in terms of the "neocortical" in the wake of "primary" needs. It may be surprising that Acquaviva should admit right at the start that "the new research (and discoveries) essentially weaken the main theories of secularization."[4]

*I should like here to thank for their assistance Roberto Cipriani and Marco Marroni.

One does not however see to what extent Acquaviva's thought on this has changed. He tends in fact to distinguish between secularization and desacralization, stressing that "as a process, secularization can by itself give rise to new, different ways of being religious. It is clear that if religion is stripped of its external forms, it ends up allowing new ways of living the experience of the saced, precisely because the rules of the game change." However, to complete the picture there enters the idea that desacralization accompanies secularization. It is thus necessary to believe that the thesis of the eclipse of the sacred is linked to that of secularization. Yet, how then can the same phenomenon be both effect and origin of another? It is amazing, too, that, unsupported by empirical evidence, he asserts that "with secularization, religiosity (like religion) changes quality and diminishes in intensity."[5] I do not see what sense there is in distinguishing quality from intensity. Moreover, is the latter really measurable and quantifiable? Acquavivia loves pioneering positions, and I share some of his enthusiasms. But the name and work of L. L. Thurstone should be quite familiar to him. They date back to 1929.[6]

At any rate, this is Acquaviva's central argument:

> A series of biogrammatical needs (that is, having a direct or indirect genetic basis and that within limits orient human behavior and social organization), which are physical and psychological—where they are not satisfied, this complex generates anxiety and frustration or, at any rate, a more or less serious state of unease. However, this state of unease can be lessened or eliminated by sublimating it. Their combined and sublimated satisfaction gives rise to religious experience, and subsequently to the sacred cosmos and the religious institution (naturally, the process may also be the reverse and start from one or more points of the chain).[7]

There remain a few questions, since the distinction between religious experience and sacred cosmos is not made clear. Is a religious experience possible without any content related to the sacred cosmos? The slight importance given to the order of succession of these processes shows a basic empirical inconsistency. If historically and sociologically the interchange between religious institution and experience is proved, the hypothesis of the separability of sacred cosmos and religious experience remains dubious. Acquaviva follows the list of needs with a logical table intended to be didactic but which is confused, given the fluidity and nominalistic nature of the linkages of the phenomena mentioned. One calls to mind the oversights of an inattentive proofreader, since nothing in the previous context seems to point to any distinction between the "mediated" and the "culturally rooted." As earlier, in 1961, the theses produced and the empirical proofs seem to form part of the logical framework of a theorization with shadows of plausibility, but only after major efforts at adjustment and "reduction." It is true the author seems aware of the sporadic and provisional nature of his data. However, he is tied to his starting point: "Religious experience exists, lives astride the ecclesial world, or at any rate the organized religious groups and the secularized world; it has deep biological roots and is linked to psychological factors that it is time to investigate.[8]

After this, with a hasty but rather strange procedure, the author throws on to the reader and potential critics the burden of proof. We should ask if the "words in the wind" Acquaviva complains of in others are not basically part of a certain parascientific armory that uses summary indices to enter, apparently in a new form, into the lists of the *querelle* on the sacred. On the other hand, Acquaviva refuses, very scientistically, to use other perspectives; he "refuses to reflect . . . on nonpertinent, or insufficient, approximate reflections (with reference to the religious experience) on astrology, invisible religion, and the like."[9]

The book's second part, by R. Stella, hinges on a careful defense of Acquaviva's thesis, throwing at me the accusation of making an instrumental case against his argument, from its first appearance subordinate to the "cry of pain" of de-Christianization, and thus guilty of a basic ethnocentrism, unable to grasp the phenomenon in its global dimensions. In throwing my own argument back at me, or at least part of it, Stella shows he has a fencer's wrist, dangerously loose and rapid, but he does not see some defects within the apparatus of his own general reasoning. *Latet anguis in herba*! In criticizing my position as subordinate to the need to set out the foundations of a "lay religion," Stella brusquely states that science must be absolutely neutral, pure, and transparent. He forgets the famous question of the presuppositions, or point of view, that inescapable and testing question for any scientific research that hopes to attain the critical level. Stella thus falls, with the best of intentions, into the flattest scientism, that is, a caricature of science.

The argument of Roberto Cipriani in *La religione diffusa*[10] seems much more convincing: even if his idea of "diffuse" religion may make one think of a diluted, vague religion, like the mainly English seventeenth- and eighteenth-century deism, or those strong currents of "natural theology" that marked the origin of (mainly) American universities.[11] Cipriani concentrates his critical force on his contemporaries, especially Robert N. Bellah, bringing out his conceptual distortions, especially concerning Italian experience. "It is as well to distinguish clearly and cleanly between 'diffuse religion' and what Bellah maintains with his religious ground bass, a kind of 'real' religion counterposed to 'official,' 'legal' religion of the institution."[12] Cipriani proposes clearly distinguishing himself from Bellah's position.

> As is well known, for Bellah the five religions of Italy are, in order: "real" religion (religious ground bass), "legal" (Catholicism), liberalism, activism, and socialism. All these are "civil religions," Catholicism itself is now, but has also been in the past, a "civil religion." These conceptual distortions are threadbare, especially if one moves on to observations of an empirical kind. Thus activism is hard to confirm as having a "religious" nature. But above all the argument of an experienced religion that is separate from the more formal theologies expressed by Catholicism, and goes on its way with no harmony (or accord) with the developments in institutional religion, does not hold; while the latter remains, on the other hand, a recurring parameter for comparison, and even a conflictual one."[13]

It would be as well to return to these problematic points, but meanwhile I do not want to end this note without recalling the themes emerging in the conference at Turin, 10–12 May 1989, organized by Professor Pietro Rossi, in collaboration with the Turin Goethe Institute, planned to focus on studies of Max Weber's thinking, also regarding sociology of religion. On that occasion it fell to professor Wolfgang Schluchter to make an interesting contribution on Weber's thought in that, in hiw view, it is a moment of transition from the "critique of religion" to the "sociology of religion."

The first part of Shluchter's paper, significantly entitled "The

Transcendence of the Critique of Religion by Means of the Sociology of Religion," traces the reasons whereby the latter is not a completion of the critique of the religious phenomenon, as suggested by Comte and Marx in the wake of Feuerbach, but rather a radical development of the analytical perspective itself. "With the transition from the critique of religion to the sociology of religion, religion was no longer seen as an historical component (we say 'historically determined') of culture, but rather as its constituent component."[14] In other words, whereas the critique of religion replaced theology by anthropology (Feuerbach and Marx), or positive science (Comte), the sociology of religion recognizes in the religious phenomenon the character of a universe of signs and symbols, with their own laws, in which there is a genuine expression of human experience.[15] Certainly they have a common background: "Both analyze the religious phenomenon in terms of an anthropocentric and sociocentric perspective. . . . But distinct from the critique of religion, the sociology of religion takes its distance from two types of reductionism, that of religious symbolization to a base (= a substratum) that is always determinate, and that of religious experience to its scientific basis."[16]

In fact, the sociology of religion—in Weber's sense, since to Schluchter Durkheim still stays in this aspect close to his master Comte—"must certainly translate [*übersetzen*] the religious experience of the believer into its frame of reference, and thus externalize [*verfremden*] it, it does not however therefore propose itself to replace it [*ersetzen*]"[17] Then, Schluchter analyzes the "metaphor" of the "struggle of the gods" contained in the "science as profession," asking himself if this does not constitute a falling back into the critique of religion.[18] After recalling how heavily the contingent historical situation (1917) weighed in determining the tone and characteristics of Weber's text, Schluchter stated that to believe that this Weberian metaphor was a development of the critique of religion would only be possible if one let oneself be blinded and misled into a superficial analysis of the text. Indeed, in his view, only to a superficial reading could Weber's argument seem a (downright "Nietzschean") resumption of the themes dear to the critique of religion. In reality, "Weber's analysis goes much deeper. . . . It does not involve mere pluralism of values, but rather an antagonism between values; not mere subjectivism, but something more: the internal pressure to decide . . . as regards the final meaning of one's concrete action; it concerns not mere secularism, but something new, the experience of a (new) dependence.''[19] The thesis Weber set out in this discussion would be completely vitiated,

> whenever one proposed to see in it an attack on religion in general and Christianity in particular. Rather, it contains an attack on a modern science viewed in the wrong way. In that, Weber attacked all those over- and undervaluing, at the same time, their own abilities—those who overvalue them [*überschätzen*] because they do not respect the limits of rational, empirical knowledge, and those who undervalue them [*unterschätzen*] because they wish to avoid the inconvenient realities ascertainable by science. The discussion is thus marked not by an attitude of critique of religion, but rather one of critique of science. He is only indirectly critical of religion to the extent that it opposes in a wholly general way a specific type of synthesis of values.[20]

One must say that, once the correctness of this analysis has been conceded, Schluchter expatiates on the exposition of a sustained Kantian analysis (he refers more precisely to the "tradition of criticism" of this type of analysis in Weber, "intended to establish the limits of rational, empirical knowledge, whose correlative is self-limitation [*Selbstbegrenzung*]").[21] Schluchter makes clear:

> This critique has an historical side and a systematic one. The historical side: the representations of science as a journey towards true being (Greek philosophy), true art (Renaissance), true nature (period of the rise of the exact natural sciences), true God (science indirectly influenced by Protestantism and Puritanism), and true happiness (Cxix) were all illusions. The systematic side: one must fight the naturalistic monism that links up in part with historicism and again produces illusions, since this produces "the decline of the gods from every evaluative viewpoint in every science" . . . and because it holds fast to an ingenuous concept of progress, and thus does not see the paradoxes of secularism.[22]

Allow me a postscript here. Admitting what Weber believed,[23] it seems to me right to make clear that this professed "critical tradition" should be somewhat recast as regards the original Kantian perspective. If it is indeed undoubtedly true that we find in Kant the need to establish the limits of rational and empirical knowledge, this necessity arose for him from the fact that it was important to guard science from the illicit intrusions of theology into its range of competence and not—as it seems here—from the fact that religion should be "guided" by science. This position of Kant was intended to limit theology and not the exact sciences, as clearly appears both from a careful reading of the *Critique of Pure Reason* and the *Prolegomena*, and especially a work like *Religion within the Limits of Reason Alone*, to any future metaphysics, as Kant not by chance received an order from the Prussian political authorities (under the pressure of the [Lutheran] religious authorities' protests) to be silent on religious matters.

For Kant, any religious or theological statement that conflicted with scientifically acquired findings should always and at all costs be rejected, along with any religious assertion claiming to have a scientific content as a result of the revealed truth of faith. Making, today, the "headsman of God" (to repeat Carducci's famous metaphor) the "guardian of the sphere of the religious" seems a courageous—I should hazard, a desperate—operation. Kant's antinomies were functional in repulsing the intrusion of theology into the field of the sciences, and not vice versa. That he argues conversely that, in the current (i.e., eighteenth-century) state of scientific knowledge it was not possible scientifically to resolve specific problems—the beginning and end of the world, the nature of human beings, the existence of the soul—did not imply this would also be impossible in the future. The claim of theology to reply to these very questions by claiming these replies had a truth content, analagous to what characterized (and characterizes) scientific truths, was to be always and at all costs rejected—and for centuries to come. In the framework of Kantian philosophy, the charge of dogmatism, not by chance, is always leveled at Berkeley, and certainly not at Hume, and this is not insignificant, since for Kant dogmatism is the chief enemy from which a correct scientific argumentation must protect itself. Dogmatism—the dogmatism of reason—claims to impose its own laws on the physical world. Kantian criticism (the famous "Copernican revolution" of which Kant made himself spokesman), by taking physical laws back to the human mind, which interpreted reality on the basis of innate a priori forms (space and time), open to experiment and verifiable, led in quite another direction.

To return to Schluchter: on the basis of these observations, he goes on to analyze "divinities in the sociology of religion" in the light of Weber's analytico-comparative itinerary. In his view, the product of this comparative analysis is the statement that in the history of religions in our time, there are only two logical and significant basic conceptions, and only three logical and significant conceptions of the relation between divine and human order (theodicies). For the former, he acknowledges the idea of an immanent, original, impersonal order, and that of a personal, transcendent God the creator. As regards the theodicies, they are that founded by Karma, that based on dualism, and that of predestination.[24] On the other hand, we have for all these currents the result "that the search by their supporters . . . for a closeness [*Nähe*] to the divine order, or even a unity with it, has led them to distance themselves from the world, and themselves. Only this distance [*Distanz*] lets men judge (= take a position toward the world themselves). . . . As Weber's studies on the cultural importance of ascetic Protestantism show, these positions [*Stellungnahmen*] were to lead in the West, and only there, to an attitude of dominance of the physical world explained in religious terms, which has become certainly not the only, but one of the founding conditions of modern professional culture."[25]

On this basis, through the intermediate phases of the Enlightenment and Utilitarianism, secularization would be reached, whereby "an era estranged from God has arrived, without prophets, distanced from the Christian God. . . . This has led to a new polytheism. This distinguishes itself from the ancient in that it recognizes [*anbetet*] divinities still in the shape of impersonal powers, or that of abstract values."[26] Modern polytheism is said to open for man, formally, a series of opportunities for choice: "You must lead a conscious life, must enlighten yourself regarding your value relations, must choose your destiny and be responsible for this choice. But in the name of what God are these questions raised? Certainly not in the name of the Christian God. Has the sociology of religion then some special divinity it serves, and if so, which? And what is its relation with the God of theology?" Do we find ourselves again at the level of Marx and Comte or, still worse, an aimless decisionism? "That finally involves the question of Weber's practical position, that concerning the basis of his practical philosophy,"[27] which occupies the fourth part of Schluchter's essay. The latter refers to the consideration (I have already criticized this in its claimed Kantian foundations) whereby "Weber opposes naturalistic monism in scientific thought . . . the moment it forcibly limits the productivity of rational and empirical knowledge."[28] It must indeed find itself embarrassingly answering such questions as "What must we do? What can we hope for?" through its being linked to purely subjective presuppositions. It would expel the religious dimension from within itself (we perfectly agree with this), and resolve the question by leaving everyone essentially free to believe what they want.[29] However, Weber was not to be content with this "simplistic" solution, which "would have the advantage that the 'God' of the sociology of religion, who would become one of the 'divinities' of science, and thus the 'divinities' of practical and technical domination of life, could leave to the 'God' of theology the ultimate questions regarding meaning (of life, human experience, etc., as in Kant, as we saw earlier)." Weber naturally is not content with such a solution, "otherwise his position would be trivial [sic]."[30] On the other hand, according to Schluchter, there are two other perspectives available for Weber.

1. Man, "in order to give concrete embodiment to his original rationality, experiences in this at the same time the fact that a conscious life should not be guided solely by reason. It certainly corresponds to his original rationality . . . to anchor his life to the ultimate, supreme ideas of value [Wertideen]. But the preciseness of the particular frame of reference of values selected is an aspect belonging to the sphere of faith, not reason. This faith can certainly be based *in* reason, but not be *inspired* by it. *Or:* only decision [Entscheidung] leads to a conscious life . . . and only faith leads to a conscious life not in contradiction with the conditions of the unity of the rational personality."[31]
2. Or—and this is in Schluchter's view the argument Weber acknowledges—there becomes clear the "insuperability [unüberbrückbar] of the tension between the sphere of values of science . . . and that of religion. . . . Only for the nonreligious man does the scientific frame of reference remain the founding one and the relation between faith and reason precarious. . . . [Religiosity] is not a 'knowledge' in the ordinary meaning of the word, but a 'having,' more exactly a positive having."[32]

Thus Schluchter arrives at what was intended to be the central argument in his reading of Weber:

> From my point of view, expressed in this commentary, we do not find in Weber
> so much a pursuit of the critique of religion by other means as a referral to the
> basic differences in the latest formulations of a religious world-picture [*Welt-
> bild*], and a nonreligious one, certainly not only on the theoretico-historical
> plane, but also on the metatheoretical and axiologico-normative one. Religion
> and theology must excise [*sprengen*] the anthopocentrism of science and a way
> of life connected to that. Only in this way do they not give in [*verfallen*] to
> secularism and an explanation of the meaning of life in immanent terms.[33]

These are quite strong formulations. On the other hand, they can
only with difficulty be attributed to Weber, who does not seem so
inclined to "excise" modern science (the translation already soft-
ens its meaning, which is better expressed as "blow up," "ex-
plode"). Schluchter is aware of this, to the extent of correcting
somewhat the weight of this assertion. Weber's merit is that of
having brought out the gap (*Kluft*, meaning abyss) between a
religious way of life and one based on scientific knowledge, one
which only a leap of faith (*Glaubenssprung*) lets one overcome.

> This leap has different premises and consequences than the choice between the
> immanent divinities of life. As Weber states, it presupposes a religious musical-
> ity. He recognized, always, he did not have this. So, he never made that leap.
> He chose for himself the conception of life and a way of life specific to an
> individualism sensitive to values, and tragic, and thus heroic. That, however,
> did not make him a critic of religion of the caliber of a Marx, a Comte, or even
> a Nietzsche. He could understand the religious point of view and give it attention
> as a basic possibility of life, even, precisely, in the context of a world marked
> by secularism, where, to agree with Peter Berger, human beings, religiously
> motivated, certainly represent a huge "cognitive minority."[34]

The question is always "What leap is it?" A leap to one's death?

Omitting here the consideration of the idea of "secularization,"
in P. L. Berger's version and others, a notion anyway soon raised
to a mythical plane, and which I think I have adequately criticized
elsewhere by bringing out above all its unconscious ethnocentrism,
I should like to restrict myself to some short final considerations.
In reality, far from toning down the critique of religion in a sociology of religions, Weber historicizes universal religions, in my view,
in that he proposes testing their effect (considered as "lived
ethics") on average economic behavior. Not only this; it may be
possible to see in Weber a more radical critic of religion-in-church,
that is of religion as hierocratic structure of power, administrative
arm of the sacred held in monopoly, and as such counterposed to

religion as religiosity, as deep, intimate experience. This is a music Weber admitted to having no ear for; but he recognized its legitimacy and importance for the purposes of an historical upsurge of professional conscience. In this sense, one might perhaps argue that Weber is a more incisive critic of religion than Marx or Comte.

A Short Note on 'Charisma'*

The concept of "charisma"—from the Greek Χαρισ, τοσ [χαι´ρω]: enchantment, grace, jubilee, festivity, grace, gift, favor, merit, veneration, and Χαριομα, τοσ [χαριζομαι]: divine gift; and from the Latin *charisma, atis*: gift, divine grace—has a deep link with the concept of "sacred," especially those aspects that make the "sacred" an extraordinary quality, inherent in objects and persons, which transform them into *instruments of mediation* with (divine) *power*. In the wider sense, charisma corresponds to *mana, orenda, virtù*. In the more specific sense, it is above all a *personal quality* containing the idea of a *relation*, an intermediation between the individual who bears that *gift* and the indistinguishable mass (tribe, people, community) that aspires to a relation with that *potency*. In my view the aspect of gift, the favor conceded by God, is basic and distinguishes charisma from any kind of acquired ability. The fact that it is an *inexplicable privilege* grounds the conceptions of *election* and the *call* that always accompany charisma.

The concepts of *relation* and *mediation*—between the individual and God, through the bearer of charisma, and between the mass and the *leader*, by way of the possession of the divine gift—are central in the definition of charisma.

The Charismatic Model

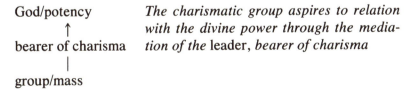

God/potency
↑
bearer of charisma
|
group/mass

The charismatic group aspires to relation with the divine power through the mediation of the leader, *bearer of charisma*

*For her collaboration I should like to thank Dr. Enrica Tedeschi, author of *Per una sociologia del Millennio—Davide Lazaretti: carisma e mutamento sociale* (Venice: Marsilio, 1989).

From the sociological viewpoint, the relation is inverted:

leader   *The contact between leader and his people*
  ↓   *is established through the charismatic*
charisma/potency   *function, the special gift with which god*
  ↑   *has invested the leader*
group/mass

Before Weber

Before Weber, charisma was defined by: a) the ethno-anthropologists (e.g., J. G. Frazer), especially in studies of primitive magic and the functions of the priest-magician-king (seen in the developmental sense and that of the progressive institutionalization of charisma); b) R. Sohm, scholar of canon law and the origins of the Church, for whom charisma and law exist in unresolvable contradiction; and c) E. Troeltsch, who used the perspective of charisma to explain the processes of transformation of religious sects into churches.

Max Weber

To Weber we owe the richest and, in sociology, the most influential explanation of the concept and the ideal-type related to the charismatic relation. Weber arrived directly at the sources most meaningful for Western culture to define charisma: the Old and New testaments. In particular, he analyzed: a) the historico-sociological development of the charismatic relation in the culture of ancient Judaism (preexile prophets, prophets of exile, prophets of misfortune, from Moses to Christ, king-prophets, and so on, and b) the sociological result of this development in the proto-Christian communities, especially through the reading of Paul's letters.

This analysis is contained chiefly in *Economy and Society* (1922), but to some extent also in the essays in the *Sociology of Religion* (F. Ferrarotti, trans. and intro., Turin: UTET, 1988); for a detailed account of Weber's work overall, see L. Cavalli, 1981). Schematically, the conception of Christian charisma, the result of an age-old development of charismatic leadership (prophetism), is as follows.

1. Charisma is the exceptional quality endowed by God to a few elect, in an inexplicable fashion, unforeseeable, arbitrary, on the basis of his secret goals (this orientation was to be basic in the theology of the Reformation). Corollary: the exceptional characteristic of charisma lies not so much in the "proofs" (miracles) that the chosen one incidentally produces, as in the contact with potency, as evidenced by them.
2. Charisma is donated arbitrarily and *unequally*. It is not possessed automatically by the community. Its members have the obligation to recognize the chosen one, the bearer of the gift, the annointed (*cristo*), and the duty to obey him.
3. The gift is personal, but to the advantage of the whole group.
4. Charisma creates *metanoia* in whoever possesses it—that is, a deep internal regeneration, transformation of the soul, death and rebirth through a new soul.
5. Between the bearers of charisma and the community there arises a *recognition*, on the basis of the *metanoia* that grounds the charismatic relation, characterized by *individuality* and *inequality*.
6. The elect feels himself *called* (by God) to a *mission* (a cause).

Essentially, Weber accepts this conception of charisma in his ideal-type, giving it an explanatory sociological trait through his *sociology of power*, which makes charisma a theoretical instrument of sociological analysis and which finds its theoretical placement in the contact between *political sociology* and the *sociology of religion*.

Perhaps this theoretical necessity makes certain aspects marginal that in my view are of basic importance in the Christian conception (e.g., that of Paul, Letters and Acts). These aspects, neglected by Weber, are: a) the plurality of charismas within the community, and b) the subsequent potential *hierarchy* of charismas in the charismatic group.

(Incidentally, I am working, in regard to the analysis of this point, toward a redefinition of the charismatic relation, or a fuller elaboration of it, which would allow me to take account of certain *otherwise inexplicable* dynamics found in Lazarettism. Weber, indeed, by focusing on the leader exclusively, as the main bearer of charisma, and on the distance between leader and group, which mediates between at the most a small circle of apostles (the charismatic aristocracy), neglects possible working hypotheses that might envisage a fuller breakdown of the chrismatic relation into a plurality of *charismatic interrelations hierarchically structured*, within the community. The search for this more accurate definition of the charismatic model would not in any case oppose individual to collectivity (as always happens in the critical revisions of Weberian theory) but would *exalt the role of the individual* more or less endowed with charisma, in group dynamics.)

Charisma/Power/Legitimation

If for Paul *metanoia* is the disturbing effect of charisma in the privileged individual, for Weber it is above all a relational process, produced by the figure of the leader, the "dominator," for the benefit of the "dominated."

Charismatic power, the other face of the relation with potency, is one of the three pure types of dominion.

1. Charisma has the function of *legitimation* of power exercized by the leader over his followers and by the charismatic group over the masses.
2. The recognition of charismatic dominion involves a *duty* for the followers in regard to the leader; there is no search for consensus, but the imposing of a will.
3. The charismatic community is devoid of amministrative-bureaucratic structures (charismatic apparatus)—a movement in *statu nascendi*.
4. The charismatic relation is exceptionally plastic. It must be continually kept alive through "proofs," confirming the justness of the mission (the cause) the leader feels himself entrusted with.
5. The fluidity and exceptional nature of charismatic power pose the problem of its *transformation into daily practise*, by way of: a) bureaucratization, institutionalization (official charisma)—sect–church; movement–institution and b) the search for a new bearer of charisma (investiture, hereditary transmission).

Social function

Charismatic power is "revolutionary," "from within," of the individual as of the group, opposed both to the power of tradition as to that of the law, and tending, once the *statu nascendi* has been passed, to transform itself into traditional or legal power.

Theory of crisis (χρι´σισεωσ: separation, choice, judgement, decision, quarrel, sentence, result, success, explanation, interpretation, divination). The historical efficacy of charismatic power lies above all in *metanoia* (history of the change in mentalities?). Hence arise the most interesting starting points for analysis in the study of charisma: a) charismatic experience as motive power of history, as historical creativity, with the significance of innovation of meaning; b) the opposition of charisma, rather than to rational practice (rational action toward a goal), to *daily routine*, "petrified" social practices; c) the link of charisma with the emergence of an orientation of the individual kind, with the birth of the individual and the concept of the *personality* (compare the culture of the Reformation); and d) the decisive role of the *word* (the vehicle of meaning), both written and spoken.

Post-Weber

Weber's concept of charisma has had from the outset a double development from the moment it was used both in the context of ethno-anthropological research and sociology of religion, as well as that of political sociology and sociology of power. T. Parsons (1951), for example, uses it in the analysis of social change (revolutionary movements).

In political sociology. For a reconstruction of the use of the concept in political discussion of society, the masses, elites, totalitarianism, democracy, and so on, the book by Luciano Cavalli (1981) is useful. He tends toward a cautious revaluation of charisma in the current political dialectic. He basically agrees with the conception of Parsons that "there cannot be a legitimate order without a charismatic element" (p. 252, n. 13), though charisma is seen as an "anomic form of the sacred" and thus as a form of transition from a legitimate order to another (see A. Piepe, 1971).

Furthermore, I suggest reading: A. Schlesinger Jr. (1962), on the current problems of the crisis of leadership in relation to contemporary democracies; E. Shils (1958, 1965, 1972), on the concept of "charismatic inclination"; and G. Roth (1973, 1975) and R. Bendix (1960) on the relation between movement and institution, leadership and domination, charisma and "derived" charisma. Of special interest in the context of relations of domination between individual (leader) and dominated masses are the studies with a psychological orientation, whose importance Weber had already indicated in using the models of W. Hellpach, a scholar of social psychology (note the concept of "influence," which Weber preferred to that of "imitation," in Tarde). In the context of contributions from psychology and, especially, from psychoanalysis to the problem of the charismatic relation, as a preliminary reading the books by D. McIntosh (1970) and E. R. Dodds (1959, 1969) are useful.

Ethno-anthropology. The contribution of students of socioreligious phenomena to the examination of the concept of charisma arises from the problematics relative to Western messianic movements (N. Cohn, 1961) and especially extra-Western ones (P. Worsley, 1957).

Weber's analysis represents a starting point also in terms of ethno-anthropological research, though a mainly critical one, for redefining the charismatic relation. Two directions of research emerge, which, for a wuite long period of scientific comparison, remained separate and not complementary.

The analysis of the charismatic process hinges essentially on:
a) the figure of the prophet, and thence on the personal, psychocultural, ultimately psychopathological, characteristics of charisma (W. E. Mühlmann, 1964) and
b) on the sociocultural and/or socioeconomic context from which in specific circumstances the exceptional individual tends to emerge (P. Worsley, 1957; M. I. Pereira de Queiroz, 1978; V. Lanternari, 1974).

For the debate in ethnology, V. Lanternari's preface to the second edition of *Movimenti religiosi di libertà e di salvezza dei popoli oppressi* (1977) is an excellent, well-reasoned synthesis of the theoretical approaches of scholars of non-Western peoples to the problem of charisma.

A very interesting comparison of the different disciplines' approaches to this problem, especially by historians and ethnologists, is in *Forme di potere e pratica del carisma* (1984).

Further, one should mention the notice attracted by the review *Social Compass* in its interest in charisma. In particular, J. Freund (1976) reconstructs the chief points of Weber's thought, and C. Seyfarth (1980) makes an accurate account of German sociology on the subject, drawing interesting conclusions on the problem of secularization and thence on the relation between rational and irrational in social phenomena. This reflection represents, along with the problem of the dialectic between individual and group (central in ethno-anthropological research), the second important theoretical question the concept of charisma in Weber still implies.

Stimulating, though secondary to the general orientation of *Economy and Society* is Seyfarth's reading of it, as not opposed to "rational" (and thus meaning secularization as mere rationalization), but rather to "everyday" (giving secularization a meaning of *routinization and bureaucratization not necessarily rational*). Moreover, as observed by many, faith in reason is for Weber only the "last" charismatic process.

Finally, it seems useful to propose some remarks about the practices of charisma in postindustrial Western culture, or that of late capitalism. In this context (of advanced capitalism), the concept of charisma tends to take on changes of meaning, or to stress certain meaning that have never been wholly absent, though not particularly dominant. In this regard, the crisis of Protestant theology in the nineteenth century and the successive movement of American theological neoliberalism in the 1960s are not wholly extraneous to certain religious manners—also Catholic ones—in the last twenty years in the West. In brief, "radical" theology tends to psychologize the religious phenomenon, which is essentially "reduced" to an "internal emotion," "ineffable experience," highly suggestive and above all incommunicable.

Aside from the dominant themes of the "new theology" (see P. Berger, 1969)—such as "Christianity without religion," the "death of God," the reading of the Scriptures as "symbolic systems" at the limit of psychoanalyzing, and so on—the accent on introspection, internal experience, and the ineffability of the sentiments seems to me to have considerably penetrated a particular conception of charisma. This is charisma as it is experienced by the neoascetic sects, but especially by the neomystical, Catholic ones (E. Pace 1983). The preindustrial Christian conception of charisma—and so too the Weberian one—seems marked by a greater *"objectivity"* and verifiability of the gift of grace, the ineffable "breath of the Spirit," as distinct from the currently prevailing conceptions.

Notes

1. Most recently in *Studi di sociologia* 3–4 (July–December 1988): 26.
2. Rome: Borla, 1988.
3. For some remarks on this, see my introduction to the second edition of H. Spencer, *Principi di sociologia*, 2 vols. (Turin: UTET, 1988).
4. Acquaviva and Stella, 7.
5. Ibid., 9; 11.
6. See L. L. Thurstone and E. J. Chave, *The Measurement of Attitudes: A Psychophysical Method and Some Experiments with a Scale for Measuring Attitudes towards the Church* (Chicago: University of Chicago Press, 1929).
7. Acquaviva and Stella, 21.
8. Ibid., 47.
9. Ibid., 51.
10. Rome: Borla, 1988.
11. See the emblematic works of John Locke, *Essay on the Reasonableness of Christianity*, 1695; for the U.S., see Milton Valentine, *Natural Theology, or Rational Theism* (Chicago: Griggs, 1885).
12. Cipriani, 71.
13. Ibid., 72.
14. W. Schluchter, *Der Kampf der Götter: von der Religionskritik zur Religionssoziologie* (Heidelberg Universität: 1988), 3.
15. Ibid., 5–6.
16. Ibid., 7–8.
17. Ibid., 8.
18. Ibid., chap. 2.
19. Ibid., 12.
20. Ibid.
21. Ibid., 13.
22. Ibid.
23. I cannot argue this with assurance, but I refer the reader here to my *A Theology for Non believers* (New York: Academic Press, 1987), chap. 4.
24. Schluchter, 17.
25. Ibid., 18.
26. Ibid.
27. Ibid., 19.
28. Ibid.
29. This is an aspect of Weber's thought that found in chap. 4 of Leo Strauss's *Natural Right and History* its tough, logical critique, though insufficiently in context from the historical point of view.
30. Schluchter, 20.
31. Ibid., 22.
32. Ibid.
33. Ibid., 23.
34. Ibid., 24.

An Essential Bibliography on 'Charisma'

With Special Emphasis on Contemporary Authors

Bendix, R. *Max Weber. An Intellectual Portrait.* London: Heinemann, 1960.

Berger, P. L. "Charisma and Religious Innovation: The Social Location of Israelitic Prophecy." *American Sociological Review* 6, no. 28 (1963).

———. *The Sacred Canopy.* New York: Doubleday, 1969.

Bord, R. J. "Toward a Social-Psychological Theory of Charismatic Social Influence Processes." *Social Forces* 3, no. 53 (1975).

Brinton, C. *Anatomy of Revolution.* New York: Random House, 1957.

Burridge, K., *New Heaven, new Earth: A study of Millennarian Activities.* Oxford, 1969.

Cavalli, L. *Il capo carismatico: Per una sociologia weberiana della leadership.* Bologna: Il Mulino, 1981.

———. *Max Weber: Religione e società.* Bologna: Il Mulino, 1968.

Cohn, N. *The Pursuit of the Millennium.* New York, 1961.

Coleman, J. A. "Church-Sect Typology and Organizational Precariousness." *Sociological Analysis* 2, no. 29 (1968).

Découflé, A. *Sociologie des révolutions,* Paris: PUF, 1970.

Desroche, H. 'Micromilléniarismes e communautarisme utopique en Amérique du Nord du XVII au XIX siècle." *Archives de sociologie des religions,* no. 4 (1957).

Dodds, E. R. *The Greeks and the Irrational,* Berkeley: University of California Press, 1951.

Dogan, M. "Le personnel politique et la personalité charismatique." *Revue française de sociologie* 3, no. 6 (1965).

Eisenstadt, S. N., ed. *Max Weber on Charisma and Institution Building.* Chicago: University of Chicago Press, 1968.

Emmet, D. "Prophets and Their Societies." *JRAI* 1, no. 86 (1956).

Ferrarotti, F. *Il paradosso del sacro.* Rome-Bari: Laterza, 1983.

———. *Una teologia per atei.* Rome-Bari: Laterza, 1983.

Frazer, J. G. *The Golden Bough: A Study in Magic and Religion.* London, 1922.

Freund, J. "Le charisme selon Max Weber." *Social Compass* 4, no. 23 (1976).

Friedrich, C. J. "Political Leadership and the Problem of Charismatic Power", *Journal of Politics* 1, no. 23, (1961).

Glassman, R. M., and Swatos, W. H. eds. *Charisma, History, and Social Structure.* Westport: Greenwood Press: 1986.

G. S. R. "Questionnaire sur les messianismes et millénarismes." *Archives de Sociologie des Religions* 5 (1958).

Hellpach, W. "Die geistigen Epidemien." Vol. 11 of *Die Gesellschaft, Sammlung sozialpsychologischen Monographien,* ed. M. Buber.

Hiernaux, J. P. and Remy, J. "Sociopolitical and Charismatic Symbolics: Cultural Change and Transactions of Meaning." *Social Compass* 1, no. 25 (19).

Hill, C. *A Sociology of Religion.* London, 1973.

Lanternari, V. *Festa Carisma Apocalisse.* Palermo: Sellerio, 1983.

———. *Messia, Enciclopedia 9.* Turin: Einaudi, 1980.

———. *Millennio.* Turin: Einaudi, 1980.

———. *Movimenti religiosi di libertà e salvezza dei popoli oppressi.* Milan: Feltrinelli, 1977.

Levillain, P., and Sallmann, J. M., eds. *Forme di potere e pratica del carisma.* Naples: Liguori, 1984.

Marcus, J. T. "Transcendance and Charisma." *Western Political Quarterly* 1 (1961).

McIntosh, D. "Weber and Freud: On the Nature and Sources of Authority." *American Sociological Review* 5, no. 35 (1970).

"Mouvements charismatiques et socio-politiques." *Social Compass* 1, no. 25 (1978).

Mühlmann, W. E., ed. *Chiliasmus und Nativismus: Studien zur Psychologie Soziologie und historische Kasuistik der Umsturzbewegungen.* Berlin, 1961.

Neitz, M. J. *Charisma and Community.* New Brunswick, N.J.: Transaction, 1987.

Pace, E. *Asceti e mistici in una società secolarizzata.* Venice: Marsilio, 1983.

Pereira de Queiroz, M. I. "Millénarisme e messianismes." *Annales ESC.* 2 (1964).

———. *Riforma e rivoluzione nelle società tradizionali: Storia e etnologia dei movimenti messianici.* Milan: Jaca Book, 1970.

Piepe, A. "Charisma and the Sacred." *Pacific Sociological Review* 2, no. 14 (1971).

Pitocco, F. "Millennio e/o utopia." *Studi storico-religiosi* 2, no. 1 (1977).

Prades, J. A. *Persistance et métamorphose du sacré.* Paris: PUF, 1987.

Robbins, T., ed. *Cults, Converts, and Charisma: The Sociology of New Religious Movements.* London: Sage, 1988.

Roth, G. "I virtuosi e la contro-cultura: Sull 'utilita' tipologica del concetto di 'carisma.' " *Rassegna italiana di sociologia* 3 (1973).

———. "Sociohistorical Model and Developmental Theory: Charismatic Community, Charisma of Reason, and the Counter-culture." *American Sociological Review* 2 (1975).

Schlesinger, A., Jr. "Democrazia e leadership eroica." In *La democrazialla prova del ventesimo secolo,* ed. R. Aron. Bologna: 1962.

Schiffer, I. *Charisma: A Psychoanalytic Look at Mass Society.* New York: Free Press, 1975.

Schutz, J. H. "Charisma and Social Reality in Primitive Christianity." *Journal of Religion* 54 (1974).

Schwartz, G. *Sect Ideologies and Social Status.* Chicago: University of Chicago Press, 1970.

Séguy, J. "Les problèmes de la typologie dans l'étude des sectes." *Social Compass* 2 (1965).

———. "Ernst Troeltsch ou de l'essence de la religion à la typologie des christianismes." *Archives de sociologie des religions* 25 (1968).

———. "Max Weber et la sociologie historique des religions." *Archives de sociologie des religions* 25, no. 33 (1972).

Seyfarth, C. "The West German Discussion of Max Weber's Sociology of Religion since the 1960s." *Social Compass* 1, no. 27 (1980).

Shils, E. "Charisma, Order, and Status." *American Sociological Review* 2, no. 30 (1965).

———. "The Concentration and Dispersion of Charisma: Their Bearing on Economic Policy in Underdeveloped Countries." *World Politics* 1, no. 2 (1958).

Sohm, R. *Kirchenrecht.* Leipzig: Duncker and Humblot, 1892.

Spencer, A. "What Is Charisma?" *British Journal of Sociology* 3, no. 24 (1973).

Stark, W. "The Routinization of Charisma: A Consideration of Catholicism." *Sociological Analysis* 4, no. 26 (1965).

Tedeschi, E. *Per una sociologia del millennio.* Venice: Marsilio, 1989.

Thomas, H. M. "Der politische besonders der revolutionäre charismatiker." *Zeitschrift für Religions und Geistesgeschichte* 4 (1985).

Thrupp, S., ed. *Millennial Dreams in Action.* The Hague, 1962.

Troeltsch, E. *Le dottrine sociali delle Chiese e dei gruppi cristiani.* Florence: La Nuova Italia, 1941.

Tucker, R. C. "The Theory of Charismatic Leadership." *Daedalus* 97 (1968).

Turk, H. "Task and Emotion, Value and charisma: Theoretical Union of Several Levels." In *Institutions and Social Exchange: The Sociologies of Talcott Parsons and George C. Homan,* ed. H. Turk and R. L. Simpson. Indianapolis: University of Indiana Press, 1971.

Wallis, W. D. "Quleques aspects du messianisme", *Archives de sociologie des religions* 5 (1958).

———. *Messiahs: Their Role in Civilization.* Washington, 1943.

Willner, A. R., and Willner, D. "The Rise and Role of Charismatic Leaders." *Annals of the American Academy of Political and Social Science* 348 (1965).

Wilson, A., and Perinbanayagam, R. S. "The Dialectics of Charisma." *Sociological Quarterly* 3, no. 12 (1971).

Wilson, B. R. *Sects and Society.* London: Blackwell, 1961.

Worsley, P. *The Trumpet Shall Sound.* London: Schocken, 1957.

Index